# The Aspen Papers

# The Aspen Papers /

Twenty Years of Design Theory
from the
International Design Conference in Aspen

Edited and with commentary by
## Reyner Banham

## Praeger Publishers
New York/Washington

Design:

Chermayeff & Geismar Associates

Photography:
Ferenc Berko

James O. Milmoe

The verse from "The sunlight on the garden" from
*Collected Poems of Louis MacNeice,* edited by
E. R. Dodds, is reprinted by permission of
Oxford University Press, Inc. © The Estate of
Louis MacNeice 1966.

Published in the United States of America in 1974
by Praeger Publishers, Inc.

111 Fourth Avenue, New York, N.Y. 10003

Library of Congress Cataloging in Publication Data
Banham, Reyner, comp.
The Aspen Papers
1. Design—Addresses, essays, lectures.   2. Industrial
design—Addresses, essays, lectures.   I. International
Design Conference.   II. Title.
NK1510.B26          745.4          73-14559

Printed in the United States of America

# Contents

# Aspen Speakers and Programs: 1951–1973

The difficulty of selecting the papers for this book may be judged from the number and eminence of the names listed below in the complete register of Aspen speakers. Some were famous then, some have become famous since, and others have passed from the public scene. Some gave formal lectures, others took part in panel discussions—where a year boasts many names, it usually means that they largely served on panels; where a few, they probably gave more formal papers; but in the free-form conferences of 1971, 1972, and 1973 almost anything could happen, and did. One almost constant feature, however, has been the guiding and responsible presence of a program chairman, organizer and animator of each year's conference. Although the role was not fully instituted until after the mid-1950's, Leo Lionni is rightly recognized as the first real program chairman, in 1953.

## 1951 Design as a Function of Management

Walter Paepcke
William Connolly
Charles S. Downs
Stanley Marcus
Andrew McNally
William M. Stuart
Burton Tremaine
René d'Harnoncourt
Edgar Kaufmann
Louis I. Kahn
Leo Lionni
Hoyt L. Sherman
Charles H. Sawyer
Herbert Bayer
Charles Eames
George Nelson
A. S. Costello
John M. Gates
Charles Zadok
Egbert Jacobson
Francis E. Brennan
Charles T. Coiner
Harley J. Earl
Theodore S. Jones
Josef Albers
Bartlett Hayes, Jr.
Faie Joyce
Otto I. Spaeth

## 1952 Design as a Function of Management

R. Buckminster Fuller
Alfred A. Knopf
Richard Gump
Walter Dorwin Teague

## 1953 Design as a Function of Management
Program Chairman: Leo Lionni

Max Bill
Gyorgy Kepes
Enrico Peressutti
Charles Eames
Nikolaus Pevsner
Dave Chapman
Xanti Schawinsky

## 1954 Planning: The Basis of Design
Program Team: Will Burtin, Carl Maas, Gyorgy Kepes

Richard Neutra
Robert O. Carlson
Merrit L. Kastens
A. Gerrard MacLeod
Roberto Burle Marx
Russell Lynes
Burns W. Roper
Albert E. Parr
Ted Parnales
John E. Burchard
Saul Bass
Edgardo Contini
Renato Tagiuri
Reuel Denney
Robert Saudek
Laurence Schmeckebier

## 1955 Crossroads: What Are the Directions of the Arts
Program Chairman: Will Burtin

Harry Bertoia
Earl C. Kelly
Sol Cornberg
S. I. Hayakawa
Arthur Drexler
Victor Gruen
Lancelot L. Whyte
Michael Farr
Williamm de Majo

Kiyushi Seike
Arnold F. Arnold
George D. Culler
Manuel Pizarro
John Houseman
Walter A. Netsch
Koiche Ho
Bernard S. Benson
Robert Osborn

## 1956 Ideas on the Future of Man and Design
Program Chairman: Will Burtin

Anatol Rapoport
Max Frisch
Mortimer Adler
Paul Rudolph
F. H. K. Henrion
Garrett Eckbo
Misha Black
Gregor Paulsson
Armin Hofmann
Jupp Ernst

Alberto Rosselli
Gordon Lippincott
Arthur Hald
Saburo Asaba
John A. Pappas
Peter J. B. Stevens
Sori Yanagi
Josef Muller-Brockmann
Jacques Vienot
Dennis Flanagan

## 1957 Design and Human Values
Program Chairman: Saul Bass

Ernesto N. Rogers
Jacob Bronowski
Conrad M. Arensberg
Robert Anshen
Bruce MacKenzie
Edmund N. Bacon
John A. Kouwenhoven
Amiya Chakravarty

James Real
Myron C. Helfgott
Lewis Clarke
Jane Fiske Mitarachi
Jennie I. Rowntree
Richard L. Meier
Richard S. Latham

## 1958 Design and Human Problems
Program Chairman: Garrett Eckbo

C. Wright Mills
Christopher Tunnard
Henry Hill
Claire Falkenstein
E. A. Gutkind
Edgardo Contini
Gordon Stephenson

Edward A. Williams
Albert T. Arai
Hin Bredendieck
Walter E. Packard
Robert Gwathmey
Morton Goldsholl
Romaldo Giurgola

## 1959 Communication: The Image Speaks
Program Chairman: Morton Goldsholl

Norman McLaren
Lancelot Hogben
Lancelot L. Whyte
Len Lye
Gilbert Cohen-Seat

William Golden
Abram Games
Jerry Schnitzer
James Real
Thomas N. Folds

## 1960 The Corporation & The Designer
Program Chairman: George D. Culler

Craig Ellwood
C. Northcote Parkinson
Bill Tara
Paul Reilly
Bryan Heath
Traugott Malzan
Leslie Julius
Paul A. Fine

Vernon Walsh
Spencer Stuart
Eliot Noyes
Olle Eksell
Blair Gettig
William Capitman
Joseph McGarry

## 1961 Man/Problem Solver
Program Chairman: Herbert Pinzke

Bernard Rudofsky
Tomas Maldonado
Richard Morris
Jay Doblin
Peter C. Kronfeld
Gwendolyn Brooks
Milner Gray
Yuri Soloviev
Roman Vishniac
Will Burtin
Harold Taylor
Hy Hoffman
Elisabeth Paepcke
William Friedman
Richard Pick

Edith Heath
R. Hunter Middleton
Bruce Beck
C. B. Sitterson
Rhodes Patterson
Jack Roberts
Herbert S. Zim
George McVicker
Arnold Rockman
Bruce MacKenzie
Edward C. Bursk
Bernard S. Benson
Merlin Krupp
Joe Sander

## 1962 Environment
Program Chairman: Ralph Eckerstrom

Robert Wallace Craig
Balkrishna Doshi
John Entenza
Bertrand Goldberg
Brinckerhoff Jackson
Louis I. Kahn
Oscar Lewis
Karl Menninger
Jonas Salk
Peter Blake
Arthur A. Cohen
Heinz von Forster
Reginald V. Jones

Herbert Muller
Theodore T. Puck
Robert C. Weaver
Justin Herman
Richard Lippold
Harrison Brown
Mildred Constantine
Robert Johnson
Robert F. McLean
Walter A. Netsch
Eric Sevareid
Robert Zion
E. M. Benson

## 1963 Design and the American Image Abroad
Program Chairman: Peter Blake

Alan Pryce-Jones
Wolfram von Hahnwehr
Robert Wool
Arnold M. Picker
Pat Want Singh
Peter G. Harnden
Donald Wilson
George Stevens
George Freedland
Reyner Banham

Martin Rosenzweig
Jack Masey
Andrew Heiskell
George Englund
Lucius D. Battle
Ray Mackland
Robert Sivard
Charles H. Clarke
Eliot Noyes

## 1964 Directions & Dilemmas
Program Chairman: Eliot Noyes

Robin Boyd
Cleveland Amory
Louis Dorfsman
Andre Francois
Philip Johnson
Dexter Masters
Wolf von Eckardt
Ivan Chermayeff
William Bernbach
Nelson C. Foote
Leon Gordon Miller

Paul Rudolph
Dwight MacDonald
Jay Doblin
Ralph Caplan
Reyner Banham
Allen Hurlburt
Georg Olden
Joseph R. Passoneau
Seymour Silverman
Richard S. Latham

## 1965 The New World
Program Chairman: George Nelson

Stuart Udall
William F. Lynch, S.J.
Philip M. Hauser
David Finn
Robert Theobald

Konrad Wachsmann
Martin Wohl
Philip Rosenthal
James Rouse
Peter Blake

## 1966 Sources and Resources
Program Chairmen: Allen Hurlburt, Mildred Constantine

Tomas Maldonado
Ben Shahn
Henry Dreyfuss
Arthur Drexler
Benjamin Thompson
Leo Lionni

Reyner Banham
Edgar Kaufmann
Richard Farson
Gyorgy Kepes
Julian Beinart
Henry Wolf

## 1967 Order and Disorder
Program Chairmen: Craig Ellwood, Jack Roberts

Jerzy Soltan
Piet Hein
Max Bill
Moshe Safdie
Charles Correa
Jacob Bronowski
Paul Weiss
Alfred Caldwell
William H. Thomas
Theo Crosby
Christopher Alexander

Crosby M. Kelly
Paul Heyer
Art Seidenbaum
Jeffrey Lindsay
Robert Lewis Propst
William Arrowsmith
Leo Lionni
Donald Resch
John Whitney
Stan Vanderbeek

## 1968 Dialogues: Europe/America
Program Chairman: Reyner Banham

Alf Böe
Misha Black
Morley Markson
John Allpass
David Gebhard
Dennis Crompton
Jivan Tabibian

Federico Correa
Irving Grossman
Richard S. Latham
Francois Dallegret
Peter Eisenman
Nuno Portas

## 1969  The Rest of Our Lives
Program Chairmen: Ivan Chermayeff, Henry Wolf

Frank Stanton
William Sloan Coffin
Balkrishna Doshi
Rene Dubos
George Nelson
Adrian Kantrowitz
Gerry Goodman
Peter Ustinov

Anthony Wiener
Dwight MacDonald
Robert Lowell
William Klein
Robert Osborn
Peter Knapp
R. O. Blechman

## 1970  Environment by Design
Program Chairman: William Houseman

Carl Koch
Stuart Udall
Peter Hall
Reyner Banham
Richard Farson
James E. Lash

Sim Van Der Ryn
Richard Saul Wurman
M. Paul Friedberg
Walter Orr Roberts
Cliff Humphrey
Cora T. Walker

## 1971  Paradox
Program Chairman: Richard Farson

R. Buckminster Fuller
Victor Papanek
Allen Kaprow
Nicholas Johnson
Lawrence Solomon
C. H. Waddington
Hans Proppe
Gene Youngblood
Warren Bennis
Robert Walter
Milton Wexler
John Margolies
Billy Adler
Karimu Kadma

Michael Aldrich
Michael Murphy
Saul Bass
Sherri Webber
Jeremy Shapiro
Jivan Tabibian
Andrew Young
Sheila de Bretteville
Bernard Gunther
James Fadiman
Caroline Bird
Keith Goddard
Nam June Paik

## 1972  The Invisible City
Program Chairman: Richard Saul Wurman

Louis I. Kahn
Ronald Gross
Leonard Finklestein
Donald Cressey
Albert Eide Parr
Jaquelin Robertson
Alan Levy
Bill Lacy
Paolo Soleri
Nicholas Johnson
Alan C. Green
Marcus Foster
Warren Bennis
Everett Reimer

Harry Parnass
Bernard Kohn
Lawrence Wells
Michael Southworth
John Holt
Farnum Gray
John Dollard
Ronald Barnes
Troy West
Simon Nicholson
Ruth Kohn
John Sullivan
Judy Seidenbaum

## 1973 Performance

Program Chairmen: Milton Glaser, Jivan Tabibian

Patricia Schroeder
David Wheeler
Robert Rauschenberg
Theodoros
Carlos Campbell
Clare Spark Loeb
Marie Casindas
Roman Vishniac
Duane Michaels
Mary Bardone
George De Leon
Richard E. Farson
Marshall Ho'

John Simon
Richard Goldstein
Brendan Gill
Reyner Banham
Robert Simon
Julian Beinart
Robert Benton
David Newman
The American Brass Quintet
James Earl Jones
Murray Gell-mann
Miralda

# I Introduction

The first I ever heard of any Aspen Design Conference was a talk by my revered professor Nikolaus Pevsner on the radio after he returned from the conference of 1953, and it was clear that for him it had been a voyage of discovery into an unknown design world that included then unheard-of names like Eames and Buckminister Fuller. The last I heard, before beginning work on this reader, was the words, "Well, gentlemen, shall we break for lunch?" as Jack Roberts, incoming President of the Board of the International Design Conference in Aspen, broke up the board meeting after the conference of 1970. Between the two dates I had become something of a regular speaker at IDCA, an adviser to the board, program chairman for 1968, and editor of the present volume.

Quite apart from my own involvement with IDCA, however, 1953 and 1970 are important Aspen dates. The former was the year of the tacit commitment of the Aspen pioneers to a regular annual design conference, although the formal incorporation of IDCA did not follow until 1955, which was also the year in which the conference really crystallized into its classic form of a week of top-flight lectures and all-star panel discussions, but that pattern was clearly emerging in 1953 at the third conference, and it did not die until 1970 at the twentieth, which—whatever happens—will be the last Aspen design conference in anything like the form on which its reputation has been built.

The beginnings, in 1951, are traceable to the afterglow of success, prestige, good-fellowship, and useful-work-done that lingered from the Goethe Bicentenary celebrations of 1949 and the quite unconnected Photographers' Conference in Aspen the following year. Emboldened by these, ideas for some sort of conference devoted to good design and good business were put together by Herbert Bayer, distinguished veteran of the Bauhaus and consultant to Container Corporation of America, and Egbert Jacobsen, Container Corporation's design director.

By New Year's Day, 1951, their proposals were sufficiently advanced for Jacobsen to write a circular letter to progressive heads of major business corporations (e.g., Frank Stanton of CBS) sounding out their responses to the idea of a "Design Seminar" at which creative talents like Bayer himself, Paul Rand, Gyorgy Kepes, and Will Burtin "could present their views to men like yourself who are already sympathetic, and especially to others who still have to be convinced of the importance of good design."

The bait offered by Jacobsen to lure the unconvinced others, "who might not come to hear a speaker like Herbert Read," was in two parts. One was that they would hear business figures of the stature of Stanton, whose opinions they would ignore at their financial peril, and would thus go away and hire good designers if he said so. The other part was that, in Jacobsen's words, "I have asked Mr. Walter Paepcke if he thought the meeting could be held in Aspen, Colorado."

Conceivably, such a "Design Seminar" might have been held in Chicago, say, since that was Container Corporation's home town, but looking back now it is inconceivable that Walter J. Paepcke could have said anything but *yes* to such a request, since this was exactly the kind of activity that interested him and fitted into his developing pattern of Aspen activities. IDCA is Paepcke's child, or nobody's.

As head of Container Corporation, which he had built up from a small family concern to a nationwide enterprise, Paepcke was a model of the progressive businessman. He was also a model of what we might nowadays call the concerned entrepreneur, one who saw good design as an essential part of good business and no less a part of a healthy public culture than the arts and music. He had been an active member of the group which promoted the Institute of Design in Chicago and invited Laszlo Moholy-Nagy to become its head. He had also put a generous slice of his own money into the institute over the years—sometimes in response to last-minute requests to save it from payroll problems and other overnight crises.

By 1950 he had also begun to commit an even larger slice of his own money, and the psychological capital of five years' personal activity, to Aspen, a ghost silver-mining town with a newly discernible potential as a ski resort, near Glenwood Springs in the Colorado Rockies. He and his wife had stumbled on the place in the last months of World War II, looking for somewhere to create "an American Salzburg"—an ambition that could be combined, in Aspen, with long-term business from the unavoidable postwar boom in skiing. Even before the first World Ski Championships had been staged in Aspen in 1950, Paepcke's instant Salzburg was a reality, for the Goethe Bicentenary had been held in 1949, and Eero Saarinen had designed, for its star-studded concerts, the first of Aspen's big tented auditoriums, which still provide the main focus for cultural activities there.

But given Paepcke's "yes" and his still-young Institute for Humanistic Studies as organizational backup, and Container Corporation as a power base, the situation was still not one in which prospective members of the first conference could simply adjourn to Aspen and bask in prefabricated hospitality. On the ground, things were still pretty raw and improvised. Those of us who nowadays jet into Denver and Hertz the rest of the way (for the sake of a four-hour drive through fabulous Rocky Mountain scenery) are too prone to forget how difficult the place was even to reach in 1951, let alone how primitive when you got there.

The most-approved mode of arrival in those days was to come out of Chicago in one of those classic old streamlined trains, the California Zephyr, and change at Glenwood Springs to one of the buses of the Glenwood Stage for the last forty rattling miles up the valley. Even Aspen Airways, that legend of scheduled bush flying, was not operating then, and the roads, for those who opted to drive over from Denver or Salt

12

Lake City, were such as often to make a jeep the most feasible vehicle. Even in the 'sixties, the road up to Independence Pass was not black-topped much beyond the city limits.

In the same years, Main Street had no curbs and only two lanes of asphalt down its center, the rest being red dust that would hang around in picturesque but irritating curtains after a bus or truck had rumbled past. The town in general was nearly all buildings of pre-1890 vintage, randomly disposed vacant lots where buildings had been removed, burned, or collapsed, and a few modern structures of post-Paepcke origin. The Jerome was the only usable hotel, the Wheeler Opera House the only permanent structure that could house a meeting.

The population was a mixture of survivors from the mining days and of the ranching economy that had never quite faded way, and new-comers of the postwar epoch—an eccentric collection of ski professionals, designers, writers, and artists. Camped out among the relics of ancient affluence and the promise of new experiment, they were at variance with the ambitions and customs of America-the-Organized. As a consequence of this ingrained nonconformity, Aspen has, for instance, no local TV; its radio station (KSNO, what else could it be?) is a law unto itself; the town has been, at various periods, on Daylight Saving Time when the rest of Colorado was not, so that the quickest way to start a high-level philosophical discussion was not to speak of Goethe but simply to inquire what time it was!

Yet discomforts, underorganization, eccentricities, and physical isolation would always sink below the threshold of complaint whenever one raised one's eyes unto the hills; the scenery of Aspen is Total Stun Country! The town itself sits on the floor of a flat-bottomed valley, into which the river has carved a gulch fifty feet deep all along one side of the built-up area. On either side of the town, closing the vistas along the north-south streets, rise the mountains—Ajax to the north, Red Mountain to the south—clad in thick stands of aspen trees on their lower slopes, pines and streaks of summer snow on the upper parts of Ajax, and the Maroon Bells behind.

The beauty of those mountains has escaped the descriptive power of pens more poetic than mine. The reader must take my word for it; but it does occur to me that, if beauty is in the eye of the beholder, then the eye that perceives Aspen may well be part of a slightly overwrought metabolism. At 8,000 feet, the air of Aspen is ridiculously clear and dangerously thin; to come there directly from the smog and soot and heat of the cities of the plain (as most of us do) is to experience an intoxication that exceeds even that caused by the hospitality Aspen traditionally offers.

So one comes down from Aspen after the conference with one's consciousness imprinted with memories that amount almost to addictions. Memories of a landscape ideally appropriate to noble and elevated thoughts, and of an atmosphere that seemed to purge the mind of obscurities and irrelevancies. But, above all, of an environment that was as much part of the conference as what was said, and who was present. The imponderable, inexplicable, incommunicable part of every design conference is the setting and atmosphere, which, simply, are not reproducible elsewhere. Proposals to put Aspen "on the road" and stage the conference somewhere else in, say, alternate years, have often been heard, especially from Europeans for whom the cost of getting there is near prohibitive. But all such proposals have come to naught, and chiefly because everyone ultimately recognizes that IDCA, unlike the scientists' Pugwash conference (to which it is sometimes compared) is not a movable feast.

The comparison with Pugwash has been made because Aspen has tried quite hard to tackle the major problems of the social responsibilities of design. But this is fully true only of the more recent conferences. Not that the early conferences were socially irresponsible—some major talents, like Buckminister Fuller, spoke seriously at early Aspens—but at the beginning it was, as Jacobsen proposed, chiefly a matter of getting designers and executives together for their mutual benefit, and the discussions were largely business-oriented. We know this from eyewitness accounts of what conferees saw and heard, rather than from transcripts of the papers actually delivered.

Fully transcribed records seem to survive only from 1955; that is, from the incorporation of IDCA as an independent entity capable of maintaining its own continuous records. Something—quite a lot, even—of the original business orientation, the urge to sell design to management, still survived in 1955, and some of it was still there as late as 1960, but a more philosophical strain was already coming through, as one can see in the rhetorical flourishes of Will Burtin's opening remarks of 1955. (It is probably just as well that his rhetoric was balanced by a sharp, perceptive paper by S. I. Hayakawa on "How to Attend a Conference," a primer that was reissued in subsequent years.) As Burtin's speech makes clear, Aspen was already beginning to wear the aspect of "the thinking man's summer camp" and to exhibit the style of discourse that has made it famous. The papers of 1955 are therefore a very proper place at which to begin the selection that forms this book, but only after Pevsner's astonished account of the events of 1953.

# At Aspen in Colorado
## Nikolaus Pevsner
## 1953

As I started thinking of what to tell you of Aspen in Colorado and the weird and stimulating conference on industrial design I have just attended there, I was flying east, leaving behind me the Rocky Mountains. And hidden in the distance somewhere, 7,900 feet up, there was Aspen. Aspen—the village has a right to its name. For the slopes of the mountains which flank and close the valley are covered with a delightful mixture of dark green fir trees and light green, fresh, rustling aspen trees, tall dark trunks and tall whitish-gray trunks. Only above 12,000 feet patches of snow appear, and the 14,000-footers are streaked with snow, carrying blankets of snow spread over the hollows. It is ideal skiing country, and indeed the World Skiing Championship was contested at Aspen a few years ago.

This and my conference and much else are due to one man, Mr. Walter Paepcke. Until he came along Aspen was one of the ghost towns of the Rockies. It flourished with mining and was slain by the great mining slump of 1893. In 1879 it had fifteen churches and twelve schools and three newspapers, and even streetcars. In 1945 there were about 500 inhabitants left and just a few townish stone buildings, among which were one hotel and the opera house. But then Mr. Paepcke got going, and chalets and cabins appeared left and right. In addition, a spacious, elegant, informal tent to hold several thousands was designed by Eero Saarinen, an excellent modern architect, for the holding of the conferences. Music festivals were started, and the conferences on design of which this year's was Number Three.

Mr. Paepcke himself uses design in the production of his forty-six factories, and he is idealist enough to use it everywhere with discrimination. Up at Aspen, for instance, lives Herbert Bayer, outstanding typographer and artist from the Bauhaus in its early days. To the conference of which I am speaking Max Bill was invited from Zürich. Another invitation—mine—was from England. The American contingent was remarkably international, too. My own name, I should say, was among the more easily pronounceable. Gyorgy Kepes, a Hungarian from Boston, for instance, was there, and Enrico Peressutti from Milan, one of the best Italian architects, and so on. Peressutti was in America to design a new shop for an Italian who takes his cultural responsibility seriously and whose buildings are as exemplary as the design of his products.

Manufacture and design was indeed one of the problems discussed at the conference. Another was the relations within one man of artist and designer, that is, free art as self-expression and design as an

Reprinted from *The Listener* (London).

aesthetic activity, directed to particular everyday purposes. Other problems were art and science on the highest level and design and technology on a more easily accessible level. All these topics might have been discussed in London as well.

What was different at Aspen? Well, first of all it was all remarkably informal. Much was done at so-called round tables—we would say brain trusts—with the familiar disadvantages of brain trusts, that is, the vagueness of the unprepared statement. It made it humanly more enjoyable but factually less profitable. For me, of course, it was ideal, for I wanted first and foremost to meet certain people, and this living together helped to do that. One went out on car trips. There were, of course, masses of cars, mostly of the bulgy American mouth-organ type; one of my own most hospitable experiences was of an open sports car of a highly successful Chicago designer with a staff of fifty, a sailing yacht, and a fine, big, handsome buccaneer presence. I loved him; he seemed as easily at home in a small discussion and in the deafening noise of the local night club, which latter, I am afraid, I could not take. After two hours of concentrated barrage, Peressutti and I pushed together and talked for the first time of the less acceptable sides of America. Youth is all very well—was it Oscar Wilde who said that her youth was America's oldest tradition— but this night club business has neither the grace of Paris or Rome nor the genuineness of Negro jollification, by which it is all the same so clearly influenced.

It is the same with many things. You buy a local newspaper and the main headline is "Bobo Rockefeller Outsmarts Husband." You buy a what I would call Penguin—that is, a twenty-five- or thirty-five-cent book—and it has (if it is not an imported Penguin) a glossy cover, and when I finally spotted *The Return of the Native* and bought it, it was called a classic novel of desire and betrayal, and on it you saw Eustacia in a very low-cut frock and bending far enough back to make that point sufficiently patent. And then there are the colored printed ties and, even more overwhelming, the colored printed shirts. They were quite popular even at the conference itself. Now you could not imagine English designers in wildly patterned shirts, could you? I am, as a matter of fact, quite ready to appreciate these shirts intellectually, and if that daring, that naive trust in novelty were not part of the American character, modern design of the best quality would not have made such spectacular progress in the last ten years—along, of course, with modern vile design. I daresay in a powerful nation the two must grow together. Britain is too timid in the popular field and too glued to genuine Georgian—or imitation Georgian, which is a form of timidity also. I had to try and analyze these different approaches a little at Aspen, with the result that the students who attended the conference gave me as a present the loudest shirt they could find. I wore it, too—sadly and sheepishly.

The students. Being bitten by the educational bug, I took over the conducting of a students' forum and made them work hard to arrive at statements a little more articulate than they would have otherwise. The audience seemed to like them in the end, and that was very noble of the audience. In form they were certainly less literate than they would be in a good English architectural school, where students without any doubt would have read more, but in content they were exactly the same: all very earnest, not a bit light-hearted, and all about society and responsibilities. One got the feeling that somewhere under a table Senator McCarthy was getting restless.

But on the whole the conference was happily free of politics. Now what were the highlights for me? First of all that wonderful contraption, the chair lift—a lift leading up some 4,000 feet, which you cover in iron chairs suspended from a wire cable. You sit down, they clap a slight bar in front of your waist, your feet stand on a small iron step like a rung of a ship's ladder, and that is all. Up you go, between the treetops, and above the treetops, exactly like a bird. In one place you are 120 feet from the ground. It is not a bit gruesome, just extremely exhilarating. Then, Highlight Number Two, gracing the conference with his presence was Bucky Fuller, or Buckminster Fuller, an architect of I suppose about sixty, adored by the students. He has spent some twenty-five years perfecting geodesic domes, domes of ever lighter materials carrying ever heavier loads. At the conference students erected one in about two hours, large enough for several hundred people to stand inside, so light that one student standing on a ladder could hold up the whole structure on a pole in the middle while others worked lower down. The dome was said to carry a snow load of 50,000 pounds. It sounds like wizardry, and Bucky is a bit of a medicine man, with an excessively obscure literary style. I daresay it is scientific, but I can never understand it precisely, and students certainly can't. But it all helps them to feel happy.

As Highlight Number Three, I think I ought to mention Charlie Eames, a youngish Middle West architect who now lives in California, with a delightful boyish face and a delightfully slow drawling speech. His fame started from the design of a chair, a type of chair that has since become a pattern for chair designers in many countries. He does not build much or design much. Indeed, he wants to please himself and considers work from that point of view. At the conference he showed some films he and his wife have made, and they were indeed among the finest of their kind I have ever seen. One was simply the play yard of a school they can see from their windows. It is hosed once a week, and all the film does in fifteen minutes or so is to show what the water does—drops, rills, streams, meandering, running, separating and uniting, forming drops or wavelets, and in the absence of anything to give scale, looking now like the wide ocean, now like the patterns in microscopic photos. Another short film (in color) was on bread, just wandering over the surfaces of loaves and rolls, and closely watching the breaking or the slicing of bread. It had the same sense of an eye adventure. These things, I think, are extremely valuable in an age of visual atrophy.

Extremely valuable, yes—but with one proviso. America tends anyway to regard picture information as a substitute for read informa-

17

tion, and does not England also? I am thinking of comic strips, of boys' papers, and so on. There is a tendency in America to think that a film on Egyptian art can take the place of books on Egyptian art, and that would be a disaster; for the volume of reading, literary and vocational, of the student in an American university is rather low anyway, I am told.

Are comments like these ungenerous to the conference that invited me? My listeners might well think so. Listeners in America would not. For the outspokenness of Americans is something that must be experienced to be believed.

As I boarded my plane to London, a man sat down next to me who, in spite of a rolled umbrella and hat from St. James's Street, turned out (after some superficially inquisitive conversation) to be a very successful American industrial designer with an office in London. I had known his work for nearly twenty years; he had read me. Well, when we found out who we were, he did not say "I have always wanted to have a chat with you to find out your point of view." He said: "I have always wanted to ask you what reason there should be for a guy like you to exist at all." It took me two hours in a well-stocked bar to explain, and would have taken more to convince. But it is on a platform of such exposedness that the designer and the manufacturer work in America, that they take risks, defend their positions, and in the end offer us, the public, a far higher volume of products for the house that are not the least bit hidebound in design. Our best designs may be more refined than theirs, but we have less, and certainly too few designs that pronounce frankly what century they belong to.

# Opening Remarks
# Will Burtin
# 1955

There are times in our lives when our heartbeats seem to quicken, when the intensity of events and the impact of thought raise our consciousness to the heights of new experiences from which new vistas open up. Gone are the doubts, and forgotten the silent hours of questioning, the many days of patient work. It all seems to have had purpose and logic in the end. One realizes that the principal motivation for going through with this ambitious endeavor is the desire for better understanding and the hope that by pooling our experiences and ideas we will have created better conditions for progress.

It seems to me that man is at his best and greatest when he looks up and beyond himself. Appreciating the reality of living through his senses, he has asked questions and tried to find answers ever since he rose from prehistoric times. The rapidity of his progress is intimately tied to social freedoms, which give him the climate in which he can present his ideas to his fellow searchers and fellow man.

We are here because we have questions. We are here because we want to test ideas that may be important to us and others. Whatever they may be, it is necessary that there be discussions, questions, and agreements which may carry in themselves the seeds of new questions already. This is the continuum of living—proceeding from question to answer to new question to new answer—in an unending chain of challenges and responses.

Thomas Jefferson stated once that education is a process in which we learn how to learn. I believe he would enjoy being here with us because his interests in philosophy and design, science and art, and the humanities parallel ours closely. To learn how to keep learning is the mark of civilized man, wherever we may look.

It is always a challenging, yet difficult task to evaluate what should and what should not be discussed here. We are living in a world which is not all good or all bad. Oversimplification and purity of a one-sided approach bring the dangers of a uniformity that is at striking variance with the diversity of living—a major source of progress.

Discussion is always based on controversy, often a bad word with some people. Yet it is axiomatic that controversy is an almost absolute essential of a working democracy as well as of any successful business. We must have moral stamina and a cool dollars-and-cents attitude in defending the need for seeking controversy even in issues where the need may not be apparent at first. And while we *must* give credit to achievement, we must never cease to question the expert. The lessons of history are too ample to permit ourselves the easy luxury of over-confidence in the established. The great discoveries in the arts and sciences have hardly ever come from the academy or university, but from a tax clerk in Switzerland, from a storekeeper in France, or a farmer in India, and many thousands of nonexpert people of goodwill, of insight, and profound thought.

In our professional work we tend to be engrossed with technical, psychological, and experience factors that of necessity limit the frame of reference on which we can draw for the inspiration that lies in larger perspectives. By reading the statements, by listening to the representations from the distinguished individuals appearing on the five panels we will expose ourselves to the thoughts and problems that they see when *they* think about our design and art profession.

As designers and artists we are daily and intimately connected with business activities, whose character in terms of social and economic ramification we must understand and appreciate. Yet in our lives we are also moved—and perhaps more profoundly—by broader issues of philosophy and an awareness of a need for experiment, for investigating directions of thought in which business as a commercial activity cannot assist, yet stands to benefit. To use business language: Before we sell something to business, we should know *what* we are selling. This cannot, of course, imply that we are uninterested in business, or arrogant, or naively unaware of its importance. On the contrary, the interest that many businessmen and concerns have in our design activities—from Walter Paepcke to Harry Baum, from Olivetti to Montecatini to the Upjohn Company and many others—cannot be praised too much and should be recognized especially in this setting.

The conference program itself went through many changes: Gropius, Eames, Mumford, and Shahn were enormously interested and agreed to come but found later that their work did not allow for a week's absence. The failing health of Wilhelm Wagenfeld of Germany, Luigi Nervi of Italy, and Lancelot Hogben of England, and the death of Einstein and the ensuing need for Hermann Weyl to execute Einstein's last will were other detaining factors.

*Crossroads: What Are the Directions of the Arts?* This title of the conference about to begin should be looked upon as more than a theme of five days of thought and discussion. It can be as well a symbol of our lives and endeavors. The crossroad quandary is *always* with us, as long as we live. It implies to us the challenge of choice.

Behind us, from where we come, are the tradition and accumulated values of the great human family, of many cultures, many professions, many trials, many errors. To the left and right stretch avenues of the sciences and arts, looked upon so often as separate entities, yet meaningless if not considered as two aspects of men's drive to give the reality of life measure and value. Forward we dimly perceive the dangers and opportunity of a new time, which we must approach with understanding and a positive philosophy.

A century has passed since Henry Adams predicted the downfall of our civilization because it would be unable to utilize cosmic instead of electric power without a new social order. Sigfried Giedion, the eminent art historian, draws a *result* line under the last hundred years of Western civilization with the statement that "mechanization takes command" in a book of the same title. Lewis Mumford sees our only future in the idea that "man must take command," that he must act now to make mechanization a servant of human welfare, not the master of his fate.

I am certain you will permit me, in concluding this address, to add a somewhat sentimental note. The five panel subjects that denote the procedures of the next five days have become something personal to me. They are like friends who have gone with me through a multitude of diverse situations—of strength and of trial—in the discussions with speakers and many other interested individuals and groups. Whether they will stand up to the final test that is yours is of deep concern to me, but now beyond my control. I give these friends to you, to your minds and hearts.

Ladies and gentlemen: The International Design Conference, the fifth in Aspen and the first permanently organized conference, is on its way.

# II  The Movies

The most complex and innovative art form of the technological century, film, has been an endless source of stimulation and bewilderment to designers. Staggering under the impact of television at the time IDCA was starting up, the movies were for the first time forced to take a straight look at themselves and their basic procedures. Veteran film, stage, and TV director John Houseman asks how they work, and Len Lye, experimental abstract moviemaker, asks where they stand. Both approach them from an essentially professional viewpoint.

# How Does a Movie Communicate?
## John Houseman
## 1955

The most compelling instrument yet devised for communication between human beings is the image of man himself. Animate this image; breathe life into it; let it move and talk at your bidding, within sight and hearing of an audience that is limited only by the size of our known world—and you have created a genie unequaled for potency and range in the history or in the imagination of the human race.

Two masters currently employ this genie: motion pictures and television. Very briefly, let us examine the uses they make of him; where they coincide and where they differ.

In one essential respect, television and motion pictures are alike. They both communicate by means of images—human images—projected upon a flat, framed surface and accompanied by the synchronized, though separately recorded, sound of the human voice. They vary technically in their methods of recording and projecting (the one electronically, the other mechanically; the one publicly, the other privately) a seemingly identical product.

But this identity is more apparent than real. Between television and movies, for all their constant overlapping of functions, there are certain deep and basic differences—aesthetic, operational, and historical.

TV was born full-grown as a mass medium, with the accumulated resources of the world's great communication systems behind it. Technically and functionally, it was an elaboration of radio, which, in turn, was conceived and originally utilized as an extension of the telegraph. In a most literal sense, therefore, television is a medium of communication.

Therein lies its strength. The nature of its electric transmission gives it a virtue all its own—the excitement of an unpredictable action recorded, transmitted, and witnessed by the viewer at the instant of its occurrence. The TV camera and its crew, recording and transmitting a scene, are at exactly the same point of observation, with precisely the same capacity for surprise, as you, the eventual viewer, seated before your TV screen. Add to this the very special and characteristic thrill to be derived from the knowledge that your emotions are shared, not only with the recording technicians but, simultaneously, with millions of other persons who are viewing and hearing the same event under conditions and from a perspective identical to your own. Here is a new and very special sense of mass participation. And it applies not only to the obvious suspense of a ball game or of a Congressional investigation but even more directly and potently to the sudden illumination communicated in a debate, in a speech, or in a casual interview by some particularly compelling or disturbing (or even commonplace) human being caught in a moment of revelation. Here again simultaneity, which is the essential and exclusive property of TV, plays a dominant part in the nature and intensity of the emotion that is communicated. It is something that motion pictures, by their very nature, do not and cannot achieve.

Movies have a very different and far humbler origin than TV. They started as a cheap sideshow with no audience at all beyond what they could snatch from the vaudeville houses and the shooting galleries. Created by gadgeteers and exploited by small businessmen, the cinema was never thought of as anything but a medium of entertainment. Beginning with the running horse and the jumping man, through *The Great Train Robbery* and the first agitated and trembling newsreels, to the full-blown epics of C. B. de Mille, the movies—short or long, comic or tragic—were created and marketed as dramatic entertainment. Historically and aesthetically, movies are a theatrical medium.

The statistical fact that, in the present state of the world's technical and economic development, movies play to audiences that are, in the aggregate, far more numerous than those that currently have access to television does not alter the fact that the *unit* of motion picture attendance is at all times limited and determined by theatrical considerations—from several thousand at Radio City and several hundreds in a drive-in to half a dozen or less at a private 16mm. home viewing. In each case, and for the duration of its running, a temporary and palpable community is formed among those who are physically gathered to view the film. This temporary community conditions the reactions of its members; repeated a billion times, it affects the nature of the medium itself.

So we have come, somewhat circuitously, to the question I was asked to answer here in the first place: How—and what—do movies communicate? Particularly our American movies, or "motion pictures," as Hollywood prefers to have them called.

One way to answer this is to take a look at the human elements involved. If you discover who made the pictures, you may also find out what they were trying to say—or you may not.

The passions behind a gold rush are confused and conflicting. And here in America, in those early days, while the film business was growing from a sideshow to a world industry, it *did* assume many of the characteristics of a gold rush. The professionals—the skilled prospectors—were few. Close on their heels came the adventurers: a wild romantic troop, violent and reckless, good for anything and for nothing in particular; actors, journalists, mechanics, and gamblers; some from the East, some from overseas, and some from nowhere at all; some educated, some almost illiterate; some middle-aged and some fugitives from college; all men of intense vitality, with nothing to lose; most of them without formal background, without preconceptions, and without inhibitions—they found in movies the perfect field for their semicreative, semicharlatanic energies. To them the medium was a vacuum in which they found themselves expressing their hopes, their nightmares, their prejudices, and their enthusiasms—all their own personal and collective versions of what constitutes entertainment.

Out of this hubbub, what *was* communicated? Energy and excitement: the moviemakers' contagious energy meeting the excitement of their audiences, most of whom had never been exposed to dramatic entertainment before, and who now rushed to meet them, uncritical and unreasoning, their eyes wide with wonder and gratitude, in this mythical and fantastic world of their mutual creation.

Many of the great names of motion pictures belong to this first wave of adventurers. With them, egging them on and sometimes impeding them, setting up the machinery for turning this great bonanza into an organized and profitable industry, came the businessmen—the promoters, the middlemen, the operators. For half a century, they and the moviemakers have lived in an intimate but ambivalent relationship.

Wherever movies are made this polarity exists, between an urge to create fine pictures and a gnawing preoccupation with their fate at the boxoffice. Between the men who make them and the men who sell them, it is the means that are at issue, not the end. Both want the same thing—audiences—and each is convinced he knows more about the public taste than the other. It is a tension as old as the movies. There is no creative picture-maker who has not, at one time or another, become deeply involved in this struggle between the artist and the businessman for control of his films. Many, like Griffith and Stroheim, were broken in the struggle and deprived forever of their means of production.

And it should not be supposed that right is always or entirely on the side of the artist. In a medium that has flourished so miraculously —"a business that is also an art form"—how much of the credit for this bewildering growth goes to the creators of films? How much to those who, by boldly exploiting their work, have developed the vast audiences that have made this creation possible? The truth is that they were all swept along by waves of technological advance and social change over which they had little control and from which they all profited. Chaplin's genius found freer expression and freer scope before a world audience of a hundred million than he ever could have realized on the stages of a few dozen variety halls. Conversely, how much did Chaplin's immediate and universal popularity contribute to the growth of this new public and to the phenomenal rise of the industry as a whole? Today, how much does the general health of the industry depend upon the risky stimulus of genius? How much upon the regular satisfaction of predictable appetites? How is originality to be measured against habit?

These are not easy questions to answer. Indeed, in this long and uneasy partnership between the businessman and the picture-maker, it is not always clear who is the progressive and who the reactionary. The picture-makers complain that if the businessman were allowed to have his way he would end up with a product entirely dominated by formula; that exhibitors and theater owners would like nothing better than a regular flow of bigger and better versions of what has succeeded before. Chronically suspicious of any intense or personal communication in films ("Is it entertainment?") the businessmen have consistently underestimated the public's ability to assimilate fresh emotional experience.

On the technological level the roles are reversed. Here it is the "businessman" who is the radical and the "artist" who tends to underestimate the public taste for change. In its brief history, three great technical revolutions have swept over Hollywood. All three were commercially inspired, all executed at the behest of the businessmen over the howling protests of the filmmakers. I am not suggesting that these protests were groundless. It has never been conceded, and it never will be, that a talking picture is better than a silent picture, or color more effective than black and white; nor is there any comparison, by any aesthetic standards whatever, between the harmonious proportions of the classic screen and the panoramic monstrosities of the present mode. Each one of these unwelcome changes was rushed through by the businessmen in a declining market, to anticipate the defections and stimulate the appetites of a fickle public. In each case the changes were followed by a sharp rise in aggregate business (which is all the businessman is concerned with), accompanied by an equally sharp drop in the quality of the films made under the new system. (It is a matter of ironic comment that of the films released in 1953 and 1954—two years in which the businessmen decided that color and large screens alone could save the industry—the two that received the highest rewards and made the most money were black-and-white, small-screen productions: *From Here to Eternity* and *On the Waterfront*).

When you view a movie today, you have to sit through almost two minutes of credits. To conform with union requirements, they include everyone from the hair stylist to the director. All these persons have, in some measure, contributed to the making of the picture. What it finally communicates is, in a very real sense, the sum of their collaboration.

Too often it is that and nothing more; what is communicated is a general tone of collective competence and a vague, not too sanguine hope that the picture will get by and pay for its overhead. Every year several hundred such pictures are produced in Hollywood. Of staple length and fairly predictable style and content, they are turned out more or less on schedule and with a fair expectation of aggregate profit. Hundreds more are made at varying costs and with varying degrees of efficiency in the other movie centers of the world.

Though they are the staples of our business, we need not concern ourselves with them here—but only with those movies, large or small, which bear clear evidence of personal expression and make some effort at vital communication. And the question to be answered is, in such cases, *whose expression and whose communication is it?* How is it realized? Who initiates and maintains the aesthetic tone of a motion picture? Who determines its content and controls its form?

Think of some of your own favorite movies. Go back quickly

over the list of the films you remember as having excited or moved you. On each one of these pictures—clear and unmistakable—is a signature. On many of them it is the signature of the director: the director performing not only the specific functions of his craft but also the wider and fuller functions of "moviemaker."

Since the director works at the very core of the project's activity, it is not surprising that, so often, he should also be its prime mover. His is the one essential and indispensable activity in filmmaking. He it is who executes the movie. At his command and in response to his personal energy the typed pages of script, the natural or constructed scenery, the lamps, the camera lens, the individual temperament, and the professional equipment of the actors and technicians are suddenly fused in that decisive and final act—the scene, whose sum constitutes a movie. That much every director must do; it is the specific duty for which he has been hired. It may be *all* that he does or is permitted to do. In that case the finished film reflects his creative personality in a very thin and limited way and communicates virtually nothing except a desire to keep his job. It does not concern us here.

You don't have to be a professional or even a movie fan to sense—when you see a picture by Hitchcock or Flaherty or Griffith or René Clair—that the director has done far more than stage the scenes. For better or for worse, the movie is *his:* His influence begins before the first word of the script is written, before the first actor is hired or the first set rough-drafted on the designer's board. And it does not stop till the last frame is cut and the last strip of soundtrack is transferred.

This is not intended as an advocacy of artistic dictatorship or a tribute to monomania. It is a sober realization of the absolute necessity of unity in an art form as mercurial as the motion picture. Making a movie *is* a collaborative act, but such collaboration functions effectually and freely only within the vital matrix of a well-integrated and unified creative whole.

How many times, in a movie, have you seen camera work that is proficient or even arresting, yet ineffectual and irritating in its irrelevance? Ask any cameraman who is not tired and timorous and he will tell you that photographing a picture with unity of style and a firm conception of its dramatic form is infinitely preferable to working on one in which he is left to his own devices.

This is true of every technical and creative element involved. It applies very specially to the actor. An actor cannot give a valid or rewarding performance unless he has been made clearly and firmly aware of the total form and final intent of the work in which he is called upon to play a part. Some actors have such strong individual magnetism that the only unity in which they can be integrated is that of their own personality. In that case it is *their* signature that the picture bears.

It certainly applies to the writer, who has always occupied a rather special and equivocal position in the movie world. For all their constant use of dramatic dialogue, movies are not a verbal medium, such as the theater or even TV. Movies are made, not written; a writer does not, properly speaking, write a movie script; he works on one. Therefore, he welcomes the opportunity to collaborate in an act of communication which he shares and approves, and in which good use can be made of his particular kind of imagination and skill. The desperate writer is the one who sits in his cell month after month banging out a script for a film of which he barely comprehends the form or the intention, one in which (as so frequently happens for lack of a firm and decisive structure) his dialogue will be expected to bear a load that words alone cannot possibly carry in an art form that is primarily visual. It is out of this despair, and out of sheer professional self-protection, that so many of the best writers have quit the business as writers to become moviemakers, by adding the functions of director and/or producer to those of their original craft.

For there are producers, too, whose signature may be found on your list. They are those few who have succeeded in turning their amorphous executive duties into a function of creative unification.

To the question, then, of who makes the movies there is, as you might have expected, no clear or simple answer. When you have analyzed and explained all the functional and organizational elements that go into the making of a motion picture, you still have not reached the heart of the matter, that unpredictable miracle of individual energy that is at the core of a movie's essential communication. It may take the form of technical perfection, as in the Japanese picture *Gate of Hell;* a range and an arrangement of color so exquisitely conceived and executed that it opens up a whole new area of visual pleasure. It occurs when a director, like Kazan in *East of Eden,* suddenly stimulates certain nerves and sets in motion certain patterns of feeling not frequently touched with quite that intensity; or when a writer, like Chayefsky in *Marty,* rediscovers simplicity. It may be a sudden, delightful sense of imbalance such as that conveyed by Jacques Tati as he moves with jaunty strides through the familiar yet unpredictable universe of *Mr. Hulot's Holiday.* It may be the emergence of a new personality of such beauty or vigor that, overnight, it creates a common mythology among audiences thousands of miles apart and with no other possible point of contact.

For such communications the movies, with their flexible and highly charged dramatic form, have always furnished a fruitful soil. It is disturbing, therefore, to note Hollywood's growing tendency to concentrate on the filming of material that has already proved itself successful in other media. According to a recent statement, "about eighty percent of our present motion picture output is based on published books, stories appearing in magazines with a national circulation, and produced stage plays."

Today, theatrical hits and best-selling novels are being acquired with little consideration for their cinematic possibilities, for no better reason, often, than that they *are* hits and best-sellers. With the gradual decline in the potency of the established star system, and considering the mass audiences' prevalent habit of concentrating their patronage upon a few hugely successful items to the neglect of all others, it may be sound merchandising for the sales and publicity departments to protect themselves with what is known in the trade as a "presold" product. But it threatens to turn Hollywood from a vital center of mass entertainment into a conversion plant or disseminating agency for other people's successes.

And that brings me, finally, to consider the *content* of our motion pictures. For reasons that are implicit in their origins and have multiplied with the years, American filmmakers have always been reluctant to inject controversial contemporary problems into their work. Save as an occasion for melodramatic action, our movies have remained comparatively unaffected by the shattering events of the past fifty years. The "neorealistic" movies that came out of Italy at the end of the last war; the revolutionary films made by the Soviets in the early 'twenties; the growing neurosis of German motion pictures (described by Siegfried Krakauer in *From Caligari to Hitler*), which found its culmination in the Nazis' epic nightmares of the late 'thirties—each of these film cycles, for better or for worse, directly reflects the political events and the mental climate of its own time and place.

Our nearest equivalent, I imagine, is the gangster film, from the badmen of the West, through Capone and *Murder, Inc.,* to the latest encroachments of the "syndicate." But it is hardly the same. Despite all the reproaches they have called down upon our heads—from well-wishers and ill-wishers alike—it is difficult to see in the endlessly repeated and long since formalized Hollywood gangster movie anything more significant than a regrettable, and apparently irremediable, national taste for violence in our entertainment.

What, then, is the total effect produced by our pictures? Is there, in fact, sufficient unity in our product to carry a consistent or perceptible ideological identity? In all these years, in all these thousands of films that we have made and shipped and shown in every inhabited corner of the globe—what *have* we been communicating? At home, because they are so closely in mesh with the general pattern of our lives, the communication of our movies is hardly separable from that of all the other social and emotional influences to which we are continuously exposed. Abroad, where they arrive as strangers, its nature becomes clearer.

I believe that, in certain ways, our films and the manner in which they are received follow those laws of energy which relate to the attraction of the greater mass. Inevitably, in the past forty years, our pictures have become identified with our position as the world's most rapidly growing unit of political and economic power. For negative as well as positive reasons, the peoples of the world are concerned with us; our presence is pervasive. The main functions of our films abroad are now to satisfy this curiosity and allay this preoccupation.

It has long been the custom to deride Hollywood films for their atmosphere of ostentatious display. The fact is that material luxury, in its most fancy and in its most practical terms, has always been an important element in our communication. To the fabulous palaces and the black marble swimming pools has succeeded the even more alluring spectacle of domestic elegance, the Dream Kitchen in every cottage and the Cadillac in every garage. In this respect, let's admit it, our movies' communication does not seriously differ from that of the advertising pages of *Life* or the *Saturday Evening Post,* except that, being dramatically presented, the siren message of material well-being is delivered by a film with a far higher degree of personal identification. To some, our films are objectionable flauntings of our good fortune; to many more, they furnish a temporary, if illusory, escape from the bitter realities of want.

Luxury and energy—if these were all we communicated in our movies, it would be a disturbing and discouraging thought. I hope there is something more, something inevitably related to these two but which, in some small measure, transcends them. I believe that, in an uncertain way, our films—for all their violence, their frequent vulgarity, and their occasional inanity—do carry to the far ends of the earth a residue of something more. It is not easy to define. It has to do with goodwill and with those rights of man mentioned in our Declaration of Independence; it has to do with the endless horizon and the open frontier which played such a vital part in our brief history; it has to do with the stereotypes of "individual enterprise" and "unlimited opportunity," which, for all their abuses and corruptions, still determine the dynamics of our society. For all that it is largely unspoken and partly unrealized, I like to think that there is communicated by our motion pictures some vague reflection and some weak echo of the American Dream.

# Is Film a Fine Art?
## Len Lye
## 1959

Advanced art and basic science have common social values. For example, in their application to environment. The graphic arts sharpen standards in applied design, and the sciences increase everyday standards of living. A second shared characteristic is that works of art and scientific works both result from a search for truth, the *emotional* truth of great art and the *factual* truth of great scientific discovery.

In this sense we can examine the relatively new medium of film. This medium has not, apparently, attracted and held the creative attention of the calibre found in other mediums. There are great films, just as there is great jazz, but both are usually felt to be great in the folklore and nostalgic, rather than in the classic, self-sufficient, continually fresh, deeply true, or absolute sense.

The durability of value in a great art object, such as a cathedral, sculpture, painting, poem, musical work, and so on, is due, in my opinion, to the philosophically insular content of detached individuality it portrays. Over and above subject matter and medium, culture and epoch, this biologically founded and psychologically transposed content of evolutionary individuality is symbolically portrayed and is extra-sensorily responded to because, no matter what our temperament and background may be, the work carries the impress of something we each carry in every cell of our body, namely, the evolutionary gene pattern of individuality. The artistic impress of evolutionary individuality seems to symbolically record its reproductive *end* in essence of itself rather than to signify its reproductive *means,* such as good husbandry, prowess, might, and so on. But, whatever this content in a work, as an expression of evolutionary individuality may be, it would seem to be symbolically represented and emotionally communicable in lasting aesthetic works. They possess a detached self-sufficiency of emotional content; a refined essence of being; a spiritual quality that endures. Generations of people *feel* that the content exists in this cathedral, that painting, composition, poem, appreciate the portrayal of the problems of evolutionary individuality in tragedy, and so on.

Works of art would seem to epitomize a durable form of self-sufficient completion; that is, a satisfying image achieved in respect to an attitude to create and finalize. Brancusi stated this epitome as follows: "Don't look for obscure formulae and mystery. It is pure joy that I bring you," and Matisse stated that he sought to express serenity.

Artists working in their craft may not necessarily think in terms of beauty and serenity. They may as readily be concerned with creating an effective image that would seem to require appreciation simply as effectiveness for its own sake, in affirmation of the experience of life and, as in theater and great novels, in an awareness of the inexorable nature of individuality and the causes of tragedy. Film is the Cinderella of the fine arts. Her beauty lies in her "kinesthesia." This is the basic element of abstract expression prevalent in twentieth-century fine arts. "Kinesthesia" is from the Greek *kinein* (move) and *aisthesia* (perception). This Cinderella is still waiting for her glass slipper in order to enthrall with her unique kinetic beauty.

The graphic arts have been visibly exploring the direct sensory appeal of both light and motion, which, naturally, must be simulated as part of their aesthetic. A decided advantage of film is that these two qualities are an integral part of it.

As a filmmaker I am, of course, begging the question, therefore an elaboration on the relation between the experience of kinesthesia and its symbolic isolation and expression in the fine arts would help to establish a logic for critical understanding of film as a fine art form. As follows:

Film, like any other medium of expression, can only contain lasting value as a work of art to the degree it carries, communicates, and stimulates degrees of the experience of individuality. For example, effects of kinesthetic empathy, such as the roller-coaster sensations exploited by Cinerama, remain mere sensation devoid of philosophic content concerning human values. They remain unrelated to our evolutionary depth. Nevertheless, these Cinerama effects, like Coney Island, remain good folklore fun.

*Film as Fine Art*. We enter highly conjectural and abstruse areas of art criticism when we try theoretically to get to the roots of art from either the psychological or the aesthetical modes of evaluation. Whatever definitions of the aesthetic emotion we may prefer (such as its "spiritual" quality or the kinesthetically sensory heightening of perception to the symbolic "essence" of evolutionary individuality), neither the imagery of classic realism in which the art subject matter depicts the protagonist nor the newer areas of abstraction in which the painter's individuality (as represented by the style of the work itself) becomes the protagonist is more fit than the other to establish lasting social value for a work.

The artist's lifelong dedication to achieving aesthetic standards of self-sufficient value within the conventions he accepts is an intensely absorbing, emotional, and idealistic experience. The content of this emotion is carried in the art object he creates. It represents his version of such experience. And it would seem to be communicable to others irrespective of what type of imagery, subject matter, and medium is chosen. The constancy of such philosophical content throughout the emotional experience and expression of humanity, not only in the arts but also in relations and behavior, is our reason for saying that there is nothing new under the sun.

The increasingly pronounced kinetic quality of twentieth-century art evokes a sensory rather than an intellectual involvement. We react to its imagery with sensory immediacy rather than conceptual analysis. It is as if the action of our physical sensations, such as spatial orientation, nerve-muscle sense of presence—in bodily poise, weight, stress, juxtaposition, and so on—creates an unconsciously felt immediacy between our inner-outer communications, with aspects of personal existence common to all. It would further seem that the sensation of the organic act can become psychologically identified with the imagery of art objects without necessarily having the imagery depict literally descriptive aspects of everyday realism.

We infer the orienting power of bodily sensation when we say we must pinch ourselves to see if we are awake. Some of our activities have been cultivated purely for kinesthetic enjoyment, such as dancing and sports. It follows that immobility, stillness, quietude have a contrapuntal effect on our senses of motion as silence emphasizes sound.

A Hiroshige woodcut makes us aware of the power and weight of a curled mighty wave about to break; we feel an emphatic response to the decorative grace of a bird elegantly poised on a branch; we respond equally emphatically to the taut spatial relationships of a Cézanne painting; we may almost quiver to the ecstatic stillness of a Zurbarán still-life—as equally we do to the glowing candescences of the Impressionists.

In almost inverse proportion to twentieth-century rejection of the classically realistic and the literally appearances-descriptive in art has been the acceptance of the kinetic or kinesthetic experience itself. It would seem as if this element has been unconsciously isolated in contemporary creative minds as one that is more important than any other for direct symbolic portrayal.

The sister arts are no less involved: the works of Schoenberg, Webern, middle-period Bartok, and our continuing pioneers in great music show this, just as does Stravinsky's statement to the effect that serious music of the future would eschew melody as we know it. Melody is perhaps allied to the psychological use of literalness to associate various aspects of compositional form and, it seems, the evocation of emotionally charged intuitive responses occurs more readily through the senses than through the intellect.

In literature we also find comparable examples. The word effects of Stein, Joyce, and others in prose; Hopkins, Rimbaud, Thomas, Cummings, and others in poetry; the nonprotagonism of Kafka in the novel and the anticlassicism of Beckett in the theater and the novel all add their weight to the break from the Cartesian dictum: "I *think* therefore I am." This seems to have been altered to read: "I *feel* therefore I am."

I believe the kinesthetic developments going on in the arts will seesaw back and forth with increasing emphasis on the kinetic. Film, or some technological equivalent to it, will be found to be one of the most telling forms of its expression.

*The Social and Industrial Value of the Experimental Film.* Industry has found it essential to sponsor basic science for technology. In the great, emphatic area of screen-presentation usage it will be found essential to sponsor creative experimentation in film.

Creative specialization in the experimental film will seep down into current programing both at the movies and at home on television.

Developments in screen techniques for the portrayal of live-action stories is long overdue. There have been none whatsoever since David Wark Griffith incepted the present-day technique at the birth of folklore movies. When he died both René Clair and Alfred Hitchcock, among others, pointed out this fact.

A current instance of the application of basic, or fine art, cinema to the popular, or folklore, screen fare was mentioned when Stephen Bosustow, of UPA *McBoing-Boing* fame, in a lecture on animation at the Museum of Modern Art, stated that he and his colleagues "were cribbing from McClaren ten years ago." UPA's Robert Cannon makes the most pronounced kinetic entertainment cartoons, as does Norman McClaren in fine art animation. In turn, the influence of UPA's cartoon standards on the plethora of television commercials is seen with some relief by entire nations—our own, Great Britain, Japan, and others.

In general, so much television programing is presented on a level of literally explicit communication that our more intuitive wit of discerning implications of meaning—which can only be sensed poetically—becomes somewhat stultified. There is danger that the use of television as an educational device may dull rather than stimulate the sensibilities of the student.

Of all fine art media, film is the only one that cannot get off the ground when it comes to notation of an original concept. For example, leaders in contemporary fine art in all media except film, no matter how advanced they may be, eventually find understanding, performance, and presentation of their work and, if they remain alive, sponsorship and institutionalized support. But the best films do not get made.

To repeat, a film concept can only be recorded in film, there are no other means for its exact notation. A Crystal Palace can be conceived on a sheet of blotting paper, a Van Gogh painting on an old sack, a poem on the back of an envelope, a dance choreographed for future presentation, and so on; but there is no way of notating the kinetic effects of a film concept other than in film itself.

The experimental filmmaker follows the ephemeral notion of his concept by shooting any aspect he fancies and, out of an assemblage of shots, edits down to the essence of his creative idea. In other words, he "messes around" until the bones of his idea, in the form of his shots, begin to take shape. This fine art approach to film is aptly termed "experimental."

(Home-movie makers are also experimental, but there are few titans in their ranks; perhaps they don't mess around enough.)

An experimental film, to have value as such, must possess style and "kinesthetic" aesthetic and, just as the appreciation of any of the contemporary arts requires time and application before we can discern standards of aesthetic value, so similar application is required before we can feel our way around in this variegated area of the arts.

American industry is at present deeply involved in show business. Investment in creative film experimentation can add kinetic sparkle and vitality to industry's theatrical window-dressing of name and product; but neither industrial leaders, private art sponsors, nor foundations can be found to give effective sponsorship of free fine art film development. There would seem to be neither appreciation of the basic nature and value of this work nor understanding of the problem that, of all media of art, the experimental film alone requires prior financing before a creative concept can be produced.

Government sponsorship for the experimental film seems to be the only way to overcome our social blind spot to its value. The governments of Canada, Great Britain, Poland, and other countries have established precedents for this. No doubt they assume that, culturally and commercially, both the public and industry will profit from investing public funds in the development of the truly twentieth-century fine art form of the experimental film.

With reference to the arts in general, the continuous drive of humanity to seek the fullest powers of individuality becomes reflected in its social evolutionary values, such as learning and the arts.

The good husbandry implicit in the positive social survival values of technology gives us, among other devices and services, the media of film and television as the most emphatic mediums of communication for inducing an immediate psychological involvement. But it will always be the creative artist, supplementing science, learning, and technology, who gives us emotional symbols that convey the depth and greatness of our common evolutionary drives.

General appreciation of great scientific discoveries of *factual* truth is always transferred to newer discoveries. The value of the discovery, as a scientific work, diminishes with time.

The value of great artistic discoveries in emotionally charged *symbolic* truth increases with time. The greatness of a work of art is proved only by generations of response to its quality. In this respect film as fine art has no terms of reference to "greatness" and unless it finds adequate sponsorship it possibly never will.

# III  World Without Instruction Manual

Bernard Benson, now aristocratically remote from the worlds of technology and design, was one of the whiz kids of early IDCAs as well as a pioneer of the electronics industry. Here, in characteristic style, he beats the hell out of a handful of metaphors to transform a perfectly obvious point into a flash of illumination.

# Leisure
## Bernard S. Benson
## 1955

An island inhabited by natives is suddenly blessed with a bevy of washing machines; electricity too, of course. There are washing machines in abundance but no manufacturer's operating manuals, nor in fact any statement as to what the machines are for. Over a period of time, one tribe comes to the conclusion that the machine is for kneading dough, makes very fine bread in fact, and they are very happy. Another tribe decides that the machine was created for separating the corn from the husks and is very well satisfied. Another group decides that the purpose of the machine is to keep the babies of the tribe happy while the mothers work. The babies are put on the inside, of course, and the mothers stay on the outside. (The machines are slowed down for the purpose.) Mixing paint and making pea soup are the obvious purposes of the machine to other tribes, and everybody in his conviction is very happy. Nobody, incidentally, has thought of using it for washing clothes.

A standard World Operating Manual, which is universal, clear, and unquestionable, did not come with the product, and as a result the customers in different groups and at different times have evolved their own.

Because of this wide diversity of human objectives and goals, it is difficult to establish criteria for the evaluation of any creative activity. Although one cannot find a common denominator at the cause level, it seems that one can find it at the effect level, and here there is universal accord that it is desirable to achieve "happiness," although the paths that lead to this effect vary tremendously among people and at different times and may often be diametrically opposed.

It is a very common human failing to pick, with surprisingly little consideration, some factor we believe will lead to happiness and then to chase this thing madly for the remainder of our days, having completely lost sight of our original objective. Financial wealth is one of the most common paths supposed to lead directly to happiness, and leisure is another. We have a marked tendency to struggle blindly to capture the elusive leisure nymph, and if we don't kill ourselves in the effort we often find that we have no idea what to do with it once we have it.

There is undoubtedly a path from automation to leisure and a path from leisure to happiness, but it will not be without careful thinking that we will go with assurance from automation to happiness. Let us not be deceived. Automation is not just the advent of more sophisticated gadgetry. It is potentially to the office worker, the factory assembler, and many other groups what the steam shovel was to the ditch digger.

A combination of the mechanization of brawn and the mechanization of brain provides the foundation for the first major effort on a wide scale to break the direct relationship between productivity and man's time. Looking ahead, we see the possibility of productivity's going off in one direction while the use of man's time is free to go off in some other direction.

There are three outlets for the increased productivity promised by automation: greater output, more leisure for all, or all leisure for some. The careful choice of the balance of these three outlets is in itself a very interesting subject. As we see the tremendous strides made in automation during the past ten years, and extend this progress over the coming twenty years, we know without a doubt that we will have the opportunity of participating in some of these choices.

Science is busy designing leisure-producing machines. Now is the opportunity to build leisure-to-happiness converters.

We are often called a progressive society. What this really means is that we are unhappy unless we are progressing. In other words, the mechanism inside us which senses whether we should be happy or not is not an altimeter but a rate-of-climb indicator. There are many societies throughout the world where people can pass a life in happiness and satisfaction given a steady, unchanging standard of living adequate for their particular needs. Leisure for them is an asset. It provides time to sit in the shade of a tree and sleep in satisfaction.

In our civilization we have a tendency to seek new and greater sensations at an ever increasing rate, and an activity or an event tends to be evaluated by its "est" factor. It has to be the biggest or the smallest or the loudest or the fastest or the brightest of anything yet done in order that we should not become unhappy for lack of progress. Music in the home, walks down a country lane, fireside talks have all become somewhat of a lost art.

With the advent of automation, it is not hard to imagine a system evolving as follows. The work of ten is done by one and the one works to support the other nine in questionable leisure. These other nine are attached to nine sensation-producing television sets and are allowed to "wear out" by a natural process of living, at the end of which period they are junked.

It may well turn out that it takes as long to train people to convert leisure into happiness as it does to complete many of the development facets of automation, that is to say, about twenty years. If this is so, then the problem is with us today.

Automation and the arts are natural marriage partners which can produce happy children, but the marriage will not happen by accident.

# IV  Man-made Environment

It may surprise some readers to discover that the environmental preoccupations of the 'fifties were so like those of the 'seventies, but the men who spoke at Aspen were, in a very direct sense, the teachers of the teachers of the generation who made themselves heard as the 'sixties ended. Paul Rudolph was just about to enter his period of greatest influence as chairman of the architecture department at Yale, and Henry-Russell Hitchcock was at the height of his powers as the world's most influential historian of modern architecture.

And Max Frisch? That mordant Swiss dramatist had started life as an architect, then turned to the wider human scene. In his words there is a humanity and moral bite that can be far more unsettling than the slogan shouting of later years—if only because they provide no easy emotional outlets as substitutes for constructive action.

# Why Don't We Have the Cities We Need?
## Max Frisch
## 1956

Most of us live in cities and enjoy every chance of escaping into the country. Why? Because we are happy to get away from our cities. Does that mean we do not have the cities we need to feel really at our ease in these modern times? That would be pretty bad, for millions of people are forced to live in cities, and not all of them get invitations to visit the Rocky Mountains.

As you know, all European cities were founded and their layout fixed long before motorization was even dreamed of. They were very well designed to meet the needs of people who went about their business on foot or used horse-drawn vehicles. Most citizens were tradesmen or craftsmen and lived where they worked. So they had no idea of the shuttle traffic between home and work that turns our cities into witches' caldrons four times, or at least twice, a day.

There is no need for me to give you a description of those medieval towns, which were actually fortresses. You all know them, at least from pictures. Indeed, it will not be long before we, too, shall know them only from pictures. For we moderns living in the cities we have inherited from our forebears have developed needs that those cities are less and less able to meet. And these vital needs are forcing us not merely to extend the limits of our cities but to destroy their very heart—if bombs have not done so already.

To console us there are cities like Florence or Munich or Paris, which are saved by their worldwide renown, or Siena and Rothenburg, whose very smallness keeps them intact. They make up the category of beautiful cities we can still show American tourists. But it is a category without a future, for as time goes on they will be less and less capable of coping with the tasks that the future will set them. They are in the process of becoming museums where everything is beautiful and nothing is of any practical use.

To dismay us, instead, there are cities like the Frankfurt of today —congeries of modern, or merely modernistic, multistory buildings, all of which have the bad luck to stand where medieval gabled houses once rightly stood. What I mean is that the rise of a modern city is impeded precisely by the presence of these modern buildings. The same thing can be seen today in all European countries, and it is a joke that does not make anyone laugh.

Frankfurt was dreadfully damaged by bombs. The inner town in particular was practically razed to the ground. Yet the layout of the old town, which will never arise from its ruins, was preserved and the old streets are now lined with new buildings. Strangely enough, the cathedral—the focal point of the old town—seems to be no longer in its former position. Of course it has not been moved, but a suburban settlement has been built at its feet. And it is funny to see a cathedral in a suburb.

To put it briefly, the hopes that wartime destruction would offer a unique opportunity for building rational new cities in Europe did not materialize. Perhaps I should say: "Thank God for that!"—otherwise it might be used to justify the production of new bombs. What a decade of reconstruction has achieved is a monument to incredible industry, especially in Germany, but it is not town planning.

And how are things in my own country, Switzerland? No bombs fell on us, or hardly any. A young man from Texas or Nevada, unaccustomed to such small countries, did drop a dozen rather heavy bombs. The United States immediately paid up a few million dollars to cover the damage. A very friendly gesture but not enough to start town planning.

What I should like to say about Switzerland is that we are doing our own destruction. We are not mad enough simply to tear down our venerable old towns to make room for modern cities. We are far madder; we widen one street after the other to make them safe for pedestrians because motor cars keep multiplying like rabbits—our public squares are only architectural at dawn, for the rest of the day they are mere parking lots—and then we erect multistory buildings that hold more people and so bring more traffic into the medieval streets. Then we invent a labyrinth of one-way streets that make our life miserable; and even that is no use. In the end we have to remove the medieval fountains, widen the streets again—though even that will not do much good—and so on, until we have destroyed the town our forefathers left us without building the city for our future descendants.

There you have the situation in a nutshell. If man were a rational being, what would he do about it?

Everyone knows that architects are chock full of ideas. There is no lack of genial projects drafted by Le Corbusier, Gropius, Neutra, Wiener and Sert, Samona, and many others. And when we study them, we cannot help being amazed. For these projects are not only capable of satisfying the vital demands of our life today but would even be more economical than anything that is being done at present. Then why are they not realized? That is the question that preoccupies me most. Are democracy and planning two things that mutually exclude each other? Or, to put it differently, who is really responsible for the formation or deformation of our cities?

One fine morning, when I was still an architect, I saw an open field, almost the last surviving field on the bank of the Limmat (which is the Hudson of Zürich). I love my home town and made the following suggestion: The municipality should purchase the field that I had been offered; we should found a cooperative society for an artists' settlement; the municipality would keep the title to the land and so be able to dispose of it in time to come, and we would merely rent it. That would prevent one of the last green fields on the river bank from being devastated by a real estate speculator. So I went to the Town Planner. "That's not a new idea", he said. "We wanted to do the same thing long ago. Go to the Mayor and tell him I agree." The Mayor also agreed. "I want the city to take the opportunity to buy the land while it is still for sale at a reasonable price. Go and tell the Town Planner I agree."

But it was already too late! Thirty-six cents a square foot was the price I was asked. The city offered forty; an anonymous speculator bid forty-five; the city agreed, so the speculator raised it to fifty. The Town Council saw how important the lot was for the town plan and accepted the price. The speculator went up to fifty-five. And so on until he got it at last for sixty-four cents a square foot. And now it is being built up on that basis and exploited without the slightest regard for, and in defiance of, all the laws of town planning we learned at school.

What is the lesson of my story?

The ground on which our cities are built has become a trading commodity. In Zürich, a town of 400,000 inhabitants, the annual profit on this commodity—which, after all, is no mere commodity but our land, our fatherland—is in excess of 20 million dollars. Where does that profit come from? Who pays it? The answer is: the inhabitants, the tenants, at a rate of fifty dollars a year each. That is not right, but I don't want to take it tragically. Let them have it, the few who still refuse to believe that money does not give happiness. But I should like to ask another question. Is it right that those few who care only for profit should plan our cities? They do so, in fact; and, as we have seen, it is a catastrophe.

Why do I prefer to live in an ancient hovel of the old town or in a village? Indeed, I am actually on the point of buying an old, old house in a little medieval town. Why? Our town planning—which is really no planning at all—estranges our towns and us. As I see it, all these settlements are ghettos for different income groups. The neighborhood is not a cross-section of the whole society. The fact that all the people who live in it have more or less the same monthly salary does not make for unity but only for uniformity. In my genuine city, instead —and I mean the sort of city that used to exist and that we must build again—I have neighbors of all sorts, both richer and poorer than myself: a lawyer, a chimney-sweep, a large family, an eccentric recluse, a toper who beats his wife, a trusty policeman, a butcher richer than all the rest of us together, a girl who had a lot of nocturnal visitors, and even a singing teacher who gets on my nerves. And yet I feel better and closer to life in its many aspects when I am surrounded by a neighborhood that is lively and real than in any income-bracket ghetto, however comfortable. The fate of our society depends to a great extent on whether we solve the neighborhood problem or not. I am not surprised that town planning as understood at present is incapable of finding the solution. For it is not based on a democratic order of society but on real estate speculation, and that cannot be called planning but rather the exploitation of development.

Here is another question. Who is really responsible for the development of our cities? The architect? Or the local authorities? Or the land owners? Or the whole body of citizens? I come from a country that I love insofar as it is a democracy and hate when it falls short of it. And I believe in the responsibility of the citizens. In other words, we have the cities we deserve.

How was it in the days when real cities were built? A prince— and that means a layman—set the problem, and the architect solved it. Of course I don't want to have the princes back again! But the same principle applies to a democracy: It is for the layman and not the expert to set the problem; the expert's job is to solve it. If we replace the word "layman" with "citizens" or "society," we obtain the following axiom: Town planning is far more a political than a technical question.

We cannot build for the past, and we want to build for the future. How are we to do it? So that we shall feel just as much at home as our forebears did in their cities.

Why do I feel more at home in Venice than in Chicago? Or, to put it more politely, why am I happier on the piazza of Santa Fe than on San Francisco's Market Street? I like just strolling about. It is one of the marks of a good city that I am glad to stop there and that I go there even if I have no business to do. The city should be a meeting place. For instance, I would hardly go to Wall Street if I hadn't any money, for after office hours Wall Street is a grave. But I do go to the piazza in Venice or Santa Fe—just to stroll about, look at the people, and perhaps meet someone. I wouldn't call it a stroll when the red lights keep pulling me up in my tracks or I am forced to hurry across the street just because the crowd does so at the beck of a green light.

Walking distance is the basic principle. Even Paris I can only feel on foot. A gallery, a bar, a cathedral, a barbershop, the library, the river, a bank, a florist's shop, the tax collector's office—they must all be within the orbit of my whim, within walking distance. For if I have to get into my car or take a public conveyance to reach a definite goal, that involves a decision. And when I have made my decision and climbed into my car I can see a lot of people who get in my way, but I feel quite alone. To stroll means to be close to people, a pedestrian among pedestrians. That makes me a member of society. I can stop when I see an attractive girl and stare into the same shop window.

Why are we losing all this?

That is easily explained. Traffic, already now and still more in the future, needs a lot of room—many times as much room as our old European cities, which were built for pedestrians, can give it. And if we let traffic have all the room it needs, the result will be that our cities will stretch out until they are no longer cities. Los Angeles is an example of this. Once I drove on and on hoping against hope to reach Los Angeles; at last I decided that I had missed it and had passed it by an hour ago. And all the time I was right in the middle of it. But Los Angeles has no middle, no inside! There are only houses, streets, gardens, streets, garages, more houses, more streets, gas stations, drug stores, cinemas, gardens, streets, houses, streets, gardens—until at last, thank God! the desert starts. It is the Tower of Babel tumbled down and strewn over umpteen square miles in a hundred thousand fragments.

Is this inevitable? That would be sad indeed.

If the alternative is so logical that no architect who reflects can help hitting on it, why hasn't it been realized long ago?

Because it can only be realized by founding a new town, or at least a new city.

Where are the founders to be found?

Three of us—a young historian, a young political economist, and myself—made an attempt to smoke out the founders a year ago. We published a pamphlet called "Look Out, Switzerland!" In it we mocked our towns. We jested over the disparity between the wealth of money and the dearth of deeds. We abused our political parties for being mere trading companies interested only in sharing momentary profits and challenged them to become political parties once more, namely, bearers of ideas, and so turn politics into a productive struggle to build our future. We abused society because it was no longer a society but a slave of the technocrats and urged it to get into a huddle and define the problem to be solved by the experts. We demanded the foundation of a new city somewhere in Switzerland, not as an architectural experiment (as I already said, the ideas have been framed long ago) but rather as a political experiment. We wanted to prove that democracy is capable of solving the problems of today.

What was the result of the publication?

Jeremias Gotthelf—a Swiss country preacher and one of the greatest epic poets in the German language—once said: "If you throw a stick into the pig sty, the sow you hit squeals." And that is just what happened. Squeals were heard from all sides. We sold ten thousand copies in two months and received thousands of answers, 90 per cent of them positive. Then came a barrage from the press, 70 per cent negative. Why was that? We asked for a proof that our democracy was really alive. Did that makes us Communists? We became the talk of the town for a day, and that was the end of it. But not quite. That same year several municipalities wrote saying they would welcome the task of adminstering the new city. Those same newspapers that had nothing but hard knocks for us during the first round wrote about town planning as never before. And from all over Switzerland and Germany we received invitations to lecture on the new city. The parties we had abused took the new city as the subject of their next meetings. The People's University started a course on the new city. A group of planners and students founded an association for the promotion of the new city —and we ourselves are curious to see the result.

It has already had one important result.

The idea of founding a city is a very uncomfortable one. For anyone who merely considers doing so cannot avoid making decisions that stretch far beyond the sphere of architecture, decisions of a political nature. Founding a city means choosing a form of life. Once out in the wide open spaces, we are stripped of all the excuses we had in our old towns, where we could always say our hands were tied. It makes us very embarrassed. Do we really know what we want? One cannot plan a city unless ones knows what sort of society will live in it. In other words, in ultimate analysis what interests us is not to have a city as attractive as all the models we have seen, but first and foremost to have a society capable of solving the problems of our age. And town planning is only one of those problems, though an important and particularly obvious one.

The mayor of a German town said to me: "It's a wonderful idea, Mr. Frisch, but take my advice. Build your city without asking the people how they want to live; build it and then, if you really must, make room for democracy." That is exactly what we do not want. We want the new city to be the product and expression of a social and sovereign democracy. That is what we boast of being every day, and we have got to prove it—for instance, by building that New City.

# Landscape and Cityscape
# Henry-Russell Hitchcock
# 1955

Both landscape and cityscape are unwieldy entities not readily shaped by the conscious hand of man. Here in the Rockies, it is at first hard to realize that landscape is much affected by man. But certain mining towns evidently have a very different physical setting from what they started out with because of the extent of earth-moving operations. Generally, perhaps, such considerable modification of the landscape is for the worse, and it is easy to arrive at the view that landscape only suffers from man's intervention, except where it gives way to or includes a formed cityscape. Deforestation, reforestation, major shifts in crops, irrigation projects, especially the dams that create artificial lakes—all such things drastically affect the landscape. But even mere occupation by man cumulatively modifies natural setting. It is also possible that this modification may be consciously controlled, if not by one designer, at least by the continuing tastes of several successive generations. Thus the straight rows of trees that line so many of the roads of France become a positive man-made feature of the landscape, and in England a hundred years of large-scale gardening activity in an increasingly "naturalistic" mode reformed the character of very large districts. Man's intervention is, therefore, neither rare nor necessarily deleterious.

Yet the standards by which to judge such intervention, with the weight of approval so long favoring the wild and untouched only, and even more the principles that ought to control human modification of the landscape, where and when such modification is necessary, are not easy to arrive at. Even if they were, it is not evident that society would accept them, since the forces that lead to major modifications of the natural scene are generally powerful and almost wholly the result of practical considerations. Fortunately, some of the most conspicuous changes, such as are introduced by the building of great dams and the formation of lakes behind them, are generally rather happy in their results. Since there are plenty of other canyons without dams in them, one need certainly not regret the dam in Shoshone Canyon in Wyoming; and in various barren landscapes in the West artificial lakes, whose contours are after all natural except on the dam end, provide notably fine individual features.

The major difficulties concerning man's intervention in the landscape do not seem to arise from major operations. Even deforestation, after long periods of time (as in Greece and Italy), while markedly changing the visual scene, does not necessarily ruin the landscape. It is the insidious piecemeal impingement of man upon the landscape in those vague areas which have ceased to be predominantly natural and yet have never received even the half-unconscious control that produces a cityscape that are most open to criticism. Worse, this is doubtless a matter beyond all human ordering.

Every age has had its *fiat* cities where cityscapes are made to order. Moreover, the characteristic pattern of all the most memorable cityscapes has generally been the creation of a relatively short period, if not of a few hands only. The Edinburgh we know was almost completely created in the century following 1760. The characteristic New York of the clustered skyscrapers took on its present form in the first few decades of the twentieth century. In the one case, two or three architects, first Adam and then several others, played a significant role. In the other case there were perhaps no individuals whose contribution was especially important, down at least to the designing of Rockefeller Center.

The creation of cityscape is man's most total modification of landscape. But great cityscapes generally owe something to the landscape they have supplanted. Venice on dry land is inconceivable; and the way San Francisco carries its gridiron over the hills of its site against the background of the Bay and the Golden Gate dramatizes the relentlessness of human city-building at the same time that it makes obvious the extreme importance of site. From Pittsburgh to Rio de Janeiro (the two cities could hardly be more different) the truth is evident that the canalization of city growth that is forced by difficult problems of terrain, problems that have to be solved by tunnels and bridges and other major surgery upon the setting, is the best insurance of a result that will have positive and individual character.

Two of the greatest architects of our time have had very opposed views on the subject of the city. Le Corbusier's vision of 1922 of a city of regularly spaced towers contrasts sharply with Wright's Broadacre City of a decade later. Neither conception has carried the day, nor is either likely to be realized by its protagonist. Chandigarh, however it comes out, will be very unlike its principal architect's vision of a generation ago, and Wright will certainly never build a town like or unlike Broadacre City. Partly through cultural convergence, partly through the notable influence of brave ideals vigorously formulated, however, both the Corbusian and the Wrightian cities are with us, at least partially, in the mid-twentieth century. The emergent cityscapes of our day, whether they are the result of building from scratch or merely of large-scale reconstruction, are notably different from those of the earlier decades of the century. At the base of the newly cleared Golden Triangle in Pittsburgh we can see the spaced skyscrapers of Le Corbusier, even to their cruciform shape; and if we must dismiss these structures as low-grade architecture when we are close to them, from the cliffs across the river we can nonetheless see a fine cityscape of a kind not envisaged before 1922.

Too many cities in those areas of the world such as Latin America, where the pace of urban growth is most rapid, are engaged in producing a generation later cityscapes of the early-twentieth-century type. But if Bogotá has imposed clusters of twentieth-century buildings on a sixteenth-century city plan, Caracas, expanding still more rapidly, has fortunately set out to re-create itself in a later mode. Its cityscape, however, is still in the making. Whether we consider the Edificio Polar of Vegas and Galis, the almost unique skyscraper at the Plaza Venezuela, or the forty-eight tall slabs of the Cerro Piloto housing development, we are presumably seeing only a foreshadowing of the city that is to be. In both cases we cannot but be struck by the difference from earlier cities in scale and in the relationship between the building and the natural setting. That a man-made object can rise to the scale of major landscape features has long been obvious in such things as pyramids and dams, or even in the smokestack of the Anaconda plant in Montana. Generally in the past, however, and particularly the recent past, cityscape has tended to obliterate landscape, even where (as at Bath or Edinburgh or San Francisco) the natural setting has most notably affected the cityscape. At Caracas, on the other hand, the lone skyscraper and the ranges of spaced housing blocks rise in direct competition with the surrounding mountains but do not sprawl over them. Indeed the cluttered shacks, whose inhabitants are to live in the Cerro Piloto blocks, will be wiped out, removing from the picture elements that blur the sharp contrast of man-made towers and mountain backdrop.

This macrocosmic sort of cityscape is as evident, I do not doubt, at Bartlesville, Oklahoma, where Wright's lone skyscraper rises above the plains, or at Chandigarh, where Le Corbusier's High Courts of Justice stand out against the distant mountains, for it corresponds to the passion for diffusion that our methods of individual transportation by automobile encourage. But there is no question that more attention is also being paid today to cityscape conceived as a kind of man-made landscape complete in itself, with little or no reference to the natural setting, than at any time during the last half century. A little desperately we are trying to bring back something of the pedestrian's cityscape as we plan squares and associated areas undominated by the automobile or carve out at the base of our skyscrapers (this is a different matter from wholly isolating them) islands of space within the solid masonry of the old cities we have inherited. Where the early-twentieth-century city was—and is—exciting for its turbulence, its pressures, its drama of man-made mountain ranges, there can be no question that we are again interested in the creation and the ordering of relatively small and confined spaces.

Considering that Perret was in his eighties by the time he designed it, it is not surprising that his Le Havre belongs architecturally to the period of a generation or more ago. But his Place de L'Hôtel de Ville there, with its orderly frame of low four-story buildings over colonnades, taller ones rising from small courts behind, with its sunken garden in the center, and ultimately with its major public buildings on the far side, will not be a place merely to pass through or to park automobiles in, but rather a place to linger and to utilize on foot.

In New York, Lever House boldly carves its own open space out of the solid wall of Park Avenue. But that space is best apprehended

49

going by in a car as the envelope of the tower. At ground level there is no positive utilization of the space and therefore no reason to linger in it. As Park Avenue changes from a masonry canyon to a series of skyscrapers, each rising from an island of space of its own (it bids fair to do so at least in the blocks just north of Grand Central Station within a few years), we shall see whether the macrocosmic ideals of the new city, most dramatically realized at Pittsburgh and Caracas, have validity where there is no visible landscape setting other than the man-made mountain ranges of the buildings of the 'twenties, also whether those ideals can be humanized by the parallel development of usable open spaces at ground level.

It is natural when considering cityscape to turn first to the problems of the big city. Despite Mr. Wright, we are evidently going to have big cities for some time to come, however much they may be influenced at their periphery of suburbs by ideals comparable to those of Broadacre City. But big cities take on character from sheer bulk, nor is that character readily changed once it is set. Somewhere between the big city of skyscrapers and the open terrain of the outermost suburbs, where individual houses can be so far separated that each makes its own terms with the landscape, lie perhaps the toughest of the problems of cityscape.

The new towns in England, at least as we see them in their present, very partially completed form, are disappointing. The Garden City tradition of extreme diffuseness dominates them, and they have seemed on the whole merely to destroy the landscape without becoming positive entities in their own right. Partly this is because they are being built from the outside in, the peripheral residential areas before the business core. But even in America the business core, the Main Street—which in one form or another, from the villages of New England to the ghost towns of this part of the world, has given focus and character to townscape—is melting away, or at least not being re-created. More and more constituents of the town are fleeing to the highways, filling stations, movie theaters as drive-ins, all kinds of eating and drinking places, hotels as motels, some kinds of shops one by one, more grouped in shopping centers. Of these emigrés from the towns, only the shopping centers are of sufficient scale and complexity to provide any equivalent to old-time townscape. On the ordinary high roads, where roadside construction proliferates (being forbidden the state parkways, throughways, and turnpikes), it is hard to imagine that highwayscape could ever be anything but a blight. But the shopping centers, meeting the passion for diffusion and yet at their best planned as a whole and organized to incorporate, in a more or less isolated location, most of the facilities that were once concentrated at the town centers, clearly have a future and deserve serious study as a new form of man-made agglomeration. Their siting in the landscape, particularly now that they are moving somewhat away from the main highways, can be carefully considered—it has not been very often as yet—and they can perhaps draw to themselves some of the public buildings, churches, say, or branch libraries, which would give them more dignity and broader functions in the diffuse suburban areas of which they are the commercial modes.

The major macrocosmic problem of landscape may well seem to be a matter of preservation. Even if it is possible to recognize that not all human impingement on the natural landscape is unfortunate and, further, that an agrarian countryside like that of much of the Middle West or large areas of Western Europe may have a positive character even though it be largely devoid of the mountains, rivers, and other heroic features that are most generally admired, it is nonetheless true that in all heavily populated areas it is the uncontrolled seepage from the cities and towns that pushes farther and farther back the frontiers either of nature unalloyed or of nature literally improved by the agricultural activities of men. It will be quite impossible in this country in this century, with its automobile transportation, ever to draw such strict lines between town and country as have existed and still exist in other parts of the world. The townsman, reaching out for the amenities of the country, cannot help but destroy what he seeks. Fortunately there is still a great deal of land in every part of this country too rough, too distant from the cities ever to be subjugated. In other countries, perhaps, the stronger tradition of differentiation between town and country, the lack of such an abundance of individual means of transportation, and stronger governmental controls will save the vastly smaller areas of untouched natural scenery or scenery modified only by agriculture.

In cityscape, also, preservation is important. It is not merely that in our towns and cities we are too often failing to add anything worthy of our own aspirations; we are also tearing down too much that once had virtue and might have still if we knew how to use it. European cities on the whole have more need of preservation measures than ours, and on the whole these have been supplied by government, if generally in piecemeal fashion, with too much consideration for the individual monument and too little for the general texture which forms the body of any cityscape. But the chorus of voices that have come to the defense of the big railway stations of New York against the threat of replacing them with skyscrapers, a chorus including many voices never raised before in praise of such architects as Warren and Wetmore or McKim, Mead and White, indicates more perhaps than the often dubious measures taken to preserve in isolation much older structures, the growing sense of cityscape as a total whole.

But preservation is a delicate matter, particularly as it becomes involved with restoration, and is presumably not on the agenda of this conference. We are more concerned here with the positive aspects of the creation of cityscape and with the directions that are being taken or should be taken in the third quarter of the twentieth century. The isolated skyscraper, the revival of the pedestrian precinct, the commercial nexus removed from the town center to the more or less open country, and the almost wholly unsolved problem, which I have barely touched upon, of the suburban residential development too dense to retain many of the values of the original natural setting and too diffuse to have any character recognizable as positive city- or townscape, these are some at least of the topics upon which such a discussion as this must center. And here among these mountains, in this little, typically American townscape, which has been preserved first by accident and then by intention, we see perhaps more clearly than in the metropolises the basic problems that the concepts of landscape and townscape give rise to when they are brought into conjunction.

Landscape has obviously a possible different meaning from the one given here. In addition to the macrocosmic landscape which it is within man's powers to modify but hardly to create, there is also the art of the garden, rechristened "landscaping" in the eighteenth century when its canons became naturalistic, but in many periods, including perhaps our own, dominated by architects and architectural considerations. The garden art has its place in cityscape, but it is a minor one. Nonetheless it is sad to see the extent to which what was for long an independent discipline has become subordinated to the broader if necessarily more amorphous concept of "planning." In theory, planners are to create our cityscapes of the present and the future, and also to exercise such control as can be exercised consciously over landscape in the macrocosmic sense. But there is a sense in which all these matters of man's relations to the settings provided by nature or built by himself are one, and I am not sure that the planners—even those who have had the good fortune to begin as architects—generally understand this. The complexities of planning are so enormous on the practical side, the considerations of physical amenities so important and difficult to cope with, that it is perhaps too much to expect that the more purely visual considerations to which this paper has been very largely confined should receive the attention they require. What happens to landscape in the broad sense and what happens to cities is so much the concern of everyone that it is well that it should be considered by many people who are only remotely concerned with the direct control of the situation. In the end it is the public who find the instruments among planners and architects—and also among builders and irrigation experts and highway engineers—to give them what they deserve. Our cities and our landscapes are a sort of surrealist portrait of ourselves, which we are all engaged in painting. When we relax our vigilance, we deserve the horrors that ensue; when we have faith in the power of human control we are on the road at least to positive achievements by which our day need not be ashamed to be measured against the achievements of other ages.

# The Six Determinants of Architectural Form
# Paul Rudolph
# 1956

Nikolaus Pevsner, writing in the *Architectural Review* of April, 1954, made the following statement: "The qualities of the modern movement were not developed to please the eye, but because without them no workable, no functioning, no functional architecture is possible in our age." This statement reflects the attitudes of the 'thirties but not our attitude today. We no longer think that when the problems of making a project work have been solved the exterior form will be found crystallized. As Mathew Nowicki stated in his famous article "Function and Form," we cannot keep on pretending that we solve our problems without precedent in form.

The early theory of modern architecture tended to ignore some problems. The relationship of one building to another and the façade were largely ignored. This attitude has produced some very ungainly buildings. As a matter of fact there are those who value disorder because it somehow seems "human," and anything else is termed pretentious, regimented, cold, intellectual, dictatorial, etc. The extremes are possibly illustrated in the United States by the so-called Bay Region style in California on the one hand, and Mies van der Rohe on the other.

Modern architecture's failure to produce understandable theories regarding the relationship of a building to its environment in the deepest sense is disastrous. The Ecole des Beaux Arts was actually very rich in this aspect. However, modern architects tend, even today, to admire merely some "human" square—preferably one located as remotely as possible—and to state that we must make our "squares" more human. This is, of course, admirable, but it still leaves us with acres of cars and buildings casting shadows a quarter of a mile long. The quickly moving vehicle and unprecedented requirements of sheer bulk have given us new dimensions of scale. Human scale must be coupled to the scale given by a quickly moving vehicle.

At mid-century the battle of modern architecture versus traditional architecture is won, but we find it a dry, limited, timid, monotonous thing, utilizing forms that are merely fashionable, without regard to the fundamental concepts behind the great prototypes. Part of our difficulties came from the concept of functionalism as the prime determinant of architectural forms. There are certainly as many as six determinants of architectural form, and each is important and must be heeded although their relative importance varies with the problem.

The *first* determinant is the environment of the building, which means its relationship to other buildings and the site, as stated earlier.

Modern architecture has been particularly weak in this respect and indeed even negative, ignoring especially the relationship of the building to the sky. We usually say that our buildings are related to others by contrast, but this works only occasionally. Of course, the danger in respecting too literally the earlier architecture, which is usually eclectic in character in this country, is that we may create a new eclecticism, that is, one approach to creating harmony with Gothic, another to early New England, another to Georgian, etc.

The *second* determinant of form is the functional aspects. I will not discuss this except to say that most of our buildings look like assemblages of workable parts from Sweet's Catalogue, with little regard for the whole. This is not to say one is uninterested in how the building works.

The *third* determinant of form is the particular region, climate, landscape, and natural lighting conditions with which one is confronted. Modern architecture is becoming the international style. The great architectural movements of the past have been precisely formulated in a given area, then adapted and spread to other regions, suiting themselves more or less to the particular way of life of the new area. We now face such a period. If adaptations, enlargement, and enrichment of basic principles of twentieth-century architecture were carried out, always relating it to the main stream of architecture, and the particular regions, the world would again be able to create magnificent cities. Unfortunately, this has not yet come to pass. We continue to ignore the particular. Henry-Russell Hitchcock has pointed out that "the utilitarian language of modern architecture as used throughout the world tends to have something of the thinness and lack of color of Basic English. We do not want a uniformity of architecture which might tend to confuse a muddled traveler into attempting to enter a house identical to his own, not just in the wrong street, not even in the wrong city, not actually in the wrong country or the wrong hemisphere."

There are several conditions that tend to limit regional expression. First there is industrialization; second, ease of travel and communication; third, the rising cost of traditional materials and skilled labor; fourth, the influence of the architectural press; fifth, the worship of that which is popular and our desire to conform; and sixth, the "do it yourself according to the manufacturer's instruction" movement; and seventh, the abstract qualities inherent in the new concept of space also tend to limit regional expression.

The *fourth* determinant of form is the particular material which one uses. We are currently going through a structural exhibitionism stage but this will pass. Buckminster Fuller domes, the latest space frames, the newest plastics, tension structures, etc., are only new kinds of bricks that enlarge our means of expression. Only buildings that need great visual emphasis should utilize such devices, and structure should always remain merely a means to the end. Many younger architects fail to appreciate this.

The *fifth* determinant of form is concerned with satisfying the peculiar physiological demands of the buildings. This is accomplished primarily through the manipulation of space and the use of symbols. We are particularly unsure in this aspect, partially because the revolution threw out much that still has validity. Thus we must learn anew the meaning of monumentality, how to create a place of worship and inspiration; how to make quiet, enclosed, isolated spaces; how to make spaces full of hustling, bustling activities and pungent with vitality; how to make dignified, vast, sumptuous, even awe-inspiring spaces; how to make mysterious spaces; how to make transition spaces that define, separate, and yet join juxtaposed spaces of contrasting character. We need sequences of space that arouse one's curiosity, give a sense of anticipation, that beckon and impel us to rush forward to find that releasing space which dominates, which acts as a climax and magnet and therefore gives direction.

The *sixth* and last determinant of form is concerned with the spirit of the times. This is perhaps the most difficult of all and is determined by the genius. Geoffrey Scott in *The Architecture of Humanism* says that "the men of the Renaissance evolved a certain architectural style because they liked certain forms of a certain kind. These forms, as such, they preferred, irrespective of their relation to the mechanical means by which they were produced, irrespective of the materials out of which they were constructed, irrespective sometimes even of the actual purposes they were to serve." We need not be ashamed of this same passion for certain forms today, although the layman does not yet always share our passion. Interestingly enough, the layman usually reacts favorably to that which is truly great. The spirit of the times is expressed by its vitality, its tension, its curiosity, its insecurity, its materialism, its desire for comfort, its glorification of the power of man.

These six determinants of architectural form might lead toward richer architectural expression. At the same time as one cries for greater expressiveness one must also heed Rudolph Wittkower, who believed that when architects depended on their sensibility and imagination, architecture always went downhill. There are few geniuses and most of us need guidance and discipline.

In one sense any classical building, with its columns, capitals, porticoes, and window architraves, is a collection of clichés. The cantilever, the superstructure perched on pilotis, the glass enclosed staircase tower, and the ribbon window are legitimate expressions of the structural methods that in the last thirty years added so much to the architect's repertoire.

The clichés, in their proper role, are not merely a means of appearing up to date, but a means of ensuring a civilized standard of design—even in the absence of genius—by providing the architect with a range of well-tried, culturally vital forms and motifs to convert the passive act of plagiarism into the creative act of building up and systematically enriching an architectural language appropriate to our times.

You will recall that *Progressive Architecture* sponsors each year a Design Award Program, based on proposed building. Last year I had occasion to analyze the thirty-four selected designs and would like to use them as a barometer of our current attitudes.

If that Design Award Program is indeed symptomatic of our present-day attitudes, then one concludes that a new tradition has indeed been established. There were striking similarities in spirit and intent in almost all the buildings selected: 95 per cent utilized regularly spaced structural systems, thereby freeing the interior arrangement. The linear qualities inherent in such cagelike construction were usually emphasized and were largely the means of organizing and disciplining the designs.

It is worth noting that a recreation building, a residence, and a war memorial are symmetrically organized, the remainder asymmetrically. One notes that the regular bay system seems more successful when the bay is wide enough to accommodate subsidiary divisions. No new light was shed on the problem of starting and stopping such bay-disciplined designs, they often resembled sliced loaves of bread with no beginning or end. In all, 22 per cent of the designs were to be raised above the ground on pilotis, and 25 per cent undertook to gain that effect by completely filling the lower floor with glass enclosing walls. One-half were related to the ground by slab construction; only two will rest on pedestals.

One of modern architecture's greatest failings has been its lack of interest in the relationship of the building to the sky.

Nine-tenths utilized flat roofs, and the remainder were to be pitched. This serves as a slight cause for concern, for there are many design problems where the silhouette is of the utmost importance. One doubts that a poem was ever written to a flat-roofed building silhouetted against the setting sun. What about its appearance on a misty, foggy day? This insistence on always building flat roofs also tends to make modern architecture, all too often, have the appearance of a doghouse when juxtaposed against the high-ceiling pitched roofs of much earlier architecture. With one exception, water appeared to be mysteriously drained from all roofs. Traditional methods of water shedding created real drama, and one longs for the modern equivalents.

Rather surprisingly, two-thirds turned the corners of their buildings by carrying the glass to the corners, with the return wall solid. This desire to reveal the essentially planar aspect of construction reflected itself in almost all of the plans, as well as in the elevation, by reducing all wall divisions to a series of rectangles. These modular constructions are undoubtedly expressions of industrialized building components, although paradoxically most of them will undoubtedly be actually constructed by essentially handicraft methods.

Again, 65 per cent utilized uniform ceiling heights, 25 per cent allowed the ceilings to follow the slope of the pitched roof while only 10 per cent varied the ceiling heights in any way. This self-imposed uniform ceiling height limitation is difficult to understand when one considers the importance of the psychological effect given by varying ceiling heights. To a degree this spatial characteristic is compensated for by the courtyard completely within the building, a device to be utilized by 45 per cent. One-fifth of the designers created outer defined courtyards and patios by extending walls out into space.

However, the paucity and limitation of spatial concepts to be utilized is extremely disappointing. Laymen almost never demand that their structures be clearly expressed, but they often describe in eloquent terms the architectural space and the particular psychological implications desired. The laymen seem more knowing about these matters. This current architectural limitation is evident from the lack of interest in handling natural light. There are all too often interior spaces that are merely flooded with light, uncontrolled psychologically or physically.

We all recognize that strict functionalism does not satisfy the need for the "sense of symbolism, the lasting monument, the vital ideas and shared emotions that are part of architecture's historical function to perform." In the design awards one finds symbols used three times (it was always a cross), while two utilized sculpture and two painting. One understands the difficulties, but it is undoubtedly up to the architect to lead the way.

Perhaps the most important single aspect of those designs as a group is the apparent lack of interest in the environment in which the building is placed and the particular role it plays in the city as a whole. Only 15 per cent, at least as presented, indicated anything at all of the character of the building's environment or surrounding structures. This continual thinking in terms of individual buildings as gems unrelated to earlier works is disastrous, creating cities whose buildings tend to brutalize rather than refine.

A truly successful building must be related to its neighbors in terms of scale, proportions, the space created between the buildings, and, most important of all, in defining and rendering eloquent its role in the whole city scheme. Should we not always indicate graphically the relationship of each design to the larger picture? Buildings such as governmental structures, religious buildings, gateways to the city should serve as focal points in our cities and could undoubtedly indulge in certain excesses, while buildings for commerce, housing, finance, and administration should not dominate our environment.

Just as the nineteenth-century architects showed so little regard for construction, we twentieth-century architects tend to disregard our role in the cityscapes.

The lack of interest in how our buildings actually appear is also indicated by the fact that only four of the thirty-four designs indicated any lettering or signs and only about one-third indicated any comprehensive landscaping treatment.

Every building, no matter how large or small, is a part of a greater whole, and the architect perforce participates in planning. Our professional journals are, to a considerable degree, a prime source for the architectural student and, as such, have a responsibility in presenting executed as well as projected buildings in relation to their neighbors—not merely as isolated gems. Park Avenue, just as every corner crossroad in the land, is being rebuilt in a fragmented way.

Indeed, at least one intersection of Park Avenue will shortly have four postwar unrelated buildings on each corner, with all-glass façades. It will be interesting to see glass buildings reflecting themselves. Much of the aesthetic enjoyment of a glass building is its mirroring quality of earlier and contrasting architecture.

We still have many lessons to learn from Rome. If one wants to create more human outer spaces, one gives thought to siting. Camillo Sitte writes in *The Art of Building Cities:* "Of the 255 churches in Rome, 41 are set back with one side against other buildings; 96 with two sides against other buildings; 110 with three sides against other buildings. Only six stand free."

We are concerned with creativity. Not the great inspiration, but a painstaking process of searching, analyzing, determining the basic values of our form of expression. Only when we become so thoroughly acquainted with them that they become a part of our subconscious are we capable of spontaneous creation.

I believe that in every cultural effort of each generation it is the Academy or the discipline, which we so anxiously want to cross out, that helps us to find and determine our basic values. These, of course, change with each generation because society and life by their own virtue are dynamic. But for the clarity of its dynamic force it needs discipline. Otherwise it becomes chaotic. In our generation we have had the stimulus of genius. Let us now analyze, organize, and determine our values and our language so that we can bring to life a clear and strong expression of our culture.

# V  The Wisdom of L. L. Whyte

Aspen made effective use of such generalist scientific philosophers as were available—Lancelot Law Whyte, Jacob Bronowski, Lancelot Hogben. This short paper shows L. L. Whyte—longtime philosopher of science—asserting yet again his basic position that the universe inhabited by man is both fundamentally simple and immeasurably rich.

# From Primitive Disorder to Twentieth-Century Visual Images
## Lancelot Law Whyte
## 1959

Though we do not yet understand the historical path from an ur-chaos to today's images, some points stand out rather clearly.

This path may have led from general atomic disorder to local inert aggregations (e.g., the earth), and by some unknown transition to organisms, and so by a quasi-Darwinian process to species with nervous systems and brains ordering records of past experience so as to anticipate possible future achievements, and the development of these ordered records into images for communication: gestures, designs, spoken and written words, the various arts. And now we find ourselves consciously discontented with the available images in relation to our experience and our need.

A study of this long path from atoms to images suggests the following thoughts:

1.  The story is a complete mystery, unless we postulate a *universal process of ordering,* of disorder becoming more orderly, evidenced in both the "physical" and the "mental" spheres. The concept of order, properly defined, is very powerful, uniting quantities and aesthetic qualities. (The relation of this ordering process to the physicist's theories of disorder, e.g., heat, is reserved for another occasion.)
2.  Images and symbols represent the ordering of various aspects of experience into convenient forms that evoke awareness of these aspects. All thought is an ordering process, leading to representations in the brain, in speech, or in visual and other symbols. The brain is not a computer but an ordering organ operating partly unconsciously.
3.  Some of the dominant images of the past, e.g., the outstanding myths, archetypes, and works of art of particular cultures, appear to me to emphasize various contrasted aspects of experience. For instance, much Egyptian work stresses permanence; classical Greek, ideal human beauty; a late medieval style, humility; certain Oriental, poetry. These images are permanent contributions to the assets of mankind because they give the highest expression to some feature of human awareness.
4.  The characteristic of recent Western culture, say 1910 to date, is clearly not beauty, humility, or poetry but, I suggest, concern with *elementals.* We have broken everything down to its elements: basic particles, the protein of organisms, ultimate factors in personality, root meanings, one hundred great ideas, geometrical elements in art and architecture, etc. We pretend that we have outgrown the superficial show; nothing less than the final analysis will do! Truth is to be found in bits. Certainly it is now in bits.

5.    But history develops in swings, and the latest craze for "richness" may conceal a deeper factor. Obsession with units implies neglect of their ordering—in subtler forms, partly ordered cell nuclei and organisms, and the beauty of nature, man, and man's creations. All the facts compel me to believe that, after forty years of elementals, an epoch of *order* is now opening—at least of the conscious recognition of the primary importance of order, both in nature and in man's desires. This has been long prepared, for example, in the recurrent recognition since about 1780 that unconscious ordering processes underlie the working of the human imagination and judgment.

6.    But if this swing toward aesthetic and scientific awareness of the role of order is to bring a real gain, some scrap of permanent enlightenment to man, it must not only recognize the great variety of specific forms, from crystals to personalities and paintings, but admit and accept the absolute inevitability of *clash* between contrasted forms (as Shakespeare did). Ordering implies clash, at any rate in this universe of sustained process. There is as yet no scientific philosophy in which both ordering and its consequence, clash, are given their proper standing as the primary agents of change. One application of this idea: The need of mankind is not for harmony, which is absurd, but for a profound understanding both of ordering and of clash that will enable us to facilitate those ordering processes which are powerful enough to prevent clash from exceeding certain disastrous thresholds.

7.    Here every aspect of culture has its own crucial role. Every organ of communication can evoke and strengthen the awareness that the species is now turning over a new page, one of challenging tasks, grand vistas, and extraordinary choices. Today the role of the image is not only to evoke past experience but also explicitly to anticipate and suggest possible future achievements. Our greatest need is an image of future greatness.

# VI  A Real Pro

Of all the intelligent, concerned, creative designers who organized or ornamented successive Aspen conferences, two alone were really capable of describing and analyzing their own distinctive business with penetration and good sense. One is Richard Latham from Chicago, who appears in Section VII; the other is his London counterpart Misha Black. The paper that follows distills Black's best experience, practice, and hopes about the most critical relationship in the working career of any design professional. With hindsight, we can see him plotting the route toward making the conference unnecessary by making the designer the client! No doubt it is that kind of thinking that has made him Professor of Industrial Design at the Royal College of Art in London.

# The Designer and the Client
## Misha Black
## 1956

It would be instructive for a client to be present, although invisible, when the designer whom he has commissioned sits down alone, or with his colleagues, to start work on a new project. He would be surprised by the transformation. The suave, genial designer who was so accommodating at the conference table and so unsophisticated a companion at dinner would have changed into a serious, engrossed man fanatically concerned with the job in hand.

This assumes, of course, that the designer has a degree of creative ability and is not merely a technician content to imitate or only efficiently to carry out instructions. The purely executant designer has his own merits, but for the moment I wish to consider that smaller band who endeavor to bring to any design problem as much originality as does the chef who slightly varies the cookbook recipe to bring the final dish more to his personal liking.

The client, now as unnoticed as a fly on the wall, would observe three unexpected phenomena: firstly, the self-criticism of the designer as he covers sheet after sheet of paper with preliminary designs, all to be discarded for reasons that would be incomprehensible to his client; secondly, the time taken in developing the finally selected basic design to a stage where drawings and specifications are completed; and lastly, the fact that he, the manufacturer, influences the designer at every stage of the work to a degree that he would hardly credit and of which the designer himself is often unconscious.

In the second-class design office, where expediency controls honesty, the influence of the client is decisive. No more time is spent on the job than the minimum necessary to satisfy the client, and if the client is incapable of judging between a solution that is properly and one only partially resolved, then it is the latter he receives. This is the path of mediocrity, to the rapid deterioration of standards and, for the designer, to an insistent sense of dissatisfaction not compensated by the increasing bank balance that often results from a willingness to produce shoddy work.

When the client is unable to see the difference between a meretricious and a creative solution, the task of the honest designer is insufferably increased. The designer then knows that the acceptance of his work will depend not on rational judgment but on his own powers of persuasion, on his capacity for convincing argument, which often must deliberately falsify the real reason for his decisions. In such circumstances, the designer feels isolated and desperate, knowing that the entire creative energy must come from him alone, with the client as useless as an irresponsible judge. It is therefore not surprising that designers who are doomed to work for blind and dogmatic clients rarely survive the unequal battle and finish up not very different from the second-rate hacks who lack integrity from the start.

Yet even when the client is sufficiently sensitive to judge between a creative and a dreary solution, and when the designer is content to produce only the best work of which he is capable, even then the client exercises so important an influence on the job as to make him almost equal to the designer in determining its final form. The independence of the designer is as illusory as would be the conceit of a motor car that imagines it decides in which direction its wheels shall revolve.

Industrial design is, by definition, creative work, which depends for its materialization on its fabrication by other hands than those of the designer. An idea restricted to visualization in the mind of the designer, or carried no further than a carefully rendered drawing, is as unfulfilled as a play written but never acted or a piano concerto played on a silenced instrument.

This argument could be countered by the deafness of Beethoven when he wrote some of his greatest music or by Cézanne unhonored in his lifetime, but industrial designers are in a different category. I have yet to meet the designer satisfied or even able to work for any length of time without the stimulus of execution, or capable of development without the experience to be gained only by seeing how the drawing-board design appears after production. But if a chair or refrigerator is to be manufactured, a shop or showroom constructed, or a poster printed, the designer must persuade his client to invest the money necessary for the product to be made or the design otherwise carried out. Then the net is immediately closed, and the designer and client are together inextricably enmeshed.

I am not suggesting that the influence of the client is necessarily harmful. The opposite is often true. When the client and the designer are in sympathy, they can together produce better work than that of which either alone would be capable. The client, particularly if he is an experienced art director, can be the encouragement and the goad, drawing out of the designer, especially if he is young and unpracticed, work of a quality and maturity he would never produce without wise, firm, and experienced guidance. These are positive contributions from the client, but the more useful they are, the more considerable a part does the client play in the production of the final design.

But more often the client lags behind his designer. When his capacity to see what has not before been known is limited, he cannot follow the designer to the frontiers of visual experience where the designer is groping for new shapes, new relationships of planes and colors, new images, which may in fact be what Sir Herbert Read has called the Icon which precedes the Idea. In such circumstances, the client is a shackle dragging the designer back to the standards of the client's world. Then the designer is the anxious leader, able to see the horizon but delayed by the weight of his reluctantly dragging companion, who is fearful to take even a step in the right direction.

This is the moment for the intelligent, farsighted client to shake his head with scarcely contained irritation, to claim that he does in fact give his designers complete freedom and is honored to follow where they lead. But this is an aspiration rather than a fact. Even the most sympathetic client has his likes and dislikes, his quirks and his oddities. Always he is at the designer's elbow, always the designer is worrying, if unconsciously, how his client will react to his proposals, how far he can persuade him to go on the fateful morning when his drawings are taken from the carefully prepared portfolio and exposed to a life-and-death judgment. Then the client, omnipotent, will decide whether the child is to be throttled at birth or allowed to grow to the full manhood of the completed job.

Always under the threat of death in the wastebasket or incarceration in the plan chest, the designer can never be free of his client. As he grows in years and experience, the influence of his client waxes rather than wanes. He becomes more sensitive to the whims of his master, more skilled in satisfying him, more sensitive to the shortness of the steps he can safely take in leadership. The experienced designer is thus able to produce success after success, yet he is always aware, while he accepts the laurel wreath of approbation, of how pitiful has been his tiptoe advance when measured against the great strides he could have taken if his client had been less timid or less restricted by the taste (as he appraised it) of the markets he serves.

It is only at a conference such as this that one is permitted to weep the acid tears of self-pity and flay the earnest features of the successful designer with the lash of self-criticism. But how many designers can truly say they have ever designed and carried to production a job that was finally just as they would have wished to see it?

We, the public designers, are, with the fewest honored exceptions, the great compromisers, the second-layer men, the translators of the real creative work of our time to a more common denominator. There is no harm in that. For every act of creation there must be a thousand adapters. We stretch as a great chain from the artist at the frontier of experience to the base camp where most of our fellow men must live. If the bridge is not weakened by deceit and excessive compromise, ours is a worthy occupation equal at least to that of a competent doctor carefully and painstakingly prescribing the cures that the research scientist has earlier discovered. While engaged in this not unpleasant occupation, let us not deny, however, that the limit of our progress is finitely determined by our clients.

*The Role of the Client.* If we are fated to live as a Siamese twin irrevocably joined to our client, it is useful if each half of this unity can contribute to the wellbeing and continued existence of his inevitable companion.

First, the client and the designer must be compatible. Here the client has an unfair advantage. It is the manufacturer who chooses his designer and only exceptionally that the designer decides for whom he shall work. But this should not be a master-and-slave relationship. If it is, the influence of the client is too strong, and his designer becomes a dim, paper-scratching shadow, drawing out only that which has been instructed. Soon, under such treatment, any creative capacity the designer may have possessed withers and dies, while he turns to gardening or amateur painting to satisfy his frustrated creative energies.

If my earlier proposition is valid and the influence of the client is as important as I believe it to be, then it follows that high standards of design can be attained only when the client and his designer are so of the same mind as to be virtually two faces that together produce the single coin.

That this is true has been shown by the major design achievements of our generation. I am not fitted to quote American examples, but for Europe one could mention Frank Pick at the London Transport Board, Sir Colin Anderson and the Orient Shipping Line, Adriano Olivetti in Turin, and the Farina car-body works, where a design standard of international importance has been established by a firm where the designer is also the director, and thus his own client.

Here lies the crux of the problem. A high design standard can be achieved only when at least one director at the top level of management really believes in design, has the visual perception to distinguish the good from the meretricious, and cares as a human being that the goods his factory produces or the physical manifestation of the services he controls should please the senses of sight and touch while satisfying those emotions which respond to efficiency and fitness for purpose.

The desire to produce good design as an end in itself is the fundamental requirement. If that does not exist somewhere along the line, then the forces of reaction or *laissez-faire* will so vitiate any new design project as to mock the creative energy consumed in its primary conception.

I am not in this sense talking about the slick adaptation of newly established formulae. This is the province of any hack manager and his hired draftsman, and they will between them manufacture and market products that will sell better than a more traditional compromise and justify the slogan, "Good design is good business." But when we look one stage ahead, there is no longer the *guarantee* of immediate trade results to justify a real act of creation. There, faith must support judgment to produce the kind of farsighted support for design that justifies tooling up. A mass produced cooker that sold only 1,100 in the first year took two years of extensive selling to reach the economic 25,000 mark.

Steps as courageous and eventually as profitable as this are the outcome of the closest liaison between the designer and the top-level management of the company that employs him. They require of the designer a stature that entitles him to entry to the board room; they require of management the imagination to employ designers of great ability, to pay them the salaries their importance in the process of production and marketing justifies, and, above all, to allow their designers the working conditions and facilities that enable them to remain capable of the creative endeavor which is their primary and irreplaceable contribution to industry.

*Stimulating the Designer.* To sustain the creative ability of the designer is no easy matter. The fact that the designer is prepared to work for industry means that he is predisposed to compromise and is willing to occupy at least part of his life with problems of persuasion, diplomacy, and administration. The transition from this normal division of the designer's working life to a situation in which the *whole* of the time of the once productive designer is occupied with talking, writing, and administering is a step so easy to take as to make it the inevitable lot of all but the most resolute artist.

This is not a reason for despondency. In such circumstances the erstwhile designer himself becomes the client; if memories of his own travail on the drawing board have not been completely buried under the avalanche of business lunches, he turns, by slow metamorphosis, into the client who is the more able to draw from the younger designers on his staff that enthusiastic, dedicated endeavor essential to the production of outstanding work.

When this happens, the full circle is complete. The designer has become the client, and his protégés no longer have to fight the soul-destroying battle of persuading the philistine. The client/designer, on his part, may be satisfied that his task has changed to that of the educator and elder statesman. He may take pleasure in the quality of the work produced under his direction and be secretly compensated for the drying-up of his personal creative work by the knowledge that he would not have turned from it had his own capacity as an artist been greater or longer sustainable.

This process is the easier and more effective if the chief designer, or design director, is on the staff of the company for which he works. Design in an industrial organization is not a question of one brilliant idea or even a series of creative bombshells. It is the slow permeation of a visual sensitivity through every aspect of the firm's work, from the product itself to the point-of-sales dispenser, from the architecture of the factory to the uniform of the truck driver, from the furnishings of the chairman's office to the fittings in the operatives' wash room.

A consultant designer working from outside his client's establishment can lay down basic principles, design a series of brilliant individual products, create a house style, and imbue management with the importance of the designer's potential contribution to the prosperity of that industry. But the consultant's characteristic is that he moves from one industry to another and thus, through the wide field of his interest, is able to act as a top-level counselor to management. He is incapable of dealing with the day-to-day problems, major or minute, that finally determine whether a firm or an industry shall grow or atrophy. That is the task of the design director, who, whether he is a designer become director or a director with the visual sensitivity of a designer, must be firmly attached to his own industry.

No business can avoid eventual disintegration unless it is aware, preferably consciously and at the least unconsciously, of the importance of design as a living, multiplying organism within it. To hang grimly to the laurels of past success is to place one's faith in a dead body already decaying. Dante said in the fourteenth century that noble origin is but a mantle from which time is ever cutting something away unless we ourselves add daily fresh worth to it, and six hundred years of history have confirmed his wisdom.

But, as a consultant designer myself, let me hasten to say that I consider that there is value in my services and those of my colleagues even to industries already well served (and pathetically few they still are, at least in Europe) by effective staff design offices.

The staff designer, if he is to be of maximum value to his employer, requires constant stimulation. The stimulation must come primarily from his own insatiable curiosity about form and function, which makes him examine and analyze each image, be it the shadow of a branch against a wall or the bulk of an aircraft standing on the tarmac, with patient intensity. To this must be added the stimulation derived from a detailed knowledge of developments in his own special industry and of the technical progress that exposes new design potentialities. For full measure he must have wide general interests that embrace the fine arts. By travel (or the second best sedentary version of travel—through the illustrated magazines), he must be exposed to the bombardment of other cultures to shatter the conceit of his parochialism.

The consultant designer can be a powerful added stimulus to the staff designer. His uninhibited criticism, his bringing to one industry the experience gained from others, his ideas—sometimes the more useful for not being immediately practicable—his support for the staff designer in his negotiation to persuade other sectors of management, are sufficient to justify his existence, but his facility for infuriating the staff designer is perhaps his most valuable asset. Here he becomes the anvil off which the staff designer strikes brighter sparks of creation than from the fuller steel of his daily companions. This is true, of course, only for the large industrial concerns. In smaller-scale industry, where the employment of staff designers of the highest caliber is not economically justified, the engagement of a consultant is essential, and he must do the best he can to fulfill both functions.

I have now posed four theses for discussion:

1.   That the client is always a partner in any design carried to production—and often the dominant factor.
2.   That only when the client and the designer are in complete sympathy can outstanding design be achieved.
3.   That only a staff designer or design director can ensure that continuity of design policy which ensures sustained achievement.
4.   That the consultant's chief merit in large-scale industry is to act as a catalyst within the industry and a stimulant to the design office.

*The Direction of Industrial Design.* If we accept for the moment that these theorems have been proved and that the client, staff designer, and consultant are working in productive harmony, then it is apposite to consider what they are trying to achieve.

If this were a conference of businessmen, I would say "Increased sales" and leave it at that. But, while we naturally admit that the rising sales graph registers the air which allows us to breathe and work, there still remain the less tangible aspects of industrial design, which—I may whisper in this fraternity of my colleagues—are to me at least as important as the balance sheet of my employers.

In an early book of criticism, T. S. Eliot wrote that we "must be quite aware of the obvious fact that art never improves but that the material of art is never quite the same." That I would unequivocally support. The diesel-powered liner is no visual improvement on the sailing vessel of the eighteenth century, the plastic-topped steel desk does not better the Chippendale writing table. The new objects are not necessarily inferior to their antecedents, but they are certainly not visually more important.

If we admit this, we need not be scourged by the need to *improve* on our progenitors, but we do need to worry about what we shall today materialize from the unchanging matrix of art.

In Great Britain there is a new growing interest in industrial design—an appreciation sufficient to have engendered governmental financial support for the opening of the Design Centre in London and to fill the popular magazines with comment about it. But as victory approaches in the primary battle for a more general visual awareness, the critics are challenging the justification for designers as we know them to exist at all.

The basis of the challenge is that design, if it is a conscious activity, necessarily reflects the personality and the cultural values of the manufacturer who commissions the design and his designers who conceive it. If the manufacturer and the designer are resolute, they will inevitably try to persuade the public to like those things which they themselves admire. Lacking confidence in the competence of manufacturers or designers to lead, the critics counsel that the public should be left alone and uninfluenced. They comfort themselves with the contention that form inevitably follows function. They argue that the only way for a designer to work is as a technician, exploring the problems of mechanics or aerodynamics or, when the object to be made is static, of production.

From what I have said it is clear that I am not uncritical of most of the things we now produce. My argument for the encouragement of the staff designer who is closely allied to the detailed problems of production reveals my own fear of the influence of those designers who are concerned only with the stamping of every product with the same fashionable style.

But to decry the best that is produced today, even if it falls far short of our images, is to retreat into the smugness of destructive criticism, which differs little from the distasteful self-satisfaction of those who consider all that is new is made beautiful by its novelty.

But even novelty is preferable to the dreariness of repetition bolstering itself with the illusion that to copy what has gone before is to inherit the glory of tradition.

Those who would sweep away all that is consciously designed today, who see beauty only in the arbitrarily produced object, or in the airplane and the radio mast, where the rigid discipline of mathematics forces the engineer to adopt solutions that leave little room for creative maneuver—those critics have lost their historical sense and, in preaching that function alone must develop form, have forgotten those great periods of the arts when the designer felt as free to carve a chair or decorate the walls of a room with molded plaster as some of us now do in designing the body of a motor car, knowing full well that an infinity of other solutions remain and that none are finitely determined by the function of the concealed engine that powers our automobile.

If Christopher Wren thought fit to build the dome of Saint Paul's Cathedral as a timber frame sheeted with lead and completely disconnected from the lantern at its crown, which it *appears* to support, then it is perhaps permissible, at a lower level of achievement, to enclose a radio set in a cabinet that also bears no essential relation to the works concealed within.

We are in a period when the scientist and the engineer have so successfully harnessed power that it no longer presents, in its purely functional form, more than a square box or an unrelieved egg. The atom is split in a structure so secreted from man's eyes that even the servants of its magic handle it by remote control. The complex excitement of the aircraft piston engine is being superseded by the roughly welded air tube of the jet. The massive grandeur of the steam locomotive is giving way to the diesel-electric, which would travel well enough if the power units were bolted only to the soleplate above the bogies, and these pioneer industries, as Dr. Bronowski has so convincingly argued, set the visual pattern for the more prosaic trades.

If the cabinet for an electronic computer must develop from its form, a rough box would serve; if the outward form of a vacuum cleaner must only express its function, why should we worry about the texture or color of the case, or obviating fixing screws, or molding the main casing so that it gives sensuous pleasure to its possessor?

Daily the appearance designer is becoming more separated from the engineer and *not* more closely integrated with him. Even in the Olivetti works, the casings of the typewriters and accounting machines are designed by artists who are in no way concerned with the mechanism of the equipment.

I know that this is only part of the problem, that in other industries the function can still control or at least substantially influence the form. However, this is only partially true of the motor car and the teacup, and it is not true of the carpet or the refrigerator, of the diesel locomotive or of a thousand other objects where scientific progress has so freed the designer that he can now model the external forms with the indiscretion of a sculptor.

The tempering discipline of an earlier decade, when the engineer, the production expert, and the designer responsible for the outward shape of a product should ideally have been so integrated as to be virtually one person, is cracking apart. Clearly the designer today must still appreciate the restrictions and potentialities of production, and it may be that eventually the engineer and the mold-maker will themselves be able, without conscious effort, to produce the shapes that express in some as yet unknown way the object they are producing. But in the meanwhile the gap widens. The engineer cares even less for appearance, and the designer and his client breathe the heady air of aesthetic freedom.

This is a dangerous situation. It calls for clients who are sufficiently aware of the problem to consult those who will advise them with honesty and sincerity. It calls for designers who are trained to the capacity which allows them to produce forms, colors, and decoration that are no longer just a cleaning up of the production engineer's failings but are a free expression of our age.

If the designer is now so free, if the machines can produce almost anything he conceives, then he is still more dependent on a client who has the understanding and the courage to allow him to be the sensitive antennae of our civilization, or at least the bridge between the artist and the public.

So we have a fifth theorem for discussion, namely, that the gap between the engineer and the industrial designer is widening, that the designer concerned with external appearances is becoming more free. If that is true, it underlines my earlier proposition that the face of our physical environment now depends on the emergence of clients able to partner their designers with the inspired judgment of a prince of the Italian Renaissance.

# VII Values

Surprisingly, these three papers align, or disagree, in the opposite ways to those one might expect. It was Hin Bredendieck, ex-Bauhaus, a European intellectual long based in Chicago, who was out of step with both Ernesto N. Rogers, European intellectual and most distinguished of Milanese architects, and Richard Latham, Chicago designer and impassioned yachtsman. His view of design problems from inside the design process is completely at variance with their insistence on seeing design as an activity that must be related to external circumstances—social or historical, environmental or product-oriented—which disclose value systems different from those generated by the current practice of their professions.

# How Do We See the World Today?
## Hin Bredendieck
## 1958

In keeping with my general approach, I hope it will be acceptable if I limit or delineate the theme and ask rather:

"How do I interpret past and current events in design in my evaluation of the present?"

*Those who are enamored of practice without science are like a pilot who goes into a ship without rudder or compass and never has any certainty where he is going.* LEONARDO DA VINCI

The majority of us still continue, to a greater or lesser degree, the age-old striving toward or longing after "beauty" and "harmony" in our environment. For the most part it is a vaguely defined goal, with few individuals able to agree on its constituents. But when we examine the emotional climate surrounding our concepts of what we call "beautiful" and "harmonious," we find a close affinity to other more precise terms, such as *integration* and *equilibrium, structure* and *order*, etc. These words can in turn be examined and made to yield still other even more precise definitions. This delineation of our basic terms is, in fact, one of the major tasks confronting us as designers. For how will it be possible to come to agreement concerning the "beauty" and/or "ugliness" of the objects of our environment unless our criteria and values are re-examined in the light of present-day knowledge and requirements? Most of us will agree that the area of "aesthetics" today seems to be little more than an intellectual free-for-all, yet we continue to use the old terms and follow the old thought patterns, often with a vague and sometimes acute feeling of uneasiness regarding their appropriateness for our times. This is just one of many symptoms of the need for change within the field of design.

In the past history of art, we find many instances of man's attempt to gain predictability in his art activity. There are numerous examples of his having devised rules and canons, laws and principles, and various other means of attaining the "ideal." We today have a similar need for predictability in our designing, whether we are conscious of the lack or not.

There are those who assume that, since the methodology of the past cannot be successfully applied to our present problems, all methodology should therefore be regarded with suspicion—if not rejected altogether.

But when we take a closer look at method as such, we find that man has always found methods for doing the things he has had to do.

He could not repeatedly do the same tasks without developing systems for coping with these recurrent actions, even though he may have been unconscious of the method he has utilized. (In science, the acceleration has been in direct ratio to the increased consciousness of the methodology employed.) In designing, all of our actions—the ideation, the preliminary sketching, the drawing, the experimentation and testing—are just so many ways and means of becoming conscious about the factors involved. What is wrong with becoming *consciously* conscious about our working habits and our surroundings, particularly since it is inevitable that we become so sooner or later? Consciousness of methodology can only be of benefit to design and, together with a surer and stronger intuition, will form an integrated approach to the problems that confront us.

*I believe that thinking is necessary in art as everywhere else and that a clear head is never in the way of genuine feelings.*   JOSEF ALBERS

During the past fifty years, we have supposedly established an adequate training for designers. But if we look at the objects around us, how many of them can we accept as satisfactory? We find on the market today a conglomerate of objects in a multitude of forms and shapes. When confronted with the problem of selecting an object, we know how difficult it is to find something we really like. Extending this scrutiny to our over-all environment, we find the same deplorable lack of integration. Object by object, dwelling by dwelling, it seems as though our surroundings are essentially ugly—this man-made world—and that we have to have to a large extent failed in the role of constructive shapers of our environment. Our physical needs have, to some extent, been fulfilled, but man-as-a-whole remains unsatisfied, in spite of the fact that our environment has been largely shaped by professionals trained in their fields, designers and artists whose sincere desire was to produce "beautiful" objects. Their whole training in the art schools gravitated around the concepts of "beauty" and "harmony," and yet even the most optimistic of us is forced to admit that, with few exceptions, the opposite has been the result. What more evidence is needed to demonstrate the fact that aesthetic concepts, into which anyone and everyone is invited to project "his own feelings," can ever result in a solution upon which more than a handful of people can agree?

Designers today will generally agree on the widespread existence of *misforms* in our environment but will often hasten to add that we today are better trained, that *we* know how to do a better job than in the past. However, is this not what our predecessors have also claimed? *Are* we actually better trained? If we are, then it can only be because we have evolved new formulations and new educational approaches.

A pretentious concern with "beauty" and "harmony" is insufficient, nor is it enough to concentrate solely on the designing of "one more object." We must cultivate a more comprehensive outlook and work toward ways and means of bringing about the realization of an environment where beauty is more than "skin deep." Too often we have created beauty spots and, soon becoming weary of them, have had them done over or have left them standing as a reminder of the transitory nature of "taste." In this haphazard manner we cannot hope to raise the level of the total environment.

Today's designing is, with some notable exceptions, the superficial correction of the mistakes of yesterday, but we should realize that, unless we revise our basic approach, the same superficial and fruitless "corrections" will continue, leaving unexplored the vast areas for new development.

All this indicates that mistakes have played an important role in the shaping of our environment. When viewed positively, as a source of learning, mistakes serve a valuable function; they indicate the degree to which we have failed at comprehension. There seem to be only three ways to avoid making mistakes—by sheer luck, by intuition, or by comprehension. Luck cannot be seriously considered a reliable method of getting things done. Intuition, which requires vast experience and/or innate ability, is also limited by personality and circumstance. The only trustworthy and educationally acceptable approach seems to be through maximum comprehension of the factors and elements involved in a given situation and the application of these data to a given problem. But, since the native ability to comprehend varies considerably from person to person and at best remains limited, a tool for extending this faculty is urgently needed. Such a tool consists of the structuring of data within a field and the subsequent building of a theory to contain the structure.

The chronology of object development may be thought of in terms of an evolutionary process from the initial research in the development of an object-to-be to the utilization of the finished product by the consumer. Of all the participants in this line of development, the scientist and engineer stand out as the most fruitful contributors. The designer, in his role of relating the object directly to man and his environment, lags far behind. In fact, his position is frequently questioned altogether. We are forced to this conclusion when we compare the theories, working methods, and end results of the designer with those of the scientists and technicians in their particular fields.

Over a period of centuries, science has built up theory and method and a constantly evolving terminology to keep pace with its stages of development. There is a never ending adjustment among "fact," theory, and terminology, one of the main characteristics of progress in any field. In the area of designing, however, we find a very different mental climate. Typical discussions usually abound in such vague and nebulous terms as "rhythm," "balance," proportion," and "harmony," with the recent addition of references to "function," "requirements," "analysis," etc. Compared to the characteristically more precise definitions of science, which make agreement between individuals possible, such terminology offers a harsh contrast. It is readily seen that the ambiguity of such words leaves them open to any and every interpretation, and that agreement between persons employing these terms becomes next to impossible. There seems to have been little effort to define terms or to come to agreement regarding conscious or unconscious assumptions.

But until such an effort is made, progress will remain slow in the field. For progress depends upon communication among the practitioners, and communication, to a large extent, depends upon agreement as to the meaning of basic terms.

Today there is little evidence of theory or conscious method underlying the practice of design. For the most part the private working habits of an individual designer cannot be considered sufficiently "methodological" to warrant the title of *method*, and this lack becomes immediately apparent when the designer attempts to communicate his particular "method" to someone else. We find often a marked antithesis to the mere notion of methodology in creative work. The contention is that ideas should spring from the intuitive faculties and that the use of system and/or method can only sterilize the imagination and result in "cold" and "depersonalized" objects. The fact that *intellect* and *consciousness* are thought of as synonymous with sterility when related to artistic creation as a whole is in itself significant and shows to what extent art is thought of as isolated from other areas of human activity —science in particular. But science owes its growth and continual development to the *integration* of intellect with intuition, and to advocate that the artist has much to learn from the scientist in no way implies that art should become intellectualized at the expense of intuition. When it is understood and demonstrated that methodology can only *free* intuition—never fetter it—then the attitude toward scientific method as applied to art will automatically change from negative to positive.

The technical consequences of industrialization now seem clear, but its cultural consequences remain obscure. In the past, when a few privileged individuals selected the forms for their time, it was relatively simple to create and maintain a coherent cultural picture. But today we deal with millions of selectors, all privileged to choose or reject. It will be a complex problem to produce an integrated environment, yet we are surely moving toward such an achievement. One thing is certain: Nostalgic longing for the cultural coherence of the past leads only to frustration and impatience with the present. Mass production and mass consumption have replaced the cozy world of the artisan and his patron.

In the preindustrial and the early industrial era, when the self-centered approach was still feasible, adherence to such a limited outlook caused no serious mischief, but the continuance of these practices in the era of mass production will have weighty consequences. A designer's own private likes and dislikes projected into the design for an object and ultimately duplicated in vast numbers through the modern machine-medium will have a much more far-reaching potential for "good" or "evil" than the object singly produced and utilized. Arbitrary personal preference for a form or a shape by an individual designer is just as haphazard as the preference for certain smells would be in the preparation of a chemical formula.

Designing for today's requirements carries with it a social responsibility, which was previously a minor factor. Such a large-scale responsibility immediately takes designing off the "personalized" level and puts it on a new plane demanding an integrated approach. This new approach in no way implies a negation of the "individual" but rather suggests a change in emphasis and will actually serve to free the creative potentialities of the individual to a degree never before thought possible.

The slow development in the design field can to some degree be accounted for by the fact that it is one of the most comprehensive professions that exists. Practitioners in the field deal with the complex problem of relating a wide variety of objects to the consumer, with regard not only to the development of a product for utilization but also to the adaptation of that object to a constantly changing, intangible group. Within this perpetually transforming sphere, the designer deals with materials, processes, problems of distribution, and the behavior of man in his changing environment. Perhaps in no other field is a comprehensive methodology so urgently needed and indispensable to further progress.

There are few areas of human activity in our present society that have not felt the impact of a more comprehensive approach. One area that has held out against this trend is the field of design. Although important advances are being made in areas related to objects, such as market research, human engineering, creative process, etc., we still lack a general approach and a structuring device by which all these and other aspects pertaining to the field of objects can be properly related to each other.

The practice and the teaching of design are today primarily a matter of experience and only to a minor degree a matter of accumulated knowledge. Competence is achieved through experience in dealing with a great number and variety of design problems.

This experience can be supplemented, broadened, and deepened through a general study of the man-made object. This study represents a new area of inquiry for which the name *objectology* is proposed. The field of the man-made object up to now, because of the magnitude and complexity of factors involved, has escaped a general study. But in every field in which man has ventured a general approach has inevitably developed from spontaneous to deliberate, finally culminating in a comprehensive theory.

# Tradition and Modern Design
## Ernesto N. Rogers
## 1957

I should like to begin by relating a personal experience which, I believe, implicitly contains most of the arguments that I shall develop later in this paper.

A few years ago I happened to be giving a course at the University of Tucumán, a city lying at the foot of the Andes in northern Argentina. There, a remarkable group of architects, unfettered by preconceptions, had been trying to set up a school of architecture that, owing to the cultural environment, proved to be one of the most intriguing human laboratories I have ever seen in my numerous travels. Many of the students, who came from the local area, had never had any direct experience with a three-dimensional work of art (which, of course, could not be sufficiently perceived in reproductions), had never seen any work of sculpture or architecture of any value. Even on the matter of pure information, they were unaware of most of the events in the history of architecture; they knew almost nothing about Michelangelo or the Gothic cathedrals or those of any other past epoch. And yet, on the subject of modern architecture—particularly Le Corbusier— they had gathered enough information to win, had there been one, a difficult television quiz game. They were like persons who had skipped infancy and had suddenly grown up. But they were grown-ups without maturity. Their lack of tradition made it extremely difficult to discuss values with them, for they were neither deep enough to be able to grasp the root meaning of any object, considering it in itself and for itself, nor vast enough to be able to express a comparative judgment between the object in question and other objects.

The most gifted of them instinctively felt their cultural insufficiency and anxiously sought to fill their lacunae by strengthening their intellectual capacity, hoping to give agility, through knowledge, to their intuition and critical reflection. At length they developed a kind of centrifugal force, which, as it could not be expanded by a real journey (during which they could have checked their intuitions against reality and widened the terms of their knowledge through direct experience), took the form of dangerous evasions, which, depending on the psychological make-up of each individual, became an inferiority complex, pessimism, or—as was most frequent—a tenuous literary delusion of belonging to the superhuman elect.

The danger for these students was that they might generalize the few notions they had and thus make it impossible for themselves to escape the kind of typological thinking that leads, nominalistically, to the identification of the formal and purely technical aspect of a given problem with the numerous solutions it really has, if one knows how to express it freely and profoundly.

I was able to observe the very opposite phenomenon at the Architectural Association School (AA) in London, where I also had the good fortune to teach. Here, the leadership of the student body was entrusted to highly cultural and intelligent persons (especially in the historical and moral disciplines), not equally endowed, however, with creative talent. Problems were faced, for the most part, from the point of view of content, with a persistent critical sense of acute dissatisfaction with every idea acquired, but all without being able to coagulate thought into form, that is, into the concrete expression of art, which is the *sine qua non* for the designer who is fulfilling the role proper to him.

The two cases I have described to you represent two extremes and show that both a primitive culture fascinated by novelty without comprehending its deeper meaning and a refined or at any rate more valid culture that merely takes the form of pure criticism of moral content without the ability to translate thought into the reality of tangible objects—both these cases are unable to grasp the fullness of an artistic phenomenon in the concrete historical process, which has established a continual relationship between the problems of form and those of content.

I might say that even beyond pedagogy, in the much vaster area of productive activity, the Tucumán school on the one hand and the AA of London on the other might symbolically represent the limits (the external limits, of course) beyond which the culture of applied arts tends to overflow (and by applied arts I mean everything from a teaspoon to a city). But every coin has its other side, and we see that, while the defect of one lies in its lack of a tradition, that of the other lies in its interpretation of reality, the product of a particular aspect of tradition (which, for Englishmen from Ruskin to the young men of our time, very often emphasizes the moral essence of an artistic object rather than its concrete plastic expression). The quality of the former lies in a kind of freshness and greater freedom from the preconceptions that the centuries have bestowed on culture and tradition; the quality of the latter lies in a greater awareness of interior richness, which, while it sometimes weighs down and checks creative impulse, is nevertheless a guarantee that, when the data of the senses fuse with those of creative activity, the result will rest on a much more solid and experienced base.

It could be said that the character of American countries tends to the limit shown by the students of Tucumán, while in European countries it tends toward the limit shown by the students of the AA in London. But it is always somewhat arbitrary to standardize, for we must take into consideration the marked shades of differences between one country and another in each group. In fact, it can be said that at the present moment architecture is particularly characterized by the achievement of a more and more precise awareness of just such shades, that is, of the data peculiar to each national culture.

The step that is being taken is a perfectly logical development of the theoretical premises of the modern movement; in fact functionalism, rather than a style in the sense of a coherent taste for the definition of a formal aspect, is essentially a method for establishing more and more subtle relationships between necessity and aesthetics (beauty is the greatest extrinsic manifestation of necessity). Therefore, at first, functionalism strove to reintroduce particularly the practical and technical meaning of the architectonic composition so that it would honestly reflect fundamental necessities common to all men; but then it deepened its content and extended the notion of necessity so as to cover not only practical but also psychological needs; from a phase of the equality of men there developed subsequently (and this without denying the achievements of a rational approach) that process of distinguishing individual from individual which had already been introduced by Art Nouveau, etc. But while Art Nouveau developed the theme of freedom of form very few tried then to give it any interior meaning, except in the case of Van de Velde, because their main concern was to free the individual artist from academic schemes rather than to create an art that suited every consumer. The second and present phase of functionalism gives attention to content and, in exploring it, draws forth the forms best suited to interpret and exalt it.

Functionalism tries to give to every man the objects he most needs, and among these objects the house, which is the most important of all, is being styled as less "everybody's" house and more "your" house.

From a movement that *malgré soi* belonged to an elite, we now see the development of a cultural operation that retraces problems to their roots, where lies the nourishing lymph from which they draw their vitality.

As it approaches the data suggested by different circumstances, design becomes less and less general and tends to interpret the values inherent in the personality of the physical and cultural environments in which the work is to take its place; thus, while it does not overlook the psychological characters of individuals, it adapts itself to the pre-existing environment.

The abstract ideology of a diffuse humanitarianism is reflected in an ideal art which, though it may take the form of a few more or less harmonic schemes, can never interpret the real aspects of existence, for these are changeable and multiple as they are *a priori* indefinable in the various cases in which that existence takes historical form.

The roots of any individual being an essential part of his personality, it becomes more than ever necessary that design, in serving society, consider that personality not only in space but also in its historical continuity in time. In other words, we must learn how to go beyond its tangible presence and penetrate into the character of the pre-existing cultural environment to which it is bound, an environment that determines a single reality (where the parameters of time and space meet). Individuals and things, the subjects and objects of artistic activity, may be considered in the light of the same critical process, inasmuch as the notion that we have of them, besides helping to evaluate them with greater precision for what they are in themselves and for themselves, creates a more subtle order of relationships both between individuals and objects and among themselves.

For traditionalist designers of the period preceding the modern movement, the problem of fitting one's works into the pre-existing environment was merely one of stylistic imitation; thus they deluded themselves that they were carrying on a tradition without realizing that theirs was a mere formalism utterly lacking in energetic content. For the first designers of the modern movement, the sense of rebellion against this state of things was inevitably to change into a bitter quarrel with the past; this went so far that every new work became an act of violence against the pre-existing environment or at best took the form of a harmonic contrast between various aspects of beauty, each autonomously valid. Today we are carrying on the very same premises as our predecessors in the modern movement, who, owing to the different conditions under which they worked, were not able to develop these premises any further. Thus, we are beginning to give much more thought to the problem of pre-existing environments, and we are not satisfied with a work that expresses our age but fails to assert the fullness of contemporary values in the context of society and space nourished by the deep roots of tradition. The modern meaning of the concept of tradition approaches that of historicism; that is, it is understood as the continuous flow of the experience of one generation into the experience of subsequent generations within the framework of one particular culture.

Tradition for us is the strain of opinions, feelings, and experiences shared by a given social group, a strain to which every individual refers his thought and action.

Thus, for the very reason that this notion is not the formulation of an abstract theory but is deduced from the pragmatic examination of facts, it acquires different meaning from country to country, and for every single problem that takes concrete form in given circumstances and in a well-defined spatial reality.

Clearly, such an outlook throws on us a responsibility that becomes more and more grave in proportion to the value of the places into which we must fit our products. For, while it is quite difficult to build where pre-existing environment is charged with evidence of an ancient but still living culture, it is equally trying to have to work within the limits of a particularly significant landscape; but it is well to remember that, just as there is no such thing as an absolute vacuum or nothingness in the order of natural phenomena (except in theory, which goes beyond normal practical considerations), so there is no such thing as a break in the complex phenomenology of history or in that of the symbols it has produced in three dimensions. Therefore, exceptional monuments and landscapes must be considered only as manifestations of the temporal and spatial vision of reality, which offers no solution of continuity. The problem of adapting new buildings to pre-existing environments may, in consequence, be more or less pressing, depending on the circumstances; but once we have put the problem—as we have done—to be examined by our conscience, it becomes an integral part of artistic interpretation at all times and in all places.

As we might expect, in Italy the problem of working contemporary activities into the texture of history is acutely felt and arouses controversy. It must be realized that ours is one of those countries in which beauty reaches the greatest of heights with respect to density, intensity, and variety because of both its extraordinary natural endowments and the heritage left to it by men during the course of its particularly dramatic history.

The great question is how to strike a balance between those who are in danger of transforming the country into a museum, embalming nature and monuments, and those others who, falling into the opposite error, would make a clean slate of everything, incredibly oversimplifying the very real difficulties before them so as to further immediate action.

In my opinion, both of them should be opposed, because both reason—perhaps unconsciously—from a superficial division of experience. Both believe that there is a break between the past and the present, or an unbridgeable gulf between the practical needs of our age and the values of culture, while it is actually a matter of creating a unity between culture and life in a fruitful cycle, a cycle in which new harmonious syntheses are continually developed among dialectic oppositions.

It will be understood that, while I defend the inalienable rights of life against any form of conservatism, these rights can be fully understood only if they are regarded in the light of a thorough examination of our entire cultural heritage. This comprises both the riches we were born to and the additions to those riches we ourselves must make with our own products, so that the society of which we are the interpreters may with dignity take its place in the great chorus of humankind.

Conservatives can to some extent be excused if we realize that their love for the beauties of our heritage is sincere and that they dread seeing that heritage ruined by new intruders, but for the most part they are sterile and incapable of any constructive gesture. Those who feel the urge to immediate action (and from this group, of course, I exclude all common speculators) may to some extent be justified if we remember that their impulses at least show vitality. But on second thought we see both of them as mere formalists who reason by generalizing from set schemes and, seeing no more than the appearances of things, fix them in immutable canons. And it is just as serious, all things considered, to believe that all the manifestations of our age are out of tune with pre-existing environments as to believe the opposite, that modern art is being sacrificed when it has to take into account that same environment. Extremes meet because they are the fruit of equally abstract mentalities.

If we grant that history has never been definable in a static system and that it has always taken the form of a succession of changes that have gradually transformed one present into another, it follows not only that it is impossible to bar the way to the expression of contemporary society but also that it is incumbent on us to make our temporal presence felt along with our natural presence in space.

By drawing the greatest possible energy from everything surrounding us, we favor the creative process of our works which, far from negatively conditioning those already present, reinforces them, for we are building a bridge between the past and the future. The future partly depends on us, just as we partly depend on the past; tradition is this perpetual flow, and to be modern means to feel oneself consciously a part, an active part, of this process.

To avoid misunderstanding, I should add that, since the masters of the modern movement are very great artists, they have implicitly achieved the value of a tradition because they were against its academic aspects only. However, later generations have felt the concept of continuity with greater awareness both because they recognize those fathers whose unexplored problems they are dealing with directly and because they are seeking to know better the ancestry of those same fathers in the long, tortuous, and dramatic process of history. We know that our statements are not the result of a denial of the preceding statements but rather acquire much greater force the more they corroborate the numerous positive values inherent in tradition. We know too that they can still be transformed into present energy. Although it is altogether logical, it is curious to note (and here I should like to return to the example of the students I described in the beginning) how certain flashy and apparently more "modern" aspects of design (especially in architecture) are seen in those countries where, though there is great economic activity, cultural conditions are less evolved (or are only the interest of small groups of elites), while the growing up of certain clichés and the consequent danger of losing one's bearings and even of relapsing into reaction may be noted in more cultured and often more socially developed countries.

In these latter countries, the search for a communicative language is becoming more and more urgent. In these same countries the physiognomy of design is taking shape because designers are rightly persuaded that the need for a communicative language cannot be satisfied by a cosmopolitan idiom; this kind of Esperanto (which actually never was a real success except as a theoretical postulation) is no longer considered a distant Utopian goal to aim at, because—owing to its very intellectualistic origins, justifiable in a certain historical climate—it could have, at the most, been imposed by some authority but could not have been useful for expressing, as we try to today, the sincere feelings of different cultural groups sprung from very different environmental conditions. The confusion and reactionary relapses to which I referred above are due to a false criticism of cosmopolitanism or, at any rate, are an erroneous interpretation of the principle (in itself quite coherent) of deepening the needs of specific cultures. I shall not mention those—of whom there are luckily very few—who have disinterred traditional styles (confusing the letter with the spirit of tradition), nor those who believe that the personalization of a design is a matter of motiveless caprice.

These are all outside the line of evolution. It is natural, however, that the attention of designers and critics should be strongly drawn to the study of popular artistic expression (folklore) and that they should seek to deepen their comprehension and uncover unsuspected values highly meaningful for establishing the relationship between form and content in those manifestations which people have handed down spontaneously, or at any rate without any awareness of the culture developed by the ruling classes.

Those who have considered these experiences without complexes have been able to draw precious instruction from them and to penetrate the content with greater human sympathy, expressing forms more in keeping with reality.

But even here, confusion between cause and effect now and then results in products that do not take into consideration the economic situation or contemporary customs, and this gives rise to another aspect of formalism aggravated morally by the attacks of demagogy of a populist kind.

What really looms at the very heart of the problem of tradition and modernity is undoubtedly that which arises from the necessity of uniting the contrasting forces of specification and standardization. This problem thus derives, to a much greater degree than it had been necessary to face before now, from the proposal to examine the relationship between tradition and modernity. For it is obvious that the more the cultural terms are specified, the more complicated the problems inherent in modern society become.

Our concept of design as method eliminates any *a priori* formulation of solutions, because it is based on pragmatic research and controls.

Therefore it is by perfecting our methodolgy and examining data case by case with greater severity that we shall discover the best ways of expressing form. Universality of method means a common conception of design, one that overlooks different traditions. The forms we shall determine—though it may seem paradoxical—will be much more suited to individual circumstances.

This undoubtedly does not exclude the standardized repetition of objects or of elements suited to the composition of a more complex object whenever conditions are such that they are required.

Cultural forces (awareness of tradition) influence the form of the design and the composition of the various standard elements, including the limits set by the consumer. Repetition is a technical act that does not involve the cultural responsibility of the designer. The designer faces this problem again when a given object is put into a relationship with other objects, that is, with an environment.

From the spoon to the town, the degree of variety in design depends on the complexity of the terms of each composition. In the design of a spoon there is a tendency toward an archetype, because between one spoon and another—considering the elementary function and the elements that determine it—variety is essentially a matter of taste, in which case the problem of tradition is, more than anything else, psychological.

The design of a house or a city may tend toward an archetype in the conception of the elements that make it up, but their combination must be left open to all possibilities; it would be foolish to think of the archetype of such a unity. Obviously, the complexity of its form corresponds to the complexity of content, so that variety must satisfy the changing syntheses of the terms that characterize a society in its historical processes.

Thus, though the relationship between quality and quantity is becoming more complex, it will find its equilibrium if we succeed in infusing design in the sense that modernity not only does not deny tradition but represents the most advanced degree of tradition itself. We shall have taken a step ahead in our purpose of giving quality to quantity.

# Communication of Values Through Design
## Richard Latham
## 1957

The problem that concerns the designer of mass-produced products is one of *value as a function of performance*. Most of the *things* any industrial designer touches perform, in one manner or another, some work for people. Some products do not actually perform a job (decorative objects, accessories, etc.) but they nevertheless perform for the owner in a very real way at an emotional level, by representing him—or what he hopes to look like—to others.

Actually, even those products that function for people also serve the second value function of expressing the owner. Both of these performance levels seem to affect the owner almost equally. Many people will accept a product whose performance is second-rate, provided it is highly acceptable socially and therefore raises their group acceptability. In some cases, this second performance means more than the real job to be done—at least it is more measurable to some people.

There is, with this emerging recognition of the emotional function of products, a good deal of confusion among consumers and designers as to how the two kinds of performance lock together. When a product is purchased purely for psychological reasons, it can be judged fairly clearly. When machines are purchased mainly for the job they do, it again is fairly easy to judge them aesthetically. In the first case we use a set of *style* values, and in the second a set of values that I call *design* enter our judgment. When the two areas are completely interlocked—in a product that must both work well and be socially correct—confusion sets in.

I have experimented with this problem of value and performance and relation to appearance in many ways in an attempt to learn how to work with it as a designer. I have sailed boats for many years and raced them in competitions. A boat is not a machine-made product, but at some point I became convinced that people judge it in much the same way they would judge a vacuum cleaner. Now, in racing yachts the standard of a "pretty boat" among men who race them is tied to performance in a seemingly pure way. In checking up on yachtsmen's opinion of "pretty boats," I encountered "length" as a factor time after time. In the class I race in, length had become the standard of performance and beauty to such an extent that the most desired boats and the most consistent winners had grown from thirty feet in length to forty-two feet in length, and the character of the hull had drawn out at both ends. It occurred to me that this sleek look and exaggerated length were not necessarily right for the job of racing. I asked the most successful designer of these boats: "Is this look the most efficient design for speed?" He answered emphatically: "No." We decided to experiment. He designed for me a boat of completely different character from the accepted long, thin norm. She was different in every way to the eye; she was shorter and higher, and even lacked the traditional detail of the deck house; finally, she had a straight spar in place of the curved mast that was the trademark for this particular class. All of these changes were made on purely technical grounds, on the basis of a theory about improving the boat's efficiency.

So the boat was built and delivered. When I first brought her out, most of those who saw her—conditioned to the old look—didn't respond well at all. By some she was pronounced ugly. Then we began to race. She began to win. As time went by, people got used to the "look" of the boat, and comments about ugliness stopped. As we won more, we heard occasional comments that "she looks very healthy." Finally we won a championship and she began to look "good." Right now the people who thought her ugly two years ago are admiring the boat and eventually, if we continue to win, she will look "beautiful." She may even become accepted as a new standard of appearance. Already some features are being copied by other owners through modifications on their present boats. One interesting sidelight is that, on all of the standard boats, a natural mahogany finish had been the accepted "beautiful" finish. We painted ours in color. This year several of the mahogany boats are being painted—including a top winner whose owner really does not have to struggle to conform.

It seems to me that the same motivating forces are working on all the things people buy and own. What they find beautiful is directly hooked to its ability to perform for them—and that, being a combination of work-doing and group acceptance at an emotional level, is often hard to pin down.

The problem is further compounded by the difficulty people have today in judging things at the performance level. When the machine separated people from things, and especially from the *making* of things, it separated them from a world of experience. A man who has never worked with his hands to carve wood or shape leather, to do any craft job, has no reliable knowledge of the performance of those materials or of their value as work-doers. When people face a car, or even a teacup, they cannot know instinctively what went into making it or whether the materials are appropriate for the job. All they can rely on is convention, hearsay, advice, or advertising. When people say, "I don't know what's good, but I know what I like," they admit this inability to judge intrinsic worth. But they know generally what the group accepts, and that is their most reliable guide, because they need to be acceptable to others in a very real way.

It seems to me that this particular fact of modern society—being separated from the real experience of inanimate materials and things—explains a great deal about the nature of fashion, fad, and taste. Social scientists point out that there are always leaders in any society who insist on being experimental in terms of *things*. These few are willing to acquire, even desirous of acquiring, new and unusual things in order to draw a line between themselves and the masses. Because those experimenters, traditionally, have also been in a position to be more knowledgeable than the masses, the very possessions they find new and daring and therefore valuable tend to become the norm of the next period. Apparently this has been the case throughout history, according to the experts, with one exception: today.

The top stratum of society today is in no better position to know the intrinsic value of things than the general public, being just as cut off from direct experience.

No doubt there is a direct relationship between our loss of "knowing about things" and our willingness to participate. People as a whole are less and less willing to participate in anything—from group singing to sanding a piece of wood (even though, from time to time, movements sweep the country that seem to fight this trend to passivity by organized patterns). By and large, this is an age that wants to be entertained, that expects to have things done to them and for them. Some people feel that the machines being created to work for men and women are reducing them to a state of nothingness. But the social scientists are not particularly worried about the evils of eliminated work *per se*; what worries them is that the machines become a substitute for a *learning experience*. You cannot learn unless you participate, and you cannot participate in television or the movies.

There also seems to be a direct relationship between credit and conformity. In a culture based on the need to be a good credit risk, it is very difficult to depart too far from the norm in either behavior or the purchase of a product. Anyone who has tried to finance a house that doesn't conform, or a car that is not average, knows this in a very real way. A man who practices design is in no better position to "not conform" than anybody else. If he wants to distinguish himself as a "character," it will have to be a very acceptable kind of character, or he will make his clients uncomfortable and run the risk of being unsuccessful.

When you superimpose these pictures—the loss of ability to judge intrinsic values and the pressures to conform—you get a new image that begins to explain the problem in design today. The next element of the problem is tradition. When people were separated from materials and began losing contact with the experience of innate goodness, they also lost contact with tradition. To be sure, Americans did not lose contact with vestiges of traditionalism, but today premachine tradition seems to be a diminishing factor in guiding people in their choice of things. I am referring to tradition not as a style but as a continuum of culture—the aggregate of mass learning about ways of living, thinking, relating to inanimate materials and objects. It is only by retracing the steps of the human learning process that anyone can build a platform of knowledge on which to base experiments with newness, to create new aesthetic expressions. Lacking this base, is it any wonder that our country, looked at abstractly, is terribly confused and ugly? We are surrounded by insensitive buildings, ungraceful things, vulgar expressions in color and form. Most of them, I might add, are considered "modern" and therefore good. It is this "newness" that is one of our most reliable guides to goodness.

But I am not talking simply about mass vulgarity. I am talking about people of so-called good taste too.

We have had, in the last twenty-five years, a modern movement. We have come to know what products are "contemporary" by the way they look. Believing the new is good, we think what came before must be bad and must be erased. Yet how do we know? How, without studying tradition, could we know? Do we dare take someone's word for it? Can we accept a show of good design without being sure, ourselves, why it's good, and without being sure we can identify bad design as readily? I am prepared to believe that there is good and bad, but I am not prepared to believe that it is a simple matter of a contemporary look, a fad, a style, a matter of good taste.

Mary Mix Foley says in *Forum* that mass taste is nonexistent and presents evidence of this in our present environment. She feels that the architect must take things in hand.

Now this question of elevating low public taste and vulgar needs is a very pertinent one. It assumes that there is also high taste, and that the low taste can be elevated from bad to good or to a level that somebody else says is good. Is this "low public" even aware of the word taste? Do they even concern themselves with it as a problem? It seems possible that in many social groups there is very little self-consciousness about taste because there is no conscious striving toward a standard other than their own. "Taste" becomes self-conscious in the mobile middle classes because it implies an awareness of a standard that is beyond their own group, beyond their own ability to distinguish with assurance between good and bad. I imagine that taste, originally referring to social manners, became a problem when it was possible to learn manners that you might not have been born with in order to convince those who mattered that you deserved to belong to a higher social group. In a contemporary society cut loose from the moorings of clear-cut class distinctions of tradition and of direct experience, taste becomes another kind of anchor; it is a sure way to know good from bad. For an aspiring middle class, it becomes a steadying rung on the way up the ladder. For a more secure upper, intellectual, or professional class, it becomes a symbol of superiority and a defense against unacceptability, against being confused with a class that is less socially acceptable.

What taste is, in all its elements, is a fairly complex question. It certainly involves the values of performance and self-expression already discussed. And it certainly is *not* art—for, in spite of the fact that taste and art may overlap at times, art is frequently in opposition to prevailing standards. Taste is at best, it seems to me, a ticket to cultural enjoyment and to art created by someone else. At worst, it is a rigid standard of values, a standard that permits easy emulation because it is detached from the more involved aspects of human existence. I submit that this problem of taste should be very much on every designer's mind today.

Suffering from the same isolation from nature and materials as others, he tends to take the same path to the security of taste that is common everywhere. He will avoid driving an American car because it is of bad design but will drive a European product that was directly influenced by America and consider it "honest" when, in fact, it is no closer to a correct expression of a motored vehicle than a Buick. What it is closer to is a set of values that shows he is more vulnerable to style than those he styles for. If he is able to go beyond momentary fashion, he may, in fact, surround himself at home with objects and works of art that are really beautiful, but, confronted with two fighter planes of distinctly unequal merit, he is unable to distinguish between them and will probably find them both beautiful.

I do not deny that this is an extremely human and exceedingly difficult problem. Designers face the quandary that everybody faces in today's society—but in allowing themselves credit for more developed sensibilities and in assuming the right to create objects for other people, they also inherit a responsibility to do the more intelligent job of tackling those problems. I observe, on the contrary, that many a designer is too content to crank out what he feels is good for people, knowing little about people and caring less. He is mainly concerned that his relationship with the maker of things be successful, and that success is based on selling the most things to the most people at a fair profit. But to do this, he sees only two blunt alternatives. He must either impose on others his own taste—the one he knows and accepts—or make a heartless stab at imitating taste levels that he basically disdains. He cannot sympathize with the patterns of other groups if he is uninterested in the basic workings of humanity. He cannot communicate with other people at a general, human level until he becomes a student of the basic elements of nature, materials, and human beings.

One of the most serious problems facing the designer of mass goods today is how to transcend this taste barrier, how to get more knowledge of the relation between social and functional values in order to achieve more creative *design* solutions. There are no easy answers. I certainly don't go along with the designers who console themselves that things are getting better aesthetically; that people are reaching "higher taste levels" and eventually it will all work out. This sounds, rather, as if the designer wants to rationalize his own desire to hang on to a set of values and hopes rather desperately that everyone will eventually learn to see things his way. It also sounds as if he is closing his eyes to the facts, believing only what he reads about a fairly fashionable subject in the fairly fancy magazines. I recently had a chance to see several hundred color slides of typical working-class homes across the country, showing inside and outside views. It was a devastating four hours. It forced me to face a reality I am generally blind to—on purpose. It left me shocked at what I saw, and just as shocked at my own lack of knowledge about mass taste, and somewhat doubtful of my ability, as a designer, to understand who "people" really are. These working-class families had tried to assemble, from the multitude of goods offered to them by designers and manufacturers, some picture of what they are. The picture was full of horror and disharmonies to any-one trained in visual values. But beneath each of those physical symbols —the lace coverlet and chenille scatter rugs and chrome dinette furniture —there was a real *emotional need* for the purchase. The symbols were no doubt confused in terms of what they were called on to do in the lives of these people; and the people's ability to discriminate and grasp the meaning of things, traditions, materials was certainly not well developed. But the needs and impulses are quite real, and who dares to scoff—without first comprehending those needs—or to insist that they substitute another set of symbols?

As designers, we may properly assume responsibility for goodness and badness in the work we create; we are called upon, and entitled, to make value decisions. We are also entitled to a pioneering spirit and a desire to see things change for the better; we need not assume that *what is* is always inevitable or for the best. I believe that change, even for its own sake, can be a good thing. But I contend that, before we dare assume this right to judge and shape other people's values, we had better first examine our own values and our own motives for wanting to exercise this control over the lives of others. In doing so, it might be helpful to go back and begin separating the truths of design from the fancies of fashion, and the truths about all people from our fancies about ourselves. The profession of engineering, born with the machine, has made logical progress ever since by daring to face facts and pursue experiment. We designers, too, can begin to build a meaningful aesthetic culture if we are willing to prepare ourselves for a new learning experience, and we cannot learn unless we participate.

## VIII  Dissent

Though Aspen often called on the services of the more formidable social critics of the day—the late C. Wright Mills, for instance—the most slashing attacks on irresponsibility and hypocrisy in the business aspects of design always came from designers who knew business from the inside, as in this punchy dissent from the myth of the corporate image by a California designer with twenty years of business experience behind him.

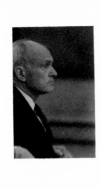

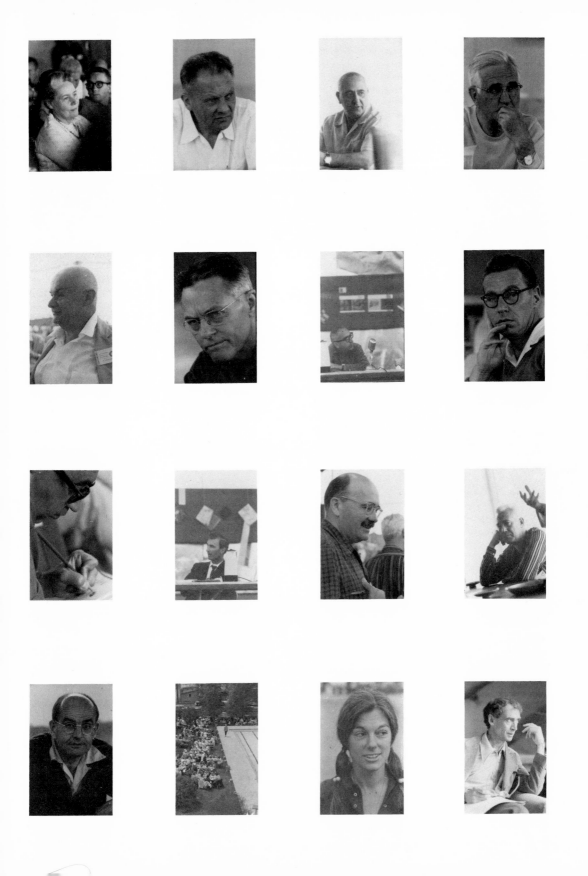

# Image or Façade?
## James Real
## 1959

Only recently the term "corporate image" has been seized upon by people in business and industry, who have been grateful for an omnibus term into which they could deposit such a wide range of meanings.

It is probably safe to say that no two of us have precisely the same image of an "image." The dictionary definition suggests that there is carried in the word an implication of accuracy of reflection, that an image is a synthesis of a truth, a recognizable and convenient representation of a person, an object, or an enterprise. Yet only in noble and uncomplicated situations is this definition completely acceptable. The majority of human enterprises are sufficiently imperfect that they submit to intense scrutiny only at considerable risk to themselves. With the exception of a handful of undertakings that are so patently good or so irresistibly powerful that they may project themselves with candor, we are talking about a *distortion* of the image.

There are numberless ways in which the image can be tampered with. The simplest and most morally comfortable method is to delineate only those aspects or components that are generally held to be good. Those less desirable are thus not contained in the image at all and, by implication, simply do not exist. Sometimes the construction of an idealized portrait involves a dual chore: A new *virtue* is introduced and then promoted simultaneously with the enterprise it is intended to enhance. Examples of this kind of construction are common in politics, wherein each candidate—being automatically *for* everything good and firmly *against* everything bad—finds his image neutralized at the very outset and starts out as a matter of course to find something new that is bad or something new that is good, in effect, to create a new virtue, which he hopes is salable to the electorate. Examples of this tortuous method are not unknown in industry. The deodorant is invented, and, as a concomitant, perspiration becomes unspeakable; the television set is produced, and you will render your child neurotic and ill-informed if you deny him access to it.

In times past the image construction has consisted of a highly complex undertaking's being represented by the controlled personal presentation of one man. There were so many pitfalls involved in this purely Machiavellian chore (which focused so uncompromisingly on the Prince) that succeeding generations of corporate-image constructors have tended to select less volatile and more easily manipulatable components within the enterprise with which to work. This has led to a search for elements that the various publics can identify with the corporation and generally accept as "good." The trouble is that in a complex technological society a common "good" is hard to define, and the striving for empathy from everyone often leads to the coining of multiple images, which merely disguise and diffuse the true nature of the institution.

In a recent discussion of the corporate image in the *Harvard Business Review,* Pierre Martineau illustrates the reduction of a complex corporate image problem to what he feels is its lowest common denominator, which he says will have far more important bearing on the image than "all the knowledge of the economists and the lawyers." In a series of quotations of unspecified origin, he gives us this picture of three of the world's most complex and visible corporations.

> In the public eye [General Motors] is not seen as a huge corporation dominating the automobile field. At the point of public contact, the GM image has filtered down to become one of pleasant people making and selling cars at retail, figuring out trades so the prospect can have a car with a radio, white side-wall tires, and blue windshield glass. 'GM bargains with me; it wants me to be happy with a new car.'
>
> Jersey Standard is not 'the biggest oil company'; rather, it handles Flit and radiator cleaner just like any small company handling small things. So people can like Jersey. 'How can you hate a company that makes Flit?'
>
> United States Steel brought itself within public awareness by promoting a 'White Christmas'; people like the notion of appliances for Christmas, and therefore U.S. Steel is simple and nice.

Regardless of Dr. Martineau's innocent, finger-painted world, Jersey Standard *is* the largest and most powerful oil company in the United States; General Motors still dominates the United States auto market and intends to continue to do so; and U.S. Steel, while it may be "nice," is scarcely simple.

The image-makers sophism is the diminution of everything—the complex is always simple; the huge is really a lot of tiny, friendly units; the hard-eyed professional board of directors is composited as a clean-toothed kid at the gas pump. Everybody is innocent, warm, and above all *simple.*

Yet almost nobody who can read believes this. They may be uninterested and let it go for what it is, a façade. But it is a diversion rather than a believable proposition. For other aspects of the nature of the corporation are apparent. The internal struggles for power, the sporadic contests with government and labor, the international power involvements, the stock raids—all these great industrial activities are reported regularly by the press to a moderately literate people. By these means the public is daily absorbing and storing impressions and counter-images, which are considerably more complicated than "Mom loves Esso."

At what point does the bland and innocent construction endorsed by Dr. Martineau become an active encumbrance to the corporate image? I suppose the rule of thumb is that it works only so long as one doesn't get caught at it, as long as it is not significantly apparent that the object and the image have suffered what Harvey Wheeler has called "product schizophrenia"—a major separation of the product's public personality from its inner nature and meaning. At that mysterious point, the public turns its back on the object, because it has become patent that the image has lied.

The image-maker's dilemma is that he has, of course, so many bases to cover. A modern industrial complex, which houses the diverse functions of production, distribution, and retail marketing, requires several public faces; hopefully, none contradicts any other. An example of this is a modern oil company in the United States, involved in foreign relations on an almost ambassadorial level; conducting complex relationships with innumerable federal, state, and local governmental bodies; and finally running a vast public relations and retail marketing operation. There are pressing daily demands to represent many kinds of "good" at many levels. At one level the company may be negotiating a foreign concession at very considerable risk to the military position of the United States; at another, it may be openly lobbying for the preservation of its hard-won tax advantages or involved in a power struggle for a tidelands concession; at still another, it may be attempting to sell a community on the virtues of in-community slant drilling; and finally, it is busy at the retail level elaborating on its minute advantages over its competition, pushing whatever consumer benefits are remotely consistent with its ability to deliver.

There is obviously built into this series of relationships any number of potentially contradictory "goods." On the retail level, where the advertising occurs, the simple and almost always rather vacant façade is maintained. Here the enterprise is portrayed as the eager servant of the individual; it repetitiously contends that it is more friendly, more sincere, more conscientious, more concerned, better equipped, and more knowledgeable than its competitors. So long as its arguments for favor stay within these traditional confines, it can generally be thought of as a hard-working contributor to the public wellbeing. At this point, the best of all worlds is that described by Martineau. But its corporate character becomes increasingly complex as it moves away from the simple retail level and attends to chores less visible to the public eye. Political negotiation on a much more private level becomes the primary tool used to forward the corporate ends. It is only when something goes wrong in the normal political relationships that the corporation is forced to bring its semiprivate problems to the attention of the public and to borrow against its wholesome retail image for political advantage. The image-tenders should sense that this revelation of part of the inner nature of the enterprise is likely to come into sharp conflict with the retail façade. A striking example of this was the massive pitting of one petroleum group against the other in a referendum brought before the California electorate in 1956. This internecine war finally involved such tactics as one industry group's portraying the other on outdoor billboards as a very carnivorous shark about to devour the tiny fish marked "public." The voters of California overwhelmingly defeated the side backed by the more powerful segment of the industry. At least one firm of commercial political manipulators went into decline, and an experienced director of public relations for one of the biggest of the firms has commented privately that the ill-conceived campaign had set back the oil industries' relations with the public by twenty years. While it might be argued that the defeat of the referendum stemmed from the complicated and ambiguous arguments presented to the voters, one could also speculate that the exposure of a part of the inner nature of the petroleum business was completely and offensively incompatible with the innocent, friendly retail images that had been so painstakingly constructed over so long a time. Even though hoary political devices such as "citizens' committees," both for and against, were employed in the campaign, it was evident that the millions of propaganda dollars being employed were not those of public-spirited citizens but were finding their way from the tills of those sparkling, friendly gas stations.

What effect did this naked power brawl have on the oil companies' relationships with the buying public? Gasoline continued to be pumped at ever increasing rates, and no particular company encountered significant losses in "share-of-market." In immediately discernible terms, then, there was no loss whatever; but it will be a long time before the petroleum industry can confidently utilize the referendum in California, no matter how pressing its needs may be or how just the cause. There is a public deposit of suspicion and cynicism that only time and good behavior can eradicate.

One can view the plight of the people responsible for this debacle with a good deal of sympathy, for it is the very nature of the managerial bureaucracy to subordinate long-term good to short-term gains. The primary function of the manager is to run a profit-making enterprise, and accountability for the efficient performance of this function is very short-term indeed. The annual report is management's recurring personality crisis, and there are few managers who can survive even a relatively short-term decline in profit performance, even though they may offer the alternative of a clearly defined long-term gain of much greater total magnitude. Thus, although the manager is committed to simultaneous "goods," both short-range and long-range, the realistic emphasis is on *now*. The day has passed when heroic corrections can be contemplated, such as the one performed by Ford when he simply shut down the factory for a year to evolve what he considered to be the best long-term solution for the company. This sort of action is now the unique prerogative of the entrepreneur and is out of the question for even the most powerful of corporate heads. Aside from responsibilities to the owners or shareholders, the modern corporation has, for one reason or another, taken on simultaneous responsibilities as a ward of the workers and a political and social participant in the affairs of the community. In some cases, it bears serious, although not necessarily welcome, responsibility for the basic economic health of the nation itself. Each of these additional responsibilities limits the functions and range of action of the managers themselves. Out of this diverse set of relationships comes the demand for a wide range of private and public behavior. Paternalism, authoritarianism, political outrage, commercial innocence, social concern —these are but a few of the interchangeable faces the modern manager is required to display with believable dexterity. When the necessity arises to display two or more of these images simultaneously, a perfectly natural crisis of personality is the price of attempting to be all things to all men.

The corporation has been led to believe over a long period of time that it could construct a composite image of itself suitable for any occasion. The one widely touted as the most effective and reasonable of achievement has been the "simple and nice" variety. But it should be apparent to the policy-makers in business and industry that this is a concept cut out for a more innocent age than the one in which we are living and are going to live. It seems to me that there is a tenable argument for depositing a great deal more direct faith in the public itself. I would argue that the preservation of the private enterprise system is dependent upon a continuous presentation of a reasonably honest image of the responsibilities of a modern corporation and the *limits* of those responsibilities. It can come as no shock to the people to be told that the primary function of the modern business enterprise is to generate profit and that anything else that it does in response to demands of the society on its behavior is extraneous to the principal business of making money. I believe this sort of thing can be done with considerable grace, with the consequence of high acceptance, and that it can be achieved quite separately from the creation and maintenance of what I have called the "retail image."

We can foresee public troubles on the corporate horizon that simply cannot be covered by hiding under the "White Christmas" or any other slick and frivolous diversion. For, as the new technological age advances, it will be accompanied by social and economic difficulties that will strain the relationships between the corporation and the public in ways not predicted by those who have been heralding the "new age of leisure." For instance, we can begin to see massive and complicated consequences to the accelerating changeovers to automation, which suggest that the nineteenth-century urban industrial city and those who live in it will suffer severe disorientation and that unemployment, relocation, and significant shifts in the nature of the labor market are but a few of the problems that the whole industrial community —the corporation, the people, and their government—will have to share. Questions and problems of this magnitude are not to be seriously affected by clean typography, neighborly-neighbor advertisements, Bauhaus factories, or lemon-yellow boxcars.

The language of vision, like any other language, can be lied in. As many frauds have been perpetrated in Bodoni as by Barnum. The central problem pressing upon the designer is the *nature* of the image. Is he helping construct an image with decent powers of reflection, or is he building masks behind which the verities and strengths of the free society are slowly eroding away?

# IX  The Word

Curiously enough, Marshall McLuhan has never made the Aspen scene so far (an omission that will surely be remedied), but the conferences seem to have managed pretty well—if only because communication was so persistently discussed there, and often with the depth of perception and robust common sense that is shown here by Lancelot Hogben, of *Mathematics for the Millions* fame, well before *Understanding Media* hit the market.

# The Printed Page
## Lancelot Hogben
## 1959

In its wider relevance to design, the story of the printed page begins with the emergence on this planet of the inter-fertile local varieties of a species that includes Eisenhower, Khrushchev, Nehru, Chiang Kai-shek, and Paul Robeson. The prince of master printers, himself a Founding Father of the American Constitution, the inventor of the first salable electrical device and the author of the terms "positive" and "negative" in the context of the electrical charge, spoke half the truth when he declared man to be a tool-making animal. The uniqueness of man depends on another circumstance. Man can uniquely communicate the experience he gains through changing his environment by the exercise of his tool-making powers, and he thereby creates a society in which successive generations start life with a new potential for further change. *Homo sapiens* can do so partly because he is endowed with the gift of speech. In some measure this was probably true of his immediate predecessors, such as *Homo neanderthalensis,* but our own species has been from the outset a picture-making animal. The deathless cave paintings of the Aurignacian hunters still speak to us in a language beyond the range of the human voice and of the grave.

For fifteen or twenty millenniums, hunting and food-gathering nomadic tribes of our own species had no chart other than the rising and setting positions of stars to guide them in the trek to new hunting grounds or seasonal sources of plant food, and no calendar other than the moon's phases or the rising and setting of stars just before dawn or just after sunset. When they blundered into herdsmanship and scattering wild grasses to harvest, a more settled mode of life made a more reliable calendar to guide their seasonal pursuits a social necessity and provided the opportunity for recording the basic data. Because time flies, we cannot number days as we number sheep in a flock. An aide-mémoire is an imperative need; and the repetitive strokes of all early numeral signs betray both their origin as a tally made by chipping marks on stone or a tree trunk and the nature of the initial impetus to a written record. Thereafter, the more primitive gift of picture-making supplied the means of labeling the items of the calendrical tally to make a script fossilized for us at the most primitive level on temple sites in the jungles of Central America.

Thenceforth, the practicability of printing as a paying proposition depends on the tortuous course which the art of writing itself pursued. The Mayan elaboration signalizes the separation of a privileged caste from the herdsmen and toilers of the soil as custodians of a calendar with a ritual whose significance is none the less utilitarian because its contemporary rationale endowed the astronomer with opportunities to exploit the superstitions of the underprivileged. As the wealth of the temple increased, the uses of writing became more elaborate to record rules of mensuration and codes of law, as well as a succession of celestial observations. Before 2000 B.C., the temple observatories of Egypt and Mesopotamia had assembled ample libraries of the written word, and the growth of private property *pari passu* with the growth of arbitrary authority had promoted the use of pictorial seals to proclaim authority, ownership, or workmanship.

In such seals, we possibly see a new ingredient for the elaboration of a pictorial script and very surely a premonition of the printer's art. In Sumeria no later than 3000 B.C. we descry another. Here the symbols other than numeral signs had relinquished any recognizable trace of their pictorial significance through the practice of punching the strokes in the manner called cuneiform with a wedgelike die on soft clay, afterward baked in the sun.

Whether or not the pictorial character of the symbols continued to be recognizable, as in the earliest form of Chinese writing, the scripts of the temple libraries of antiquity, like the script of contemporary China, consisted of symbols for individual words, having as such no connection with their constituent sounds. Independently, in many parts of the world, peoples who came in contact with the possessors, while unfamiliar with the meaning of the signs, interpreted the signs of monosyllabic words as symbols for sounds from which it was possible to build polysyllabic words, as with the Kana syllabaries of Japan. This adaptation is easy and satisfactory if the words of a language, as is true of Japanese, Swahili, or Fijian, consist of strings of simple monosyllables, as in familiar place names like Na-ga-sa-ki or Ho-no-lu-lu.

In such languages, the total number of different syllables may be no more than fifty. In an Indo-European language, such as Greek or our own, it runs into tens of thousands, so a syllabary could never serve its needs. Owing to the happy accident that a root word with a unique meaning in the Semitic languages has a unique framework of three consonants with two changeable vowels intervening, it was possible for Semitic slaves in the Egyptian mines to carry the breakdown further by using Egyptian word-signs for consonants. This first consonantal alphabet came into being about 1800 B.C., distributed by the Semitic Phoenician traders throughout the Mediterranean and eastward from the seaboard of Asia Minor. For a millennium at least, it was of little use except for short inscriptions or annotations. Seemingly it had little prospect of superseding the hierarchical scripts of the great temple libraries of the period. Its wider usefulness became speedily apparent about 650 B.C. through a unique combination of circumstances.

The Greek-speaking, seafaring trade rivals of the Phoenicians had hitherto had no script other than the syllabic writing of Cyprus and Crete, both grossly inadequate to do justice to the phonetic structure of their language. By completing the Semitic battery of sound-signs with vowel symbols seemingly taken from the syllabaries, and by adopting the use of papyrus from Egypt, they equipped themselves with a script fitting to their linguistic requirements and with a writing surface easy to store in a small space. A new literate class of master navigators eager to exploit and to advance astronomical knowledge with a new end view thus emerges in the same social context with a tribal dance institutionalized as a dramatic spectacle. For the first time in history, the *compère* of the spectacle could produce a script that was not merely a record of events, observations, or rules. It recorded the spoken word as such and set a standard for the dialogue form, in which the writings of Plato persist to remind us of the follies his teachings have perpetuated.

Such is the first milestone in the slow advance toward making our world literate. Before the beginnings of printing, the only other notable incidents in the story are the creation of the great library, which harvested all the lore of the priestly astronomers and mathematicians in Alexandria (*circa* 300 B.C.), and the emergence of a trade in scrolls during the reign of the successor of Julius Caesar, who had been inadvertently responsible for the destruction by fire of much of the contents of the Alexandria library. When the latter passed out of the picture, China had taken the first tentative steps toward the creation of a press.

In the country that first used silk as a fabric and learned to make paper early in the Christian era, the transition from the use of seals to stamp patterns on silk to block printing of pictures was a short step; but a cumbersome battery of signs could offer promise of no advance toward the wide literacy that the alphabet sponsored in the Western world. There, the introduction of block printing along with paper from China about A.D. 1200, initially for producing playing cards or pictures of saints for sale at religious festivals, was a more encouraging invitation to the assembly of movable type amenable to repetitive use—if disarticulated.

Happily, the art of the armorer and the goldsmith could accomplish this innovation as soon as the Renaissance painters began to use oil pigments that cling to a metal edge: The production of thousands of copies of a book was thereafter possible in the time taken by one scrivener to complete a single copy for the library of a Florentine nobleman or a German monastery. We thus pass the second milestone in the advance toward literacy on a global scale. How vastly printing stimulated the advance of anatomy, botany, map-making, navigational astronomy, musical notation, dictionary-making, secular instruction, political and theological controversy, and drama and fiction in the three centuries after the beginning of printing from movable type is a threadbare theme. Nonetheless, a book was a precious possession even among the more prosperous classes of Europe and America in 1750, where the unprivileged majority without the means of purchasing the written word had neither incentive nor inclination to read or write.

After the introduction of steam power, a congeries of circumstances coalesced in the succeeding century to inaugurate the aspiration to universal literacy in the countries that successively adopted mechanization of manufacture and of transport. The power-driven press immediately made possible the production of daily newspapers recording topical events for the more prosperous, and the telegraph made negligible the delay between event and transmission. By the middle of the nineteenth century, the production of paper, hitherto made from rags, first from grasses and later from wood pulp, vastly diminished its cost. Meanwhile photography had given a new impetus to the production of pictorial matter.

Before the end of the century, the linotype had cheapened and speeded up the rate of type-setting for the daily. By then, advertisement had come to stay, and advertisements could finance pictorial newspapers, which gained the ear of a vastly greater market by equipping it with a new incentive, as well as out-of-school opportunities to become literate. With the implementation of universal literacy in the more highly industrialized communities of the West, we pass the third milestone in the advance toward worldwide literacy for all; and we may hope that the efforts of UNESCO will help us to complete the last lap of the journey before the present century comes to a close.

Let us therefore now turn to an examination of the impact of means of communication of more recent origin than printing from movable type. *En passant,* it is relevant to anticipate that the introduction of photostatic reproduction and of a typewriter that justifies the line will soon make mechanical assembly of movable type as much an anachronism as hand-setting; but if the compositor's job becomes a clerical task, the make-up of the printed page will not necessarily wear a new look. The issues I invite you to consider next strike at deeper roots:

1.   Can other means of communication adequately replace the printed page?
2.   Will their rightful exploitation diminish the demand for the printed page relative to the size of the literate public?
3.   How far does a plan of peaceful coexistence for the two call for a new program of book design?

In the first question, *adequately* is the operative word. I have great sympathy with those who deplore the intrusion of radio and television on time formerly free for home study from the printed page. One may admit that many, of whom I am not one, derive stimulus from the drone of the human voice; that the level of illustration in most educational books is appallingly below the level of screen technique; and that dynamic concepts are far more easy to grasp when presented by moving images than by a static picture. Nonetheless, I submit that no sound or screen record can adequately replace book work in the foreseeable future, unless tapes and films with devices for reversing, slowing down, and speeding up at will the direction in which flow of information proceeds collectively become as cheap as books with the same content. In reading, one can skip what is tediously familiar and ponder at length on what is more difficult to grasp. One can turn the pages backward or forward to interpret the author's meaning in the light of previous statements or of what occurs later. This freedom confers an incentive to concentrated attention and acts as a brake on superficial assent. By making it possible to devote the same time more profitably to the same task, it entails a vast economy of effort and attention profitably expended.

To regard reliance on mechanized instruction without reliance on the printed page as calamitous does not, however, mean that we should also regard more extensive use of sound and television with disfavor, nor that their more extensive use need curtail the need for book learning. Two considerations overlooked in discussion about the need for recruiting more and better teachers will clarify the prospect:

1. Countries such as China or Nigeria, now aspiring to a much higher level of literacy, do so because there are urgent tasks for which there is a shortage of highly trained manpower, even for ordinary clerical tasks;

2. Countries such as Britain, which is extending the scope of educational opportunities to a much larger section of the population than heretofore, are also providing an increasing number and variety of outlets for highly trained personnel to meet the needs of advancing technology in general and of automation in particular.

Clearly, Ghana cannot have many home-trained (and better) teachers for its Northern Territories if it is to have enough agricultural experts to raise the level of soil productivity; nor many home-trained professors, if it is to have many home-trained engineers for the Volta project. Clearly, Britain cannot both have many more and at the same time sorely needed better teachers to expand its educational system when industry offers such increasing and varied prospects of more remunerative employment. Since we cannot have our cake and eat it, the only way of insuring against a deterioration of the quality of instruction is to solve a new problem in a new way. The depressing results of school films and broadcasting offered as a way of keeping children quiet while the teacher corrects test papers is not a reason for being pessimistic about what should be achievable within the framework of a program deliberately designed with a *curricular,* in contradistinction to an *apéritif,* aim.

How far it would be desirable to replace formal instruction of the sort we now have in countries such as America or Britain by exploiting the new means at our disposal is an issue about which I feel neither confident nor sufficiently competent to express an opinion. Both because of the expansion of educational opportunity in the new society and because of the circumstances attendant on, or resulting from, this expansion, it is clear that there will be a diminishing reservoir of talent from which to recruit teaching personnel. In short, there can never again be such good teachers for the many as there were for the few at a time when, for so many of them, teaching was the one avenue to creative self-expression open to gifted but underprivileged individuals.

Whether we like it or not, we shall therefore have to exploit new means of instruction. I have long seen this. Indeed, I anticipated in print more than ten years ago America's tentative lead to Britain in this matter; and I should be as happy if Britain responded to America's lead, as I deplore the havoc the Columbia doctrine of free discipline has wrought on British education during the last twenty-five years. Unhappily, there is a Gresham's Law of Educational Bimetalism. The baser currency drives the better out of circulation. Thus it has been that America and Europe have each copied the worst features of the educational system of the other to the disadvantage of the best. If I state my opinion strongly in favor of a new trend I advocated before there was any imminent possibility of its realization, I must repeat what I have already implied. I believe that radio and television can solve the modern problem of shortage of talented teacher personnel in a world of wider educational opportunities if, and only if, we can give it a curricular orientation entirely divorced from the prepossessions of the entertainment business.

To do so, we must enlist in the effort people who know the fundamental difference between clean, wholesome fun and genuine hard work. Certainly on this understanding, the exploitation of the newest visual aids will not mean that there will be need for less books in the immediate future. In territories where our fellow world citizens have not as yet passed the third milestone of the saga of the advance to universal literacy, there will be vastly more customers for the book trade if we can use the new means at our disposal to speed up universal literacy; and where literacy is already well-nigh universal, the new means at our disposal can so expand the appetite for learning that the output of new informative literature will receive a powerful stimulus.

The word *informative* in this context is my own clue to a tentative answer to the third question I have stated, that is to say, will the exploitation of the new means at our disposal change the aspect of the printed page? The answer is surely affirmative. Most professional parents are beginning to realize what publishers already know. In the wider world of modern literacy, teen-agers will no longer lap up Jane Austen, Charles Dickens, Thomas Hardy, George Eliot, etc.; and it is very difficult for anyone to write a historical novel with a larger reading public than that of *Science for the Citizen*. The enormous sales of the version of Toynbee and Trevelyan's *English Social History* show that there now exists a reading public that is too avid for historical knowledge to imbibe information diluted with erotic irrelevance in the grand Victorian manner.

Still looking at the issue from the viewpoint of the publisher, we can, I think, forecast one way in which the exploitation of the new aids will change the character of the printed page. I shall give only one example. There is an enormous market in the high school for textbooks of mathematics. Almost every publisher would agree with me about the one criterion of successful salesmanship of such a book. Lazy teachers, who cannot be bothered to make up their own examples or take the trouble to mark test papers under their own steam, like a book that contains hundreds of examples for dictation and answers duly vetted as correct. The expository content of the book is utterly irrelevant from their viewpoint, partly because they know that their pupils are not sufficiently literate to take any notice of it, partly because the expository content is far above the heads of its ostensible readers, and partly because the good teacher knows that he or she can do the job not much worse.

What is true of mathematics is true of school books in general. In so far as the charity is in aid of anything, it is in aid of the teacher, and in so far as it is in aid of the teacher, the Telly-Talky could do most of the expository part better, though only part of it if the pupil is to have any way of going back to what the Telly-Talky lessons have taught in order to check up on whether he or she has got the gist of it. To sum up my answer to the third question I have propounded, I think we may say that, though there is no reason to anticipate that the exploitation of the new means at our disposal will diminish the demand for the printed page, and ample reasons for believing that it will increase it, we may certainly foreçast that it will increasingly change the content of what printed matter is sought and set a new standard of design for books, which satisfy an abiding need. Clearly, the exploitation of new aids to human communication based on radio transmission will neither immediately curtail the demand for the printed page nor tolerate its present aspect in a large and lucrative contemporary domain of publishing. By speeding up the liquidation of illiteracy in parts of the world where millions still have no access to the written word, its effect during the coming century will be a vast expansion of demand for printed matter, albeit for a printed matter with the new look. This new look signifies a new relation among publisher, author, and illustrator. Vis-à-vis the production of educational books, the publisher is still too commonly an inert middleman, with or without ostensibly expert advisers, between the printer and the author. Most publishing firms on my side of the Atlantic hold the author responsible for producing the illustrations, execrable in themselves if the author, like most of his kind, has no talent for visual aids, and otherwise deplorably executed because the author cannot afford to commission a commercial artist to give visual copy an attractive appearance on the printed page.

The likely outcome of this will be more evident to experts of industrial design than to most publishers or authors. The production of de luxe catalogues with attractive illustrations in color has brought into being the new profession of the book designer, whose job it is to coordinate intelligently the work of author and illustrator. Only by enlisting the good offices of the book designer will it be possible to supplement what the Telly-Talkies can do usefully with what only the printed page can do at all. As with all innovations, this will mean hardship for the old firm. The young author will not, with unusual good luck, graduate to best-sellership overnight. The old family firm of publishers who are merely somnolent middlemen will go out of business.

On the other hand, there will be new opportunities for young authors to learn the art of authorship at less sacrifice of the many for the few; and publishers with vision will be able to design books at a cheapening cost, exploiting the additional dimensions of color by disposition of visual material. They will be able to plan the simultaneous production of foreign translations, sharing the major items of production costs.

The lucrative possibilities of this for the publisher who is not merely a middleman are inviting. I have long foreseen the possibility of producing books for a continental or world market by gearing visual and printed material into editions that could subserve two educational objectives. If one produced the printed *commentary* in sentences of one-line length, it would be possible to repeat the same message line by line in several different languages, as is already common on matchboxes and canned commodities. A pan-European and pan-American edition with one-line sentences in Spanish, Russian, German, and English, with or without French, could convey to a high school pupil or sophomore the elements of physics or geometry while painlessly directing his or her attention to the linguistic problems of the atomic era.

So we pass by easy stages to the second of the three most pressing problems of a world in which there need be no irksome toil, no poverty, and no likely prospect of death before our appointed term of threescore years and ten. The immediate challenge, that of sharing the benefits of the printed page, we may hope to solve on a global scale in the lifetime of some living, if we choose the path of peaceful coexistence. There remains the common dilemma of the printed page and the newer means at our disposal. Not even the imaginative genius of H. G. Wells could have foreseen, when he published his first book in the year of my birth, the possibility that every person on this planet could listen to the same human voice transmitted to every continent, and to every part of a continent, with the delay of less than a second. Today persons living as far apart as Melbourne, Minneapolis, and Manchester can interpret rightly the same message; but few people living in cities so near as Middlesbrough, Marseilles, and Munich could do so.

In the light of what I have just said, the printed page is from this viewpoint still one step ahead of electronics. Thus a second challenge of an age of potential plenty is the unification of mankind at the level of speech in the most literal sense of the term. This has now become so important that the governments of the Soviet Union and the United States are willing to allocate vast sums for the design of a translation machine. From one point of view I welcome this, both because we shall certainly learn a lot about the nature of language in the attempt to understand what language an electronic brain can understand and because I am willing to entertain the likelihood that the publication of world editions of the result of contemporary discoveries would step up if scientific writers accepted the discipline of writing with a lucidity intelligible to a machine, which can never possibly interpret muddled intentions. On the other hand, it seems to me silly to pass the buck to machinery when the issue involved is one that calls for an intelligent decision possible at top-level agreement, without a delay of more than six months.

Many peoples of the world, like the Welsh of the mountain village where my wife and I spend our weekends in readiness for our imminent retirement from professional life, are bilingual or multilingual. In all countries except the United States, where John Dewey nearly wrecked education on the rocks of free discipline, every child has some instruction in a second language. A top-level decision to adopt one and the same second language everywhere would confer as a birthright on every world citizen what every child in Wales already enjoys: the use of its home language for love-making, religion, and other inexact topics, with the privilege of a second language in which even the most nationalistic Welshman prefers to discuss atomic physics or the gold standard.

I have stated the two priorities of a new era in which the first challenge to intellectual effort is how most expeditiously to make the printed page available to all persons everywhere. The second challenge is how to make accessible to all both one and the same printed page and one and the same human voice. In the context of human communications, there remains a third challenge. A quotation will put the spotlight on one aspect of it. An eminent American mathematician has stated that mathematics has advanced more in the last fifty years than in the previous five thousand. This may be, and in my view is, a fantastic overstatement; but it draws attention to an overwhelmingly important challenge to educational technique in the forthcoming century. It seems to me that the intellectual contribution of great civilizations in the past came to a halt because no society could advance when understanding was available only to a few clever people. Such was the fate of the Temple civilization of Mesopotamia. Such in a more enlightened age was more evidently the fate of the Alexandrian episode. Our own educational techniques have not yet made available to more than a small part of our community the intellectual achievements of the Newtonian era. If Professor Bell is right in the verdict I have just cited, the prospect of human enlightenment is therefore bleak.

Thus a third great intellectual challenge of the age of potential plenty is how to disperse over an ever widening field a deepening understanding less of the mechanical techniques at our disposal than of the peculiarly human innovations. I am too old to take a pessimistic view. So I will conclude by leaving this thought with you for discussion. We have in our universities departments for the teaching of Polish, for teaching communication theory to electrical engineers, for teaching symbolic logic to philosophers, for teaching taxonomy to zoologists and botanists, for teaching mathematics to physicists. All these topics are minor aspects of the one great problem of human communications, but in no university of the world is there yet, though MIT has made a modest beginning, a program for anticipating a way of escape from what has hitherto been the fate of all our predecessors.

# X  A Private Memoir

Myself, I finally reached Aspen in 1963, after a false alarm when I nearly got invited in 1959. Even so, I got there only by means of a certain amount of self-promotion and by conning Peter Blake, that year's program chairman, into inviting me under slightly false pretenses. In Aspen terms I am one of the second or third generation, a man of the 'sixties rather than a pioneer. By 1963, the smart thing was to fly up from Denver with Aspen Airways, then in its vintage years. Yet when one got to Aspen, things were still pretty pioneering—Main still had only two lanes of blacktop, and a bond issue for curbing a few blocks in the center of town was being hotly debated. The Wheeler Opera House was still being used for some evening shows ("Remember; no smoking in this fire-trap!") and Eero Saarinen's tent, albeit looking a bit tattered, still had a couple of years to go before being replaced by the present structure designed by Herbert Bayer.

Of the social encounters of that week, the one that sticks most vividly in my memory was none of the conference engagements, not even the celebrated fish-fry at Difficult Camp Grounds, but an impromptu after-dinner visit to an early Paepcke-period Aspenite who had finally and tearfully decided to leave. Whatever the personal reasons for her tears, it was also clear that she suffered some sense of betrayal by the place itself. It was very hard for her to tear herself away, yet Aspen had somehow, somewhere lost its charm. Large and irreversible changes had taken place; most notably and symbolically, Walter Paepcke himself had died. The whole nature of the Aspen community with its specialized cultural organs—the Institute for Humanistic Studies, the Music Associates, the Music Festival, the Design Conference—was either altering or having earlier alterations made plain.

Much of this was obviously too subtle for a first-time visitor like myself to appreciate. To me it was interesting historical information, not an upheaval calling for a gut response and tear-soaked Kleenex. But as a third-time visitor to the United States I could appreciate how much had already changed since John F. Kennedy's inaugural speech, and how fast the Aspen conference was moving with the new tide of affairs. The gray flannel years of Eisenhower regime and the "progressive corporation" mystique—which had given us Lever House and the Seagram building, as well as IDCA—were irretrievably over, and the new liberalism was in the air.

As early as the 1960 conference there seems to have been a new feeling of beginning again; the first decade of Aspen was already something on which Herbert Pinzke could look back as the past, recounting (in a memoir for the London magazine *Design*) his own part in the creation of the IDCA corporation and selecting pertinent quotes from conference speakers of 1955–60.

If Pinzke could feel the 'fifties as a coherent whole, I myself feel the 'sixties to be all of a piece as well, beginning with demands to "get back to basics," from Craig Ellwood, who later organized the 1967 conference. Already in 1960, the conference can be seen to have embarked on a course of social awareness and liberal experiment, and the black poetess Gwendolyn Brooks was a speaker in 1961. Indeed, the only break in that trend was when I myself, as a nondesigner, tried to get the conference talking about the profession of design in 1968—and even then we finished up talking high philosophy: pragmatists versus dialecticians, with a few observations on alienation thrown in for good measure. If the period has a motto, it must surely be Arthur Drexler's crack, in 1965, that "frightening ourselves to death is as good a reason as any for having a conference."

Unfairly, perhaps, it is remembered as the decade of constant doom-warning, of a rising sense of the design profession's inadequacy in the face of a world run—and overrun—by demented or careless amateurs. No longer were professional designers and professional managers getting their knees together under the seminar table to investigate mutual advantage. Instead, up to a thousand designers, architects, artists, and students were sitting down in the tent to have their ears burned off by crusading biologists, fault-finding philosophers, subversive sociologists, and peddlers of every variety of apocalypse from pollution to black power. Curiously enough, this trend peaked out during the five years that the board met under the presidency of Eliot Noyes, Jr., calmest and most professional of all the tribe of corporate consultants in whose image IDCA was originally created.

Noyes, however, is not only the thinking man's designer; he is a thinking man in his own right. The thoughtful cast of the conferences of the late 'sixties reflects a trend he sensed in world design as well as something of his own philosophy. The brashly elitist self-confidence of the early 'fifties, when designers apparently held it a self-evident truth that it was the manifest cultural duty of the world to owe them a living, dissolved before the social introspection and cultural awareness of the 'sixties.

The quality of a design could be measured no longer by the approval of "the guy at the next drawing board," as Richard Latham put it in a last bid for purely professional standards in 1968, but by the objective consequences of the design when it entered the public realm. Increasingly, the old principle of guilt by association found the design profession culpable of complicity with big business in the corruption of society and the pollution of the environment, until the activists' resolutions of 1970 invited the conference to vote commercial design virtually out of existence—and thus withdraw the very foundation on which IDCA had been created in 1951.

To say that 1970 marked the end of the road for the Aspen that most of us had known and valued is to imply nothing sentimental or even regretful. The original format had enjoyed a remarkably long run—when I joined in 1963, it was already past that mystic ten-year mark that sees most vital design organizations in post-climacteric decline; yet it was flagging neither in intellectual content nor in prestige and pulling power. Audiences rose from an average of three hundred at the beginning of the decade to around seven hundred toward its end, with a peak of one thousand. Contributing corporations pitched in cash not only for the conference proper but also for special causes such as bringing in parties of foreign students as well as groups from U.S. colleges, and the Graham Foundation contributed cash for student sculptures and other devices around the tent.

In the same decade—and especially in the Eliot Noyes years up to 1970—press coverage around the world built up to make IDCA the most heavily reported design conference on the calendar, outranking even the Triennale di Milano, let alone the biennial congresses of the International Council of Societies of Industrial Design—indeed, in 1966–68, the whole fate and future of ICSID could be seen to depend on certain earnest breakfast conversations on the terrace of the Aspen Meadows Hotel, as IDCA know-how and contacts were deployed in the service of ICSID finances and organization. The consequences of Aspen were truly international, even if the number of conferees coming from outside the United States remained a disappointingly token trickle.

At this point a cynic might inquire (perhaps justifiably) what value lay in the boast of an "international" design conference when over 80 per cent of the world's design fees were being earned in the United States anyhow, or by overseas branches of American offices? Wasn't the token attendance by foreigners a fair representation of the world distribution of design business? Could be; but if that were so, then the attendance of foreign *speakers* more than justified the boast of internationalism, since overseas voices accounted for well above 20 per cent of most years' hearing.

How did Aspen's prestige work upon so many outsiders to come and speak? The money one can set on one side—for most foreigners an Aspen speaking engagement was a break-even affair generously funded but nothing like the massive honoraria that many could have got at more specialized conferences in their own fields. Designers came, I think, out of genuine concern for their profession and its future (and because they were flattered to be asked!). If they were nondesigners, they came because they were curious to find out what designers were like en masse, because they were crusaders in search of an audience, because they thought design was something that ought to be encouraged (and because they were flattered to be asked!). And, whether they were designers or not, because IDCA appeared to be addressing itself to problems that needed attention—Aspen's first attempt to tackle the problems of the environment, for instance, was as early as 1962, long before the topic had become hot and sexy.

These, however, are one-shot reasons for coming the first time: why did they—overseas and domestic speakers alike—come back again?

How to account for the fact that almost 30 per cent of Aspen's papers over the years have been delivered by second-, third-, even fourth-timers? The answer must lie in the uniqueness of the IDCA experience; not just the fabulous setting of Aspen itself, but the style and tone of discourse that had been developed over the years by a unique body of people. They were professionals, but not from a single chartered profession. Since this was not the congress of a single chartered profession, its meetings were not lumbered with hours of boring elections, minutes, and other business. It was not a conspicuously democratic body (the International Olympic Committee is the obvious comparison), hence its deliberations were not lumbered either by points of order, protocol, and constructions of the constitution—though by the same token any resolutions it passed were (I am advised) of doubtful legality.

Freed of all that, its discussions could really take off for the far blue yonder (which always seems much nearer at that altitude), and, with five days in which to orbit the topic, could re-enter with a rich payload of ideas from which the last day's summing-up speaker could extract a final uplifting message that sent everyone away braced, stimulated, and "resolved to do better in future."

Braced and uplifted with what? Often there is nothing to account for that mood in the printed record. Sometimes it doesn't survive the translation from spoken to written word; sometimes the psychic energy was generated in loose seminars and private encounters that were never destined for the permanence of print. But it would grow and build over the week until, by the last morning, it had become an emotional charge that could bring the summing-up session to the brink of a mob scene. This may astound younger activists of the Woodstock generation, who always complain that IDCA's procedures have been too dry, academic, and formal, yet the Aspen conference has always tended to be a slow-burn commune, a people-contact scene, even if it was not visibly "together" until the fish-fry on the very last afternoon.

However, I concede to the young that this was nothing like the instant release and contact for which they have trained themselves; this was the slow dissolving of the inhibitions of a generation that took professionalism and professional status more seriously and for granted. Once a distinctive student culture began to emerge, taking neither seriously nor for granted, and began to replace the deferential boy-scoutism of students at earlier Aspens, there began to be some sense of strain about many human aspects of the conference—not least its relations with the worthy burghers of the business community in Aspen itself, who had a well-nourished paranoia about long hair, bare feet, and all the rest of it.

Yet the strain never broke the conference, even in 1970 when the techniques of confrontation were deliberately deployed, and the board subsequently decided that the classic format of IDCA had no future. In most years the effects of the strain were more stimulating than distracting, and student irruptions on the platform or in seminars could be salutary (if only becuse they said things that older people felt but were too gentlemanly to utter). And above all, good humor prevailed.

111

It may seem smug for IDCA to congratulate itself on having dealt fairly and nonexplosively with the revolt of the young, but the fact remains that it managed a lot better than many other organs of the liberal establishment. But then, so it should, with no particular vested interest to guard, no social position to defend, the lingering tradition of bohemianism that attaches to all bodies connected with creative labor, and the attitudes of questioning open-mindedness that are proper to any organization that takes its intellectual activities seriously. The result, looking back in tranquility, was an operation so genuinely nonoppressive that it never felt the need to boast of its liberties or parade its freedoms, and was genuinely offended when a certain dignitary in 1970 had the misplaced gall to congratulate it on having invited a black woman speaker that year, almost ten years after Gwendolyn Brooks.

But such openness required much private background effort as well as public goodwill. A workable format for continuing student participation was not easy to achieve when students rarely came back for a second year, and much of the effort had therefore to be "design" in its most critical and valuable form—"endeavoring to produce a desired future effect on the basis of incomplete knowledge of the variables involved." Insofar as IDCA achieved this end, imperfectly but nondisastrously, it could indeed call itself a *design* conference.

# XI  Problems, Problems

The 1961 Aspen conference, "Man the Problem-Solver," was a vintage year in terms of the quality of the papers. There follow, from that year, a characteristically trenchant sociological analysis by Richard T. Morris of UCLA; the first paper given at Aspen by the outstanding postwar design-theorist, the Argentine world-citizen Tomás Maldonado; and Peter Kronfeld's intriguing paper on ophthalmic problem-solving, a classic contribution from a visiting member of a totally different profession.

# So Who Needs a Sarsen?
## Richard T. Morris
## 1961

A cartoon in the *New Yorker* not long ago showed a pair of Druids looking up at the giant stone crossbeam laid across two rough columns and asking, "I wonder how we got that up there?" The sarsens at Stonehenge have stood since about 1700 B.C. and weigh about 28 tons each. The technical problem involved in their erection was enormous and seems to have been solved by building a mound of earth between the uprights, dragging the crossbeam into place up the incline, and then scooping the dirt away. Perhaps a more pertinent question today, however, might be: "I wonder *why* we put that up there?"

*Value Problem-Solving.* The theme that I will try to develop in this paper is that modern man has reached the state in his problem-solving ability where some of the important problems to be solved are not questions of "how" but questions of "why." The environment is largely tamed today, or at least can be if we apply and combine the proper techniques that are already available. I have no doubt that, if we wanted to expend the time, effort and tools necessary, we could burrow under Mount Everest, jack it up, roll it across China, float it across the Pacific and set it down neatly next to Disneyland. Other engineering, designing, and technical feats that we have recently and successfully performed seem no less impressive. The question becomes "why"? What shall we choose to work on, how shall we allocate our energy and our skill? What is worthwhile and what is not? These decisions, this kind of problem-solving seem paramount to me and can be talked about in terms of value decisions.

As control over the environment increases, the possibilities for choice increase, and the direction of choice depends more and more upon our values rather than upon stark necessity.

To talk about values, particularly about those we know the most about—our own—is a dangerous and complicated thing. There is so much variation, so many shades of difference between individuals, between groups, classes, regions, etc., that it is hard to make valid generalizations. But since this country came into existence—from Dickens and Tocqueville to Brogan and Barzun—there have been hundreds of illuminating attempts, by outsiders and insiders, to try to characterize and interpret American values. The rather amazing fact that emerges from a review of these analyses is the very substantial amount of agreement that seems to run through them. The interpretations of the values may vary: For example, Gorer's view that the large number of Americans who go up into the Statue of Liberty each year represents a return to the womb, and the improper retort asking for the significance of the thousands who enter the Washington Monument. The interpretations vary, but the values listed remain basically the same.

For the sake of the argument here, let us pick a rather limited but representative list of values that Americans are traditionally supposed to have. We will then look at how these values are changing, or are supposed to be, and set up these changes as dilemmas or choice points that we must face. Finally, we will look at some of the implications for design that seem to flow from these value-problem solutions.

*The Fading of the Protestant Ethic.* Traditionally, Americans have been characterized as placing a high value on *individual responsibility and freedom, equality of opportunity, and success, rationality, and work.* There has been a good deal of controversy lately, however, and some evidence presented, on the problems of whether many Americans are shifting their values away from the standard model, in some cases supporting the opposite extremes.

*The Shift from Individual Responsibility and Freedom to Group Responsibility and Dependence (from Fourth of July to Mother's Day).* As the proportion of entrepreneurs to bureaucratic employees diminishes—at latest count about three out of four people in the labor force work for large organizations—it becomes more and more difficult to implement, and perhaps to place a high value on, individual responsibility, responsibility to yourself and for yourself alone. We are increasingly responsible to the organization, to the work group, to our supervisors, chairmen, presidents. And they in turn are responsible to us, to the stockholders, the public, or the larger organization. Freedom and independence shift to dependence—dependence on the group, dependence on the organization. Looked at another way, this could be called a shift from selfishness to altruism. The tremendous growth of welfare activities and the development of a welfare morality to match could be cited here.

The development of the Help Syndrome is a case in point—we want to help the insane, help the criminal, help the delinquent, help the alcoholic, the addict, and the African. Man's responsibility now goes far beyond himself and his own family. More than ever before —except perhaps in primitive societies—we are locked into a network of interdependencies. Should a man feel pride or guilt in getting what he wants for himself, by himself? This seems to me to be a very important value choice for each of us: Which way do we want to go, which way do we push, how do we solve the problem?

*The Shift from Equality of Opportunity and Success to Status-Leveling and Security (from Robber Baron to Group Dynamics).* Traditionally, the American value on equality did not mean that at a given point in time everybody *is* equal, but rather that each person at birth should have an equal opportunity to rise to the top of a very unequal hierarchical structure—to climb the ladder of success. Vance Packard points to increasing evidence—from polls of high school and college students for example—that the young man of today does not want to risk getting to the top but rather heads for a nice, secure position somewhere in the middle, upper middle perhaps, but still middle. And the middle is getting bigger all the time. Differences in status are being decreased, not increased, on many levels—education, income, social groupings, automobile styles, and the like. Increasing informality in dress and address are part of this trend. Gone are the days when you could tell a millionaire a block away by his costume alone (Daddy Warbucks excepted, of course). It could be argued that there is just a shift to more subtle indicators of status, but this shift itself has very important implications for value change and implementation. Status-leveling is occurring in many kinds of social relationships: parent-child, employer-employee, husband-wife, teacher-student. It is symbolized in familiar ways: Dad-as-a-pal, the suggestion-box and brain-storming, the democratic family decision, the core course, the problem-census, student rating of teachers, and all the other educational techniques so bitterly attacked in Barzun's *House of Intellect*. These two shifts in values—from success to security and from equality of opportunity to status-leveling—are, of course, closely related. If the ladder has only one gigantic middle rung, that is the place to go, or more often to stay. And once you are securely fastened on it, you are no better and no worse than almost everybody else. This value shift can be stated in positive as well as negative terms: equality, democracy participation, flexibility, getting along well with others, not feeling superior are all terms that are honestly and deeply valued by a great many people. Here then is the second main value choice; to dare the pinnacle and take pride in being superior, or to head for a nest in the middle where we love and are loved by our equals.

*The Shift from Rationality and Work to Credit and Enjoyment (from Calvin to Dichter).* The traditional value placed upon rationality by Americans has been variously described—and criticized or praised—as hard-headedness, materialism, pragmatism. The main belief involved is that hard work, careful planning, frugality, and efficient use of resources and tools will result in successful achievement of goals. The world is rational; there is a better or best way to get there; there are clear means to clear ends, and if you apply them effectively and sedulously the ends will be accomplished. If they are not, you simply have not tried hard enough or long enough. A part of this syndrome is the very high value placed upon work as a moral good in itself, and the corollary belief that idleness is evil. Man should be active at all times, and every activity must have a useful purpose. History is bunk, so is art, so is contemplation. Waste is evil (especially waste of time), so is debt, so is intemperance. Here again there is great controversy as to whether Americans have moved away from these central values and whether the move, if it has taken place, is a Good Thing or a Bad Thing—with increased leisure time and with more money to spend in it and on it, the emphasis has shifted in many areas from production to consumption, from work to play, from thrift to credit, from delayed gratification to continual enjoyment of the present. The work week has shrunk from sixty-six hours to forty hours in the last hundred years; only twenty years ago, 40 per cent of production workers had paid vacations, now 95 per cent have them; the length of retirement life has tripled; the leisure market (1955) was $30 billion, half again the amount spent on clothing or shelter, double the amount spent on automobiles or home-furnishing and equipment. The amount of money spent on gambling—and this includes only legal gambling—has shown over a 2,500 per cent increase in the last twenty years. The credit-card phenomenon, the house mortgage rate, the fact that Sears makes more money from its "revolving charge accounts" than it does from the sale of products, the fact that you buy, fly, or die now and pay later, are all cases in point. There is a good deal of discussion over the cultural quality of all this leisure explosion. Admissions to concerts, operas, and ballets doubled in the last ten years, money expended here soared over $50 million per year—almost the exact amount spent on popcorn in movie theaters—but still $5 million more than was spent on professional baseball games. Aside from the equivocal interpretations that can be made as to quality, there is no doubt about the tremendous increase in the quantity of leisure-time activities and expenditures, mostly on the installment plan. It is logically indefensible to infer value changes from behavior changes. If we see a society where everybody works an eighty-four-hour week, we cannot jump to the conclusion that they *like* to do so or place a high value on it. Neither can we automatically assume that, because Americans have a high standard of living and are being progressively freed from the daily, grinding task of subduing the environment, they *like* so much leisure or know what to do with it in a deeply satisfying fashion. The plight of the retired person is a case in point here. There is a good deal of guilt and confusion accompanying these changes, and some evidence that there are attempts to hold on to or return to the earlier values—do-it-yourself plywood sales are up 160 per cent in five years. The value problem to be solved may be summed up as the question of how best to spend and to manage our time and resources when present necessity does not completely dictate our decisions.

*So Who Needs a Sarsen?* What are the implications of all this for the designer? It seems to me that the designers, perhaps more than any other occupational group—with the possible exception of those in the entertainment and education occupations—must make very clear and thoughtful decisions in these three areas of value problems, both for themselves as creative individuals and more indirectly, but more importantly, for the other members of society who are dependent upon them in so many ways.

A recent two-page spread in *Time* magazine (May 26, 1961), in a section called "Modern Living," will serve as an illustration of society's dependence upon the designer and as a focus for some preliminary remarks upon the implications of value-problem-solving for the designer.

The first article discusses a renewal plan for Welfare Island (to be renamed East Island, in a blinding burst of creative neology), designed by Victor Gruen. The "new kind of big-city better living" involves building a concrete platform 22 feet off the ground over some 160 acres of land. On top of the platform are service areas, shops, schools. All motor vehicles are banned on the island, except for fire and police. Gardens and recreational facilities are on the tops of the lower apartment buildings. The air-conditioned pedestrian concourse below the platform would be lit by glassed holes in the roof and made undulating to kill the monotony of long, straight corridors. Says Gruen: "It's the first twentieth-century city. It would mean unscrambling the melee of flesh and machine." Some 70,000 people will live on the island, if the plan goes through, and will be the most direct beneficiaries of this design decision.

Individual responsibility and freedom or group responsibility and dependence? Can a man cut his own grass, raise his own flowers on the roof? Can he see it from the window even if he could raise it? Can he walk through a park by himself, look at the moon or the sun, except through a porthole over his head—16 feet over his head? Can he even get into his car and go for a ride when he wants to get out of the place? At least his child might have fun, for a while, playing coal miner as he walks to school.

Equality of opportunity and success or status-leveling and security? Here at last seems to be the ultimate in production-line conformity and security. You pop out of your pneumatic door, get on the conveyor belt, are moved to your proper office building, underground school, or store, delivered, and picked up by another machine at the appropriate time. Although this is not mentioned in the article, I cannot imagine Gruen's two-mile-long, car-free concourse without a moving sidewalk. At least, though, you are safe and secure, you cannot be hit by a car, unless it is a fire engine, and then have to be unscrambled from the melee of flesh and machine.

Rationality and work or credit and enjoyment? At first glance, Gruen's design may seem eminently practical, efficient, and rational—given the assumption that it makes sense at all to work, much less live, in an area of such dense concentration, and given the assumption that this valuable acreage is going to waste and it would take only $450 million to save it from the evils of idleness. I wonder what fraction of this amount it would take to make Welfare Island into the world's greatest park?

The second article deals with the fortress bathroom. In his search for freedom and independence at home, man in order to escape from his equal-status children has first retreated to his master (hah!) bedroom (which tends to share articulated space with a food-preparation area), and now must flee to his bathroom in order to legitimately close the door on his loved ones. The garden bathroom, with one glass wall and a walled garden attached, seems to be the answer. There are drawbacks to the overdevelopment of this symbol of freedom. *Time* quotes a dismayed woman: "Using a bathroom like that is like being caught in the middle of a prairie." In the shift to consumer-enjoyment and the escape from Calvinistic plumbing, architect William Beckett has designed bathrooms with magazine racks, reading lamps over the toilet, and ultraviolet lights for toothbrushes. On the other hand, the psychiatrists, with their usual teleological parsimony, interpret this behavior as a desire to "glamorize the basic functions."

The third article deals with the fashion designers' development of the "little nothing" dress "leaning heavily on the neutral shades—the wet-sand and mushroom colors" and running from two hundred to five hundred dollars for designer originals. "It's almost like walking around in a slip. As soon as a dress gets busy, it moves out of the little-nothing class." Does this suggest some value decisions in terms of status-leveling, rationality (one argument is that this design is in response to the difficulties of getting in and out of taxis in more elaborate, bulkier dresses), or independence?

The fourth article deals with the opening of the new House of Revlon on Fifth Avenue. Dedicated to the arts of beauty, it features such attractions as sunken sea-water baths, pre-warmed towels, pedicures on red velvet couches, spouting perfume, music from soft-speakers. The decor is Pompeiian—on the eve of destruction!

The last article raises the interesting question as to whether the growth of stereo means a decline in language (and maybe thought?). Says George Steiner: "When one is tired, music, even difficult music, is easier to enjoy than serious literature—where the library shelves once stood, there are proud, esoteric rows of record albums and high-fidelity components." We might well ask why everyone is so tired, and whether the designer is at the seat of it. These final articles have a weird resonance that project us into a science-fiction world that is already almost upon us. With our feet in the pedicure machine, our heads resting on a red velvet reclining toilet chair, we immerse our brains and souls in waves of beautiful music as the curtain slowly falls.

The designer giveth, but he also taketh away alternatives. He makes it possible to have a martini 15,000 feet in the air; he makes it impossible to drive slowly on a freeway. He makes it possible for a whole family to get away from it all in a home on wheels; he makes it impossible in a permanent house to get away from that family except in the bathroom. He makes it possible to wash dishes and clothes in a machine; he makes it impossible to make a bed in any other way than it has been done for the last two thousand years. He makes it possible to bring the world's greatest music into the living room; he makes it impossible to eat, and often to work, without music. He makes it possible to make doughnuts at home without mixing the dough; he makes it impossible to buy a string of figs or a salami or a pickle without a plastic sheath.

The designer already is, and will become even more so, a very central figure in the processes of value transformation and value-problem-solving in our society. His choices affect the possibilities of choice for all the rest of us, perhaps more than he realizes.

# The Problem of All Problems
## Tomás Maldonado
## 1961

My contribution to this conference will not consist in a description of
how I have succeeded in solving some concrete problem in my field of
activity—basic research in industrial design—but will be a description
of my ideas on the present difficulties and future possibilities of the
industrial designer as problem-solver in general.

Before starting to speak on this subject, I think it will be opportune
to refer, although rather fleetingly, to the more comprehensive subject of
man as problem-solver. This will facilitate a better understanding of the
following considerations on the industrial designer as problem-solver.

One thing which, at first sight, appears most fascinating is the
fanatic obstinacy with which man has forever borne such an arduous
and not always pleasant responsibility as that of solving problems.
Perhaps the phenomenon could be explained phylogenetically. In fact,
all would seem to indicate that man's rare passion for solving problems
is connected with his will to survive. Being basically premature, weak,
unstable, and defenseless, man had to face the following alternatives:
either turn himself into an obstinate problem-solver or resign himself
to extinction. His option is known: He prefers to survive, and to survive
as a problem-solver.

This has led to the opinion that man as such is defined and distinguished exclusively by this ability. Recent progress in science and
technology has sufficiently demonstrated that this opinion is unfounded.
We know now from the experimental contributions of comparative psychology that some animals, particularly subhuman primates, are also
capable of solving problems. In order to be more exact, we might say
that these animals are capable of changing operatively the quantitive or
qualitative relations of determined real factors for the benefit of a
determined purposive behavior. On the other hand, electronic data-
processing machines are able, as is well known, to solve certain problems more effectively and more rapidly than man can.

Therefore we may say that *for the moment* the most distinctive
characteristic of man is not his capacity to solve problems but more his
capacity to set them. I stress "for the moment" because the future
development of automatic mechanism could show us that machines also
are capable of setting problems. The phenomena of autoregulation and
internal determinism in the field of the homeostatic mechanisms have
already sufficiently demonstrated that theoretically and practically it is
possible to reach forms of automatism that are still far superior to the
present ones. However, for the time being, let us recognize that setting
problems is a very distinctive characteristic of man.

But what does it mean to set oneself a problem? To set a problem does not mean only the ability to state its existence, but also, and principally, the capacity to foresee the means to its solution: A problem, the statement of which seems to be disassociated from the concrete study of the possibility of its solution may well be, and often is, a fictitious or "pseudo-problem," as the logical positivists would have it called. The first task is always to avoid the trap of pseudo-problems, and this we can do only if we are careful not to separate the methods of observation from the methods of solution. I am well aware that on certain occasions, solutions are found without being sought, that is, problems are solved without being set. Art, poetry, and sometimes even science itself provide us with examples of this; but these are exceptional situations: Normally the merit of solving a problem—above all, if it is a relatively complex problem—corresponds to a great extent with the merit of having known enough to set it.

In the philosophy of science it is theory of methods that has been occupied with investigating a more adequate way of setting problems. The first difficulty and perhaps the greatest one in the study of methods consists in finding out which is the best method to study methods, that is, which is the best way to set the problem of setting problems. This difficulty has not been definitely resolved, but at least it has been temporarily disregarded by differentiating between "general methodology" and "particular methodology." The former is principally occupied with the logical and operative foundations that justify the selection of determined methods for determined tasks. This we could call a metamethodology, a methodology about methodology. The latter consists of the study of the specific procedures of application of methods that are selected for a determined field and for this field only. This is, finally, methodology proper. It should, however, be stressed here that in general methodology as well as in particular methodology there exists a series of notions that have not yet been definitely agreed upon and for which may be stated only partial progress.

Let me mention at least one of them. I want to refer to the notion of type or class. It is quite evident that every methodology begins as a typology, a theory of classifications. Before we strive for a more or less operable axiomatization, it will be necessary to group the existing variables into types or classes. However, the logical function of the concept of type or class—as was noted by Hempel and Oppenheimer in 1935—is extremely vague. Very often types and classes are constituted by means of analogical, purely quantitative relations between the different variables. However this procedure may not remove the difficulty of the varying intensity in the relationship between individuals belonging to the same types or classes. Thus, it happens in certain circumstances that new types or classes of fluctuating nature are formed. They render invalid their classification and above all, their operability. These are the pseudo-types or pseudo-classes, which are also known as neutral or void types or classes. Hempel proposed to get rid of the procedure of quantitative relations between variables and to replace it with the procedure of qualitative relations, in other words, to pass from the quantitative, analogical, and metrical typology to a qualitative, homological, and ametrical typology and to leave the metric formulation to a second phase.*

Nevertheless, this new theory of classification, principally because of the old conflict between formalists and operationalists within the philosophy of science, has not yet succeeded in reaching general recognition. The few opportunities of application so far offered have hindered the verification of many of its assertions. And this is not a single case. The same can be said of other important theoretical and practical contributions in the methodological field. Scientific methodology is not, and cannot be, a closed system. Nor is it a prescription for curing all possible ills. Some philosophers of science, above all the French, are inclined to think that the actual state of methodological studies should not be judged as abnormal and transitory but as normal and permanent. They argue that only the open methodologies, which are always in a crisis, would be fertile for the development of science. I quote, for example, Gilles-Gaston Granger: "The scientific edifice is necessarily in a lack of equilibrium and in constant progress. The error does not play the part of a psychological accident, it is—as it were—an integral part of the movement of the mind, which generates science."

Let us now examine finally to what extent it is necessary and possible to develop a particular methodology of industrial design, that is, a combination of formalizing and manipulative procedures that will help us to set and solve the specific problems of this field. I do not at all intend to set up the basis of this particular methodology but wish merely to introduce into the subject some ideas that are still only provisional. The necessity and possibility of a particular methodology for industrial design has recently become—above all in Europe—an object of polemical discussion among industrial designers and educators dedicated to the training of industrial designers. On the one hand, there are those who believe that methods are more important than results, and, on the other hand, there are those who maintain that the results are always more important than the methods. The first group tends to believe that to formalize a problem mathematically means (or nearly means) to have it already solved. The second group assumes that all problems in this field can be solved with common sense alone.

Evidently this polemic, at least in its present state, cannot be fruitful. The designers of the first category seem to have a much more intransigent opinion on methods than the scientists themselves: The scientists sometimes have doubts about scientific methods, but the

---

* Between the date on which the lecture was delivered and today (1972), many contributions have been made to the theory of classification that come to modify some of the issues raised at this point in the text. Specifically, I am referring to Robert R. Sokal and Peter H. A. Sneath, "Principles of Numerical Taxonomy" (1963), and Nicholas Jardine and Robin Sibson, "Mathematical Taxonomy" (1971).—T.M.

designers never. The partisans of common sense, for their part, do not resign themselves to accept that industrial design involves certain types of tasks that no longer may be solved only with common sense.

Both positions suffer from a very alarming lack of realism, and I believe that this results from the fact that both groups understand radically different things as industrial design. The main problem today is that we constantly operate with the notion "industrial design" as if it were one and only one reality. And this is the reason for all the misunderstandings. There exists not only a single but many realities of industrial design. Finally, that there are as many realities as degrees of structural and functional complexity may be verified in industrially produced objects. A coffee cup, an infrared grill, a lawnmower, a tractor, a helicopter, and an electronic data-processing machine do not constitute design problems of the same nature, problems that could be set and solved in the same way. In fact, there are tasks for which common sense can be sufficient, and even more than sufficient. Scientific methods are sometimes applied to such tasks, but often they only serve to show that the designer knows the scientific methods. Yet there are other problems with such an unpredictable number of variables and such rich and subtle mutual relations that utilizing a more objective methodology is not only desirable but even indispensable. If this procedure is not followed the designer will be unlikely to master his problem; indeed, the reverse may happen. As you can see, very practical considerations have obliged the designer to ascribe—in certain fields—great importance to the use of scientific methods. Therefore, the fetishism of the methods in the field of industrial design, that is, the assumption that the methods have an absolute value independent of results, is not justified. The methods in the field of industrial design, and in any other field, are not more important than the results that may be achieved by their application. There is no doubt that, in a certain phase, the methods may appear more important than the results, but the ultimate objective of a method—as indicated by its etymology—is always to be the means to an end. In certain cases we may even say that the methods are as important as the results, but never more important.

The debate between rationalism and intuitionalism in the field of industrial design—for in the end it is nothing but this—would lose its reason for existence if one were able to offer a polyvalent—and not, as today, a monovalent—definition of industrial design.

This will be possible only with a new classification of industrial products. The commercial and industrial exhibitions classify products according to purely economic criteria (production goods, consumer goods, investment goods, etc.). The new classification should operate with criteria allowing establishment of the different degrees of structural and functional complexity of the products.

Such classification of technical and industrial objects could reach the same operative meaning, as did for more than two centuries the *Philosophia Botanica* of Linnaeus, for classification of natural objects. While, however, the classification of Linnaeus has been one of the most brilliant examples in the history of analogical classification, the classification of technical and industrial objects will have to be necessarily homological. The quantitative relationship therefore will be less important in this case than its qualitative relationship. The aspect of the objects will be less interesting than what they are really like, that is, how they are fabricated and how they work. The similarities of their physiognomies will be less important than the relationship of their construction and their behavior. This new systematic of industrial products will open not only new perspectives for the definition—or definitions—of industrial design but also for the way of setting and solving problems in this field. With this systematic, it would be possible to state with relative exactness at what degree of structural and functional complexity a particular methodology will begin to be indispensable. And it would also help to judge at which degree of structural and functional complexity the industrial designer, for example, should begin to use the methodological contributions of the human sciences and at which degree the contributions of the engineering sciences.

But I must state here that I am not at all of the opinion that such a methodological elucidation alone might help to overcome all the difficulties that industrial design has to face today as an activity and as a profession. Besides the questions how the industrial designer can better set and solve his problems, there is another much more dramatic question of the responsibility of the industrial designer as problem-solver in our society. The industrial designer is in fact a problem-solver, but seldom a problem-solver who is free to decide which problems should be set and how they should be solved. It is certain that the problems are frequently set for him from outside, and no less frequently the solutions as well. In most cases the designer wants to set and solve problems for human use, but in most cases he feels obliged to set and solve problems for human abuse. This is, without doubt, the problem of all problems.

# Problem-Solving in Ophthalmology
## Peter C. Kronfeld
## 1961

The ophthalmologist's role may, for the purpose at hand, be defined as the maintenance of the complicated piece of apparatus that enables mankind to perceive, understand, and enjoy the creations of the designer. A large portion of these maintenance workers are graduates of medical schools who have devoted a minimum of three years of post-graduate work to the special study of the normal and the diseased human eye.

The recipients of the ophthalmologist's services are usually called patients. Actually and happily, a fairly large percentage of these recipients do not have an eye disease in the ordinary sense of the word. Their eyes are organically sound but represent variants with regard to their dimensions (length, width, and height) or with regard to the relative strength of their muscles. These variations probably are within the normal range but may cause excessive fatigue and low visual efficiency. Corrective or adjustive measures are available, in most instances, to alleviate ocular discomfort and to improve visual performance. The contact with these patients tends to keep the ophthalmologist's thinking within the realm of physiology during a major portion of his working day. Some ophthalmologists actually keep one foot in the field of physiology during their entire professional life. Thus, the definition of the ophthalmologist given at the outset may be sharpened somewhat by describing him as a highly specialized physician, highly specialized in the surgical and technological sense of the word, with a strong background in the basic sciences (physics, chemistry, physiology, and psychology). Thus, it luckily turns out that the spheres of interest of the ophthalmologist and of the designer overlap to a very considerable extent. The laws of the country have made the ophthalmologist's upbringing somewhat more formal than that of the designer, but in the end it is visual sensations with which both professions are concerned.

How various professions go about solving their problems is the official assignment given to this panel. There is hardly a method or an approach that ophthalmologists have *not* tried in their search for solutions to their problems, which range from purely academic aspects of vision to the cruelly realistic issues of impending blindness. A few examples taken from the present or recent past may serve as an introduction to ophthalmological methodology.

Designed for the reception of light rays to kindle visual sensations, the eye is unique in its accessibility to the searching light rays of the ophthalmological examiner. There are only small portions of the human eye that cannot be examined in their natural living state by means of visible light rays. This has been accomplished by a process of exploration that has taken about 150 years. The door to the inner sanctum—the retina, with its light-sensitive cells, and the underlying, highly vascular choroid—was opened when Helmholtz solved the problem of the black pupil in 1856. Since it permits light rays to pass into the eye, it should permit passage in the opposite direction, and thereby make the inside of the eye visible. A coaxial or almost coaxial course of the ingoing and outcoming rays was the answer to the problem and became the principle of the ophthalmoscope, the major diagnostic tool of the ophthalmologist.

Aside from its role in the process of vision, the territory disclosed by the ophthalmoscope holds information of great interest and importance to many specialists in the medical profession. The normal retina is almost as transparent as glass and is placed against a dark reddish-brown background. This creates an excellent set-up for the observation and examination of the only opaque elements in the retina, which are its blood vessels. These observations become much more meaningful if one realizes that the retinal blood vessels are derived from the same large vessels as those of the brain. What one sees with the ophthalmoscope represents a sample of the blood supply to the brain.

Some of the limitations of these methods are obvious. The smallness of the essential components of the eye calls for magnification, which must not be in excess of the examinee's ability to hold his eyes still. Under the best possible conditions of fixation (the ophthalmological term for holding still), the human eye describes oscillatory movements of about thirty seconds' amplitude. The illumination has to be kept within physiological limits so as to avoid discomfort on the part of the examinee or, what may be worse, changes in the tissue under examination resulting from excessive light.

Despite these limitations, diagnostic instruments built on the principles described in the foregoing have been invaluable aids, principally by permitting close, direct observation of the normal eye during the performance of its normal functions and of the diseased eye during the kaleidoscopic phases of disease.

In all the apparatus described so far, a human eye also plays the part of the receiving system: The ophthalmologist's eye receives the images and interprets them against the background of his knowledge and experience. (Both the seeing and the interpreting of these images take a measureable amount of time, which accounts for the examinee's feelings of having spent endless hours at the ophthalmologist's diagnostic instruments.) For lasting and often more objective records of these images, our profession is deeply indebted to the small number of artists who have become interested in our subjects and have taken the trouble of learning our methods of examination.

Photography has played an important role in the recording of the form and structure of the living eye. To the ophthalmological examiner, there is something extremely satisfying in a good color or black-and-white photograph of any portion of the living eye. This satisfaction stems from the fact that the photograph has stopped the physiological state of unrest of the living eye and thereby allows the examiner to study and appreciate at his leisure all the minute details of form and structure.

There is no denying that, as a receiving system for a mass of detailed information, the human eye—this time the examiner's eye—is a fairly slow piece of apparatus which starts to skip if too many, too dissimilar images arrive per unit of time. This slowness is due to the complexity of the nervous processes elicited by even the simplest visual stimulus, such as a flash of light lasting ten milliseconds (.01 second). The same slowness becomes a true asset if slightly dissimilar images are offered at regular intervals, such as twenty-four times a second. The human visual apparatus fuses such images into a continuous sensation, converting dissimilarity into motion.

The development of faster photographic emulsions and better motion picture cameras has been a boon to ophthalmology. The movements of the pupil and various flow phenomena in its retinal and choroidal blood vessels have been recorded by cinematography with a degree of resolution far in excess of that afforded by the ordinary diagnostic instruments.

The latest development in the field of problem-solving by more accurate observations has been the introduction of electronic image-processing. The principle of the method is the conversion of an originally visual image into an electronic signal, which lends itself to processing in a number of ways. Most useful are the possibilities of amplification of the electric signal, which is tantamount to greater size, brightness, and contrast of the original visual image. In the amplified form, the electronic signals may be reconverted into a visual image to be viewed by an audience or turned into a permanent record by cinematography. The new super-sensitive television camera tubes made it possible to view the inner sanctum of the human eye at light levels that entailed no discomfort (no "blinding") whatsoever. With such tubes, a number of circulatory phenomena in the human retina and choroid have been picked up and recorded on color motion picture film. This television ophthalmoscopy offers the particular advantage that the spectral sensitivity of the original viewing instrument, the television camera, is different from that of the human eye and variable within certain limits. There are situations in which the television camera is a better diagnostic instrument than the ophtalmologist's eye looking through the regular ophthalmoscope.

Ophthalmological concepts and methods are quite characteristically and poignantly revealed by the profession's reaction to the new theory of color vision, the originator of which is Edwin H. Land of Polaroid and other fame. (In a scholarly, detailed analysis of the new theory, G. I. Walles of the University of California introduces Land as an "undoubted inventive genius in the Edison-Burbank-Kettering tradition.") The basis of Land's theory is a series of simple experiments. Two black-and-white photographs are made of a colorful still life, one through a red filter (the "long record") and one through a green filter (the "short record"). From the black-and-white negatives, positive transparencies are made and superimposed on a gray screen by means of two projectors. In this reproduction, the red filter is used for the projection of the long record; no filter of any kind is used in projecting the short record. The long record projected through its red filter produces a picture showing various shades of red. The short record by itself yields an entirely achromatic picture. Superimposed on a screen and with subdued extraneous light, the two records seem to render the still life in full color. In addition to the anticipated red and pink, the screen image contains orange, yellow, green, blue, and purple. For the production of this complete range, the classical color theory, which goes back to Newton, Young, Helmholtz, and Lord Kelvin postulates three primary colors acting, in varying proportions, as additive coexistent stimuli. This classical theory Land considers disproved by his experiments.

To this interpretation the ophthalmologist raises the violent objection that the classical color theory was based on the results of color-mixing experiments in which the stimulus or stimuli were offered in a field of limited size surrounded by blackness, that is, absence of stimuli. The polychromatic rendition in Land's experiment is critically dependent upon (1) the human eyes acting as the viewing instrument and (2) the whole or total image's being taken in.

The basis of Land's polychromatic image lies, according to physiological and ophthalmological concepts, in the phenomenon of simultaneous color contrast, which is a characteristic of the human eye and distinguishes it clearly from any objective color rendition. Under natural conditions, when the entire retina is under the influence of some light stimuli, adjacent portions of the retina influence each other, through their nervous connections, in the sense of creating sharper borders and greater contrast. In the realm of color, this means that if a broad ring of color and an infield of white are projected onto a screen the human eye will induce color in the physically colorless infield. If the ring is red, the infield will to the human eye appear blue-green. Such simultaneous color contrast, the opthalmologist believes, has been most elegantly demonstrated by Land, without in any way disproving the classical color theory.

But why talk to the designer about simultaneous contrast? He was using it instinctively long before there was an official term for his profession.

More appropriate as an example of problem-solving in ophthalmology might be the story of a recent, largely American, disease. During the period from 1930 to 1950, we gradually became aware of two phenomena concerning premature infants. Their survival rate improved approximately 30 to 50 per cent while the rate of blindness among the survivors increased by 500 to 1000 per cent. The blindness was due to a disease that could be followed closely with the ophthalmoscope and ended up as retrolental fibroplasia (RLF), namely a formation of fibrous scar tissue behind the crystalline lens. The disease had undoubtedly occurred before 1930 but had not been recognized as an entity. It was given the name of retinopathy of prematurity.

The higher survival rate from 1930 on could be attributed to better facilities and better care for premature infants; the better care, in turn, was based on better understanding of the specific handicaps of prematurity. The increased rate of blindness became a problem of the first order. It was immediately made the subject of many investigations, and few, if any, congenital or environmental factors associated with either mother or infant escaped consideration as possible causes. The investigations were partly fruitful in that a good many factors could be eliminated as likely causative agents. Gradually the ophthalmologist's attention became focused on the oxygen which the pediatrician understandably and justifiably used in the treatment of premature infants, particularly if they showed signs of cyanosis, that is, inadequate oxygen content of their blood.

Oxygen therapy, that is, the inhalation of gas mixtures containing oxygen in higher concentration than in air, was at the time a well-established form of treatment for various diseases of heart or lungs in patients of all age groups. In a number of "premy-stations"—as the hospital units in which the premature infants were cared for in especially designed incubators were called—the observation was made that the incidence of retrolental fibroplasia increased with the duration of the exposure to oxygen. Confirmation of this observation was received from Australia and England by the fall of 1952 and from the first controlled clinical trial made in a hospital in Baltimore. Caution in accepting this clue at full face value seemed indicated, for three principal reasons: (1) The incidence of retrolental fibroplasia in the various hospitals of the United States and abroad varied within unexplainably wide limits. (2) There was but little unanimity in the medical literature with regard to other possible causative agents. (3) An over-all policy of cutting down on the oxygen received by premature babies seemed very dangerous to a good many pediatricians.

In the midst of this furor—the term used by one of the most careful and most objective students of retrolental fibroplasia, V. E. Kinsey of the Kresge Eye Institute in Detroit—the idea of a nationwide controlled clinical study of the role of oxygen or any other promising agent in the retrolental fibroplasia problem was conceived in October, 1952. Under the auspices of the National Institute of Neurological Diseases and Blindness, an organization consisting of physicians and investigators from eighteen hospitals was set up to work out the details of the clinical trial. Because of the urgency of the situation, the effects of oxygen were made the immediate and primary target of the investigation. The facilities of the eighteen participating hospitals were pooled and an uniform policy agreed upon. The effect of oxygen upon the incidence of retrolental fibroplasia, it was hoped, could be determined by comparing two groups of infants, which were to receive oxygen in different concentrations but otherwise would be maintained under as nearly identical conditions as possible. The first group was to receive oxygen in concentrations over 50 per cent for twenty-eight days, a procedure which was then considered routine for premature infants weighing less than three pounds, five ounces at birth. The second group was to receive either no oxygen (in excess of the 20 per cent contained in air) or limited amounts prescribed only on the basis of clinical urgency. The two groups were designated as "routine" and "curtailed" (with regard to oxygen intake). Throughout the planning of the clinical trial, its potential Scylla-and-Charybdis nature was realized by the physicians in charge. The administration of substantially lesser amounts of oxygen than were customary might significantly increase infant mortality, while the continued use of the customary amounts of oxygen might result in an unnecessarily high incidence of retrolental fibroplasia. The planning committee resolved the dilemma by assigning to the routine oxygen group only one-twelfth of the total number of infants expected to be in the study. This one-twelfth, it was calculated, was less than the number of infants in the participating hospitals that would have received routine oxygen if no over-all guiding policy had been instituted.

Carefully as all this was thought out, the planning committee, every so often, needed the reassurance that a controlled trial such as they were devising was the fastest possible way of removing the doubts and uncertainties.

Fortunately for all parties concerned, it took only three months of the clinical study to determine that infant mortality was not increased by curtailing oxygen administration. The mortality rate was practically the same in the "routine" and in the "curtailed" group. This gave the planning committee the courage to recommend that during the second three months of the study all infants be assigned to the curtailed oxygen group. Analysis at the end of the six-month period of the combined results of all participating hospitals clearly showed that the incidence of retrolental fibroplasia is positively associated with the use of oxygen and that much of the deleterious effect is due to exposure to oxygen during the first ten days of life.

The observations on human premature infants were confirmed by laboratory experiments in which newborn or very young mice, rats, kittens, and puppies were exposed to high concentrations of oxygen. Retinal lesions practically identical with retrolental fibroplasia developed and led to blindness of the animal. Newborn animals and premature human infants have in common that their retinal circulatory system is not completely developed. These immature systems, in contradistinction to the fully developed systems, react unfavorably to high concentrations of oxygen—which is the principal hard fact about retrolental fibroplasia.

The planning committee announced the results of the study at a National Meeting of Ophthalmologists in October, 1953, and recommended the cautious use of oxygen in situations where it seems absolutely necessary, and there only in concentrations below 40 per cent. Since October, 1953, retrolental fibroplasia has been an extremely rare disease. And more than that, a number of other important lessons—by-products, as they are called—have been learned as the result of the controlled clinical trial of oxygen.

Lest the reader be misled, this introduction to problem-solving in ophthalmology should end with the statement that our libraries are full of accounts of unsuccessful and fruitless attempts at problem-solving. As guides for future investigation the negative results are almost as valuable as the accounts of our successes.

# XII  Sometimes a Great Notion . . .

. . . or: What happened in 1963? That was the year when the program chairman came up with a topic that fitted the nature of Aspen like a glove: "Design and the Image of America Abroad." Unfortunately, it was too good a notion that Peter Blake had, too strong an invitation to political power plays. The week began with systematic microphone-hogging by right-wing elements (in genuine tennis shoes, yet!), progressed by way of a complete change of the Washington personnel present—from "observers" to, frankly, spies—and finished with an attempt by one of the Senate committees to impound the tapes and transcripts!

The papers from that year have never been published as part of the regular record, and I have not been able to find a complete set so far. Those that have come to light, either in their entirety or in partial quotation, have confirmed my suspicion that what was said in 1963 was either windy, frightened, or purely anecdotal. Even if the complete record had been published I have a strong feeling that none of it would have justified inclusion in this book. Yet it was a stimulating and often disturbing conference that left us all with a lot to think about: for instance, that the Washington political machine could make a repressive regime even out of the aspirations of the Kennedy Administration. Or that flying by Aspen Airways could be, in the words of Patwant Singh, "worse than the flight up to Katmandu!"—as I reported to British readers of the *Architects' Journal* on my return.

# Don't Just Stand There Trembling
## Reyner Banham
## 1963

Don't let anyone kid you that people traveled more thoroughly when they traveled more slowly. That is just mistaking hard work for virtue in that grand old British way. Pre-jet travelers were too saddle-sore, too bone-tired, too foot-weary, too unwashed, too soot-caked, too worried about bandits, too sure they had been cheated by hotels, to prostrate with seasickness, dysentery, heat-stroke, or bilharzia to notice anything short of a shipwreck, a Bulgarian atrocity, or some dirty great avalanche in the Alps.

However, if you *must* experience the full horror of the terrain you are traversing, even though time compels you to fly, there is one collector's piece of a flight that ought to be in every jet age Baedecker: Denver to Aspen, in Colorado. An air of mystery surrounds even the preparations for the flight, because you can't find Aspen Airways. It may be obvious to the Denver locals that you inquire at the Hertz Rent-a-Car counter, but it wasn't obvious to me—or seemingly to the airline, for it took more than an hour before anyone at the other end of the line would admit to any connection with such an organization. And when it was finally located—in a prefab hangar on the other side of the airfield—the entire personnel seemed to consist of two laconic characters in impenetrable sunglasses and impeccable white shirts who did all the admin. and doubled as pilots. In the light of what happened I am relieved to be able to report that they are said to be the two best mountain pilots in the United States.

The plane was an Aero Commander, a tiny high-wing twin, which holds six passengers and a pilot in conditions bordering on promiscuity, with the tips of the dumpy propellors just clearing the windows. Though quite securely assembled, it is small enough to be upset by thermal currents caused by cigarette stubs and sunbathers, so we had a couple of practice plunges before we even got to the real downdrafts in the Rockies. Climbing steadily over the Denver suburbs, we cleared the first ridge and emerged into a broad brown valley of hypnotic lunar beauty. While we were gawking at it, the first Rocky crept up craftily on the blind side and suddenly stood up in front of the plane.

Calmly adjusting everything within reach, the pilot flew round it—and the next six or seven mountains as well, until the Rockies' manager started to throw in his back-row forwards, in the shape of the first ridge that couldn't be flown around. From where I sat, it looked as if we would just clear it comfortably if we could keep up our rate of climb, but just as it came to the point the plane seemed to fall

Reprinted from *Architects' Journal* (London).

several hundred feet in a downdraft caused by a gale blowing from the other side, and we scampered over with what looked like ten feet to spare, seeing, as we did so, that the bare rock of the top of the ridge had been hollow-ground on both sides to a coarse Wilkinson cutting edge.

There was thirty minutes more of this sort of stuff, with the plane falling about the sky among some of the handsomest scenery in the world, and about this time I became uncomfortably aware that the pilot didn't seem to be looking where he was going. Busily chatting with the customers on such subjects as geology, elk-hunting, and other local lore, he spent most of the time looking back over his shoulder. Maybe he flies by ear, listening to the echo of the motors bouncing back from the rock face, or maybe those sunglasses are mirrored on the back instead of the front and work like the "Sebackroscopes" of my youth. Not to worry, anyhow, Aspen Airways doesn't have accidents. Suddenly you arrive, the plane falling out of the sky on purpose for once and screwing round to line up with a half-finished runway in the valley.

Pack mules will never replace this.

# XIII  Beetle Country

Neither of these two papers mentions the word "Volkswagen," but that of Dexter Masters, founder of *Consumer Reports*, represents *par excellence* that stern, serious, and humane tradition of product criticism that had fundamentally undermined confidence in the Detroit automobile long before Ralph Nader bustled on to the scene, while William Bernbach was head of Doyle, Dane, and Bernbach, whose advertising did almost as much as personal recommendation to establish the VW as the radical's preferred alternative vehicle.

# Quick and Cheesy, Cheap and Dirty
## Dexter Masters
## 1964

The dilemma that designers face has tended to be defined in a way that seemed to me somewhat limited, at least if we are to take designers' work seriously. I take it seriously. Partly because over the years of directing a consumer testing organization, I have had an unusually close look at the increasing numbers of badly designed, shoddy products that get to market, there to confound me and many other consumers, and partly because I respect the potential of the designer's contribution, which may be to bring order out of disorder and to make rational that which is irrational, and God knows we all stand in serious need of that. But there has been, I think, a little excess inclination to view design in its fun-and-games aspects, or in terms of the useful but limited contribution it can make to an effective promotion of a product that may or may not be really worth the effort of promoting at all. With the kind permission of our moderator, and with the indulgence of all of you, I should like to err on the other side, correctively I hope, and in the general interest. I should like to express the broad view that the first and urgent need of a good designer, perhaps more than other professionals, is to know and to work out of the prime realities of the second half of the twentieth century. I should like to provide some documentation of my charge that many designers don't do this, and I should like to state my claim that the failure has ceased to be funny. It must be noted for example that Newtonian mechanics is not ultimately precise. We cannot take it with us as we penetrate the nucleus of the atom; we need another physics in the subatomic world. We do not yet have all of it and we do not know for sure how it will work or what the consequences will be. We know, to be sure, that they will be the same for everyone alive. One of the new realities is simply that this is so, and that it calls for a rather steady reflection.

The ships of the ancient explorers moved slowly and erratically; the maps were crude and inaccurate; the explorers could tolerate both. At 2,300 miles an hour, to pick a perfectly reasonable figure more or less at random, any lack of precision in the design of any part or any minute gap in the planning means death. At higher figures, on farther-ranging trips, we do not know what might happen. That is, we are not yet sure of the nature of the death. But distance, at least terrestrial distance, has almost lost its meaning altogether and will lose it more. One of the effects of this is that the American and the Russian and the African are going to be even more alike than they already are.

These penetrations—of matter, of time, of space—coupled with the seemingly endless increase in ourselves, have moved contemporary civilization, for better or for worse, beyond the real comprehension or the actual reach of all generations but one. That generation may be described as the one that can think of a light year, for example, in personal terms; can imagine, for example, a fire of 15 million degrees; and knows that from now on all wars are civil wars. None of these thoughts, in the world of today, can be held very long without threatening many other thoughts with absurdity. Planning and criteria that were designed for the relatively simplified mechanics of the eighteenth and nineteenth centuries do not work for the period of the rise of the biologic sciences, the searching of the subatomic mass, and the dissipation of distance as a meaningful concept. The danger is that absurdity will come to tinge all planning, all criteria, all designs.

And the danger is real. For we have been badly prepared for the breathtaking show we face. Perhaps there has simply not been enough time, or perhaps we have been too slow. I have been reading the last book of Norbert Wiener, in which he reminds us that cybernetics was a pious hope only fifteen years ago. It is now, he noted last year, a working technique in engineering, biology, medicine, and sociology, impinging on ethics and religion. Its consequences cannot be foreseen, although they will, of course, affect us all, under whatever name.

I am not of the proper generation nor am I a designer. So you can see that I am presuming in all directions in being here. But one does not have to be a fireman to give the alarm. Among other conclusions to be drawn, and I can draw it as well as another, is this one: Simple speculation is no longer adequate. A task imposed on all generations now is to seek out the fixed points of this turning world, as many as can be found, remembering that they sometimes wear masks and remembering that nature does not ever withhold what Fermi called its sheer cussedness. Still, the fixed points must be sought for such guidance as they can provide, and they must be sought now through the slow spread of waste, decay, destruction, and the withering of our resources, natural and man-made, that has passed alarming and reached desperate in many areas of our life. Certainly at a conference on design, that problem cannot be blinked. And yet the main problem goes beyond.

Design works with external objects, but design is a product of the upper brain power and its working out affects the senses and the nerve ends. In another book I have been reading, a book written ten years ago by the architect Richard Neutra, this appears:

Design, the act of putting constructs in an order, or disorder, seems to be human destiny. It is the specific responsibility to which our species has matured, and constitutes the only chance of the thinking, foreseeing, and constructing animal that we are, to preserve life on this shrunken planet and to survive with grace.

But if our species has matured to this, it remains immature and unsure in other respects. Toxic emanations from old dualities penetrate us daily. The useful opposes the beautiful as though it must. The expedient diminishes the moral as though the other alternative is not worth trying for. There are many such. But the sense receptors of mankind report back an indivisible world. In such a world the environment we put together—which must contain us all—must be an extension of ourselves that is organically possible, that meets our physiological and psychological imperatives. And to that end it must now submerge the old dualities in unities consistent with 2,300 or 23,000 miles an hour, with a world of three and a half billion going on six, with fires of 15 million degrees that can blind eyes 300 miles away. If not, it is quite improbable that this species, experimenting with its surroundings like General Turgitson in *Dr. Strangelove,* will survive. Instead like General Ripper, mouthing spectacularly private dualities, it will die.

The life or death of the human race is a heady topic for a fifteen-minute statement, and I propose now to back off from it. The designer, however, cannot back off from it. It is along the horizon of the future thus considered, it seems to me, that the real world presents itself to the serious designer. In the balance of forces that affect the working out of design, it is along this line that the cultural and the social influences spread.

It may not have been so once. In the comfortable days when it could be believed that man lived by truth and the truth would make him free—in those times, the designer not too concernedly may have relegated truth and beauty to a designer's Sunday and spent his weekdays fashioning a supposed separate utility out of ugliness, shoddiness, and compromise, all with the general consent. But the fact is—and it has been staring at us ever since Galileo—that man has lived almost entirely by myths and illusions, and the truth may very well destroy him. At least it must be lived with all seven days of the week if it is to be lived with at all.

Concerning the technical forces that affect the designer I will say nothing, knowing nothing. But I would like to say something about the economic forces, for here, in this earthier realm, I have both some experience and some thoughts, and here I think many designers are working very close to one side—and the wrong side—of the scale of survival values, which is the same on this level as on any other and hence may be worth some attention for our possible instruction.

For some years, as director of Consumers Union and editor of *Consumer Reports,* I manned an interesting observation post overlooking one sector of American design. We bought at random and tested comparatively products of all kinds—automobiles, travel irons, shoes and diapers, refrigerators, seat belts, fishing rods, food-mixers, and a few hundred other things. We often have had a dozen or two dozen or even three dozen competing brands of such products—washing machines, for instance, or cameras—sitting together in our laboratories during the tests, or automobiles standing side by side at our test track. I think it is probably true that nowhere else in the country could one see all together in one place at one time so many different brands of a given product. We were thus provided with, among other things, a kind of showcase of the output of designers, and some years ago we used to prevail on Eliot Noyes to come in from time to time and ponder the showing and write up for our readers what he thought about what he saw.

Well, Eliot Noyes got very busy and he couldn't do that, and we tried to get other designers, and then we ran into a rather curious thing. We couldn't get a designer to do the criticizing. Now it seems to me that *Consumer Reports* is one of the few places where you are going to get objective, disinterested design criticism. We carry no advertising and this is about 95 per cent of the reason why it's one of the few places. And we do buy the products and report on them and we are interested in telling about them. We can't get a designer to write for us though because the Society of Industrial Designers doesn't approve of designers' commenting on the work of other designers. I respect the professional reasons for this; I think they are practically inescapable. Still, I think there are other views possible from other levels when the subject is viewed from other levels. The view is not quite as handsome from those levels as it is from Aspen.

This was important information for our readers, along with the test findings, because we reported things of a sort that the manufacturers of the products did not regularly provide. Indeed, it saddens me to say that manufacturers regularly conceal much from our readers, who are among their buyers, and the product design is as often as not a means of the concealment. It is concealment of a sort, of course, to streamline as though for aerodynamic efficiency such a product as a can opener, or to pretend that a television set, a complex mechanism known only to this century, is a piece of French Provincial furniture. But I do not mean this sort of thing, of which there is a great deal, and all of it depressing. My concern here and now is with corruption in designing that has the effect of economically cheating the buyer or endangering his health, or possibly his life, and insulting him as a fellow human in the process.

A gas range that has a control panel made of plastic and so positioned that the heat of the range's burners can melt it is an economic cheat in the sense in which I mean to use the term. It is bad design and it is corrupt design because it sets out to cozen the buyer with the look of efficiency and it ends up exploiting him. Why was one of the ranges tested by Consumers Union designed that way? An electric skillet with neat little handles that cannot be held without making the fingers touch hot metal is a stupid design, and the well-known product of which this was true was down-rated because of the fact. But an electric toothbrush that sets up a lethal shock hazard under reasonable conditions of use is something worse than stupid, and I am happy to report that our findings concerning this eventually led to getting the toothbrush off the market. The answer to why it was put on the market in the first place, I suppose, is that it was an example of old-fashioned weekday designing, or designing for sale, or designing by a designer who was not concerned with survival values, at least on an individual scale. Designing for sale is one of the forces that work on designers, and one which can put us all in jeopardy, on the broadest scale, when we are indifferent to it.

The best definition I have encountered of designing for sale is one contained, by implication, in a statement made a few years ago by the manager of the Boeing Airplane Company's Pilotless Aircraft Division. "When we first started to work on missiles," he said, "we thought they would be a breeze compared to airplanes. We said, in effect, here's a product that's expendable, that lasts only a few minutes, so we can forget the rigid quality control of the airplane business and make missiles quick and cheesy, cheap and dirty, like a mass-produced consumer product."

Last year, of thirty-two automobiles bought for testing by Consumers Union, thirty-one broke down or needed repairs of one sort or another—some minor, some major, but all needed to keep the cars in order—before they had been driven 2,000 miles. The thirty-second car went almost 5,000 miles before trouble set in. These were not unimportant products made by fly-by-night companies on the fringe of the American economy; these came from the production of the largest corporations in the greatest of our industries—from every company that made a car.

What a ridiculous record! But the contempt and the hostility or indifference contained in such a record are, in my view, quite serious and precisely what we can no longer afford. Too much shoddy gets to market. Too many tricks and gadgets are used to seduce the buyer; and too many bad designs and too much bad workmanship turn the seduction into rape. The designer, to whatever extent he bears responsibility for all this, and certainly he shares in it, is diminishing the moral and besmirching the useful and beautiful. A gas range that has a tendency to devour itself may not be calamity, but the thinking behind it is akin to the thinking that precedes calamity. A toxic emanation is a toxic emanation, and the indifferent or contemptuous product designer is not likely to harbor the thoughts that can help us when he turns to larger matters.

There is simply ceasing to be room, in a world approaching 6 billion people, all a few hours from each other, for the divisive act at any level of life. Here may be one of the dilemmas that designers face, recognizable in microcosm in the narrow world of man's goods. I trust that any such dilemma can be explored with due regard for both the restraints and the freedoms that apply, and relative to the former I submit the following for your consideration: Anything that does not serve the slowly emerging unity of those who live on the one known populated planet is now false, is truly absurd, and will be continued to our peril.

# Sometimes I Play Things I Never Heard Myself
## William Bernbach
## 1964

When Eliot Noyes invited me to appear at this design conference, I asked him if he knew what he was doing. I am not a designer. I am an advertising man, and my knowledge of design is restricted to that field of communication. As a matter of fact, I have strong reservations about design, so strong that I informed Mr. Noyes that the theme of my talk would be: "Design can get in the way." He said, "Come anyway." So, here I am. At least, you know whom to blame. All I ask is that you remember my references to design are to design in advertising, and, if you see a relationship to design in other fields, that will be your doing and not mine.

Some time ago, in an interview, one of our great artists said: "Some people mistake neatness for art." With his usual genius this man brought to life for me, with one stroke of his brush, the danger in design. The danger is a worship of technique, a preciousness, a preoccupation with good looks. What I fear, and so often see, in an over-concern design is a bloodlessness. The goal seems to be the presentation of a neat package, instead of a revelation of its contents. There seems to be a striving for a gentility, a good taste, a good manners. Well, there is nothing gentler or better-mannered than a well-dressed corpse. The only trouble is that it's dead and inspires no one.

You just can't squeeze life into a package. It's going to ooze out here and there. I think it's terribly important to be aware of this. Not to be aware of it may lead to an overvaluation of rules and techniques, a tendency to distort and ignore life when it doesn't nicely fit into your system or theory. About a year ago a son of mine was graduated from prep school, and the main speaker was the Dean of MIT, and he told the story of this young man who just fascinated him up at MIT. This young man had a great design for living. He had divided his day not into hours, but into minutes. He knew precisely what he was going to do every minute of the day: so much time for study, so much time for socializing, so much time for sports, and he said he even knew precisely what kind of girl he was going to marry. He had this design down pat. She was going to be a girl about five-six, straight white teeth, black hair, her father had to have a certain income.

His design was pat. And even a year later, the dean couldn't get this boy out of his mind. He came across the boy and said, "Well, John, how is everything going?" John said, "Just fine. Everything is working out just as I planned. I even met that girl I told you about, the one I designed. She has black hair, white teeth, she's five-six, her father works down on Wall Street, but I don't like her." Design can be dangerous.

In advertising, it takes more than a good design to provoke and persuade the consumer. I can remember—and it wasn't more than twenty years ago—when all an ad had to do was look good for it to be turned down by the client. He was suspicious of good-looking, well-designed ads. And he had every right to be. The early designers had begun to enter the field. They felt they had an easy job. It was no trick at all to make ads look better. Any change would be an improvement. The copy was to them merely a graphic element that must balance beautifully with the other elements in the ad. Making the copy inviting and easy to read was never an important consideration. Everything was lined up so evenly and neatly that the parts of the ad were completely overpowered by the total graphic configuration. Well, that may be good design, but it's bad advertising! And I question that it's good design. If you measure the effectiveness of any effort by how well its purpose has been achieved, then you cannot call some of these early efforts at advertising design successful. The purpose of an ad is to persuade people to buy your product, and everything, however expert, that slickly distracts from that idea and those words is, for my money, bad design.

About 85 per cent of all ads today don't get looked at. This statistic was just revealed in a study made by the AAAA. This study was conducted by the advertising industry to find out what the public thought of advertising. We were worried about whether or not the public loved us. Our problem is they don't even hate us. The sad thing is that business is spending too much time and money on making advertising boring, and we're achieving this boredom with such great American efficiency. The scientific way we're going about it, we just can't miss.

Design is not the answer. This deplorable statistic—about 85 per cent of ads not getting looked at—exists despite the fact that in the last ten years there has been a tremendous increase in the demand by business for more expertly designed advertising. As a principal in an agency that has won more than its share of art and design awards, I say I wouldn't hesitate for a minute to choose the plain-looking ad that is alive and vital and meaningful over the ad that is beautiful but dumb, whose vitality is buried in the neatness and self-consciousness of technically perfect design.

Of course, the ideal combination in an ad is beauty and vitality. But, the real danger is that we will be blinded by the beauty and forget that what really touches people and moves them is the idea and the warmth and sincerity and insight which we ourselves bring to the ad. Just because an ad looks good is no insurance that it will get looked at. How many people do you know who are impeccably groomed but dull?

I have seen firsthand the development of some of our industry's greatest art directors. And I am talking about industry and commerce. The pattern was always the same for these art directors. In the early stages they were preoccupied with design—and their work was self-conscious and pretentious. Then, they became concerned with the object of their design. They studied it; they analyzed it; they looked for ways to improve it. And then they searched for a way to put it down simply, believably, so that nothing would come between that product and the reader of the ad.

We have recently run a rather successful campaign for a firm called Avis Rent-A-Car, and people are coming to buy this product. And I'd like to make a very important point about the approach we took on this. We don't think just saying nice things or saying provocative things is going to make a product succeed. As a matter of fact, we believe firmly that a great advertising campaign will make a bad product fail faster—it will just enable more people to know how bad it is. We tell people in our ads that our windshield wipers work; our ash trays are clean; we are only second, but we are trying harder; we want to be first. We took this campaign around to the people who deliver the cars to the consumer, the car washers and the mechanics. We told them we were completely dependent upon them; unless they delivered what we promised in the advertising, we would fail, and never did a company need its employees as much as we needed them. They then felt important for the first time in the company. They went to work; they produced a better product, and we have had rather a big success with this.

A few years ago I spoke before an art group in New York, art directors, and I said to them:

In the last decade we have seen a revolution of good graphic taste, so that today it occupies a position of unprecedented eminence. Today everybody is talking creativity, and frankly that's got me worried. I am jealous of the position you and I have reached in our profession, and I fear lest we lose it. I fear lest we keep the good taste and lose the sell. I fear all the sins we may commit in the name of creativity, and I fear that we may be entering an age of phonies. No one believes in you more than I do, no one has been helped by you and made you look good more than I. From my early work with Paul Rand about fifteen years ago right through the years, working with such commercial graphic giants as Bob Gage, Bill Taubin, Helmut Krone, and many others, I have watched you breathe vibrating life into my ideas with your talents. It is out of this great indebtedness to you that my concern springs. It can take very little time to lose all the ground we have gained. All we have to do is forget that good taste and advanced techniques are not ends in themselves, but wonderful tools with which to make vivid the advantage of a product. The purpose of an ad is to sell, and unless we sell, people will be suspicious of our ads once more. The primary responsibility of good creative people in advertising is not just to exercise creative freedom, but to know what is good creative work and what is merely pretentious acrobatics. With the tremendous increase in political and social pressures, with violence confronting us at every turn, with the fierce competition among advertisers, more and more it will take tremendous artistry with words and pictures to touch and move the reader. So exposed is he to banalities, to self-conscious, artificial attempts to arrest his attention, that he looks, but he does not see; he listens, but he does not hear; and what is worse, he does not feel. There has never been a greater challenge to your talent. To those of you who can meet that challenge, who through the magic of your artistry can make the reader see, hear, and feel, the rewards have never been greater, for you are the insurance an advertiser takes out on all the facts that he wants to tell the public, for only you, working honestly and imaginatively, can bring those dead facts to life and make them memorable to all who see them. And as a last word I'd like to quote my favorite philosopher, Thelonious Monk, when he said, "The only cats worth anything are the cats who take chances. Sometimes I play things I never heard myself."

146

# XIV  Molded Nearer Heart's Desire

The 'sixties also produced a new kind of speaking talent at Aspen: men who were by profession not designers but commentators on design. Peter Blake was a speaker, a program chairman, a board member, and editor of *Architectural Forum* (though he may regard himself still as an architect). Arthur Drexler had not long before joined the staff of the Museum of Modern Art when he gave his paper of 1962, expressing a vision he was to realize in a great exhibition at the museum two years later. And the name Banham had come to the notice of the conference by way of published words alone. The papers by Drexler and me therefore represent something of a new Aspen genre—specifically about design, but from just outside the business.

# Perfecting the Earth
## Arthur Drexler
## 1962

For the last ten or twelve years, I have been spending my time trying to sort out architecture on a qualitative basis. This presupposes that one is actually able to define the qualities that make a building a work of architecture. It supposes that this knowledge or this view of things can be communicated to other people. One tries to select buildings as works of art on the double basis of intrinsic quality and of significance of the moment. This is another way of saying historical significance. It assumes again that judgments can have a certain consistency. It also assumes that there is a purpose to this activity, and that ultimately one will help to produce an audience for good architecture. If there is already an audience for good architecture, one hopes to enlarge it. One also hopes that some architects might even find this process helpful. The process is usually regarded as helpful to the public and sometimes even to architects, but there is, alas, one fact that simply cannot be ignored. The world has not become more beautiful; architecture has not become noticeably better; in fact, the world has become conspicuously uglier.

All of us here presumably believe there is something that can still be done. In this sense, I guess, we are all optimists; at least, I feel myself to be an optimist. It is true that today we are all of us one day closer to death than we were yesterday. We may perhaps lengthen life, but ultimately we must all die. Beyond this fact, it seems to me that not much else really matters terribly seriously. And yet, while we live, it does seem better to be fully alive than partially alive. It is, in fact, the certainty of death that makes me an optimist, since I view the possibility of being really alive as within reach.

The purpose of this talk is to suggest what seem to me to be some of the reasons why we are in our present difficulties in terms of the architectural environment. It is also to propose an attitude toward architecture that might yield, if not a world of luminous beauty, at least a different set of difficulties. This might be an improvement.

In ancient times, architecture was the representation of what men took to be the order of the universe and of man's relation to God. Building forms represented those events in nature and in human experience by which life could be measured and understood. If properly used, those forms could bring benefits. What are some of those forms? Well, the axis on which the universe revolves. The road that men travel in time. The gate that marks the transition from youth to age, or from life to death. The place which is the end of the journey. It might be a mountain, a cave, a garden, or an island in a lake. All buildings or groups of buildings that portrayed these events or acts could be described within two or three categories of forms. Journeys, which are processional ways, roads, colonnades; and destinations, which are mountains, pyramids, masses that may or may not look the same from all sides but which do have a meaning that resides at the top and involves an ascent. The top of a pyramid is noticeably different from the bottom. The meaning also resides, in most of these so-called destination forms, inside rather than outside.

There is a possible third category: the object. The useful object. The magic jewel, the sword, the efficacious instrument that enhanced life and warded off death.

Greek and Roman architecture, it seems to me, substituted (largely by means of a column) an image that we are pleased nowadays to read as the human body in upright possession of the self. Gothic architecture, it seems to me, presented the universe as a path, a road defined by stone lines and colored lights. At the end of the path are some very important efficacious objects, but it is in the transforming light that we find, I think, the true meaning and power of the cathedral; its power to suggest the nature of heaven.

The history of modern architecture is generally thought to begin in the mid-nineteenth century. There are two building types that make their appearance around the 1850's. They might, for purposes of convenience, be described as factories and fantasies. The factory represents the rationalization of labor, the manipulation of human energy, the quantification of work, the distribution of effort in a pre-scribed cycle of events, predetermined by men for specific ends. The cast iron column, the large span, the slim linear structure, which is in itself no end but only a means to an end, is the significant building type that emerges in the mid-nineteenth century. It is the building as an instrument, not as an end in itself. It is an instrument for labor.

The very techniques that made possible both this instrument and the work to be done within it also yield the fantasy of the famous Crystal Palace, the building designed to house the great Exhibition of 1851, an instrument for the display of efficacious objects. The Crystal Palace, indeed, had more useful objects than anyone knew what to do with. And, thank goodness, most of them have vanished, if only to be replaced by fresh waves of unnecessary useful objects. The beauty of the Crystal Palace, and it must indeed have been a beautiful building as far as one can judge from the surviving photographs, must have resided largely in the demonstration it gave of the abundance made possible by the new techniques. The Crystal Palace, among other things, introduced the age of statistics in architecture. Here was a building that could be valued because it employed so many thousands of identical columns, so many thousands of panes of glass, so many thousands of identical beams, and, in a way, so many thousands of identical useful objects. Sheer abundance. A source of joy and reassurance. But if one tries to define the Crystal Palace, a building of the most compelling magic, one cannot, I think, describe it as anything other than a Thing—not a Journey, not a Place—and of dubious utility. It was a Thing, a manufactured artifact, visibly proclaiming that its component parts came from a place of labor, were assembled with labor, and reflected only the briefest escape from labor in its final finished form.

It seems to me that it is possible to describe the history of modern architecture as the shift in our attitude toward buildings—a shift away from the sense of Place to the sense of Thing. We live in a world in which buildings are instruments. We value them according to their efficiency. This means that as our ends change, the means to the ends are devalued. Today's perfectly functional solution to the problem of the design of a laboratory, for example, may be devalued within two years because the ends will have changed, and the means will be required to change anew.

The recent history of architecture seems to have involved a double effort to make effective instruments: functional buildings, and at the same time buildings to endure beyond the period of immediate use-fulness. In the 1920's the style formations, the visible shapes of build-ings, were tested, altered, and abandoned; and in the hands of two or three architects of phenomenal talent, they achieved a certain durability beyond mere utility. I think, for example, of the early work of Le Corbusier, the Villa Savoye. Here was a house intended to look as if it had been made in a factory (a very French factory), carried perhaps from Paris and set up on a lawn like a picnic table. On top of the table, if you recall this building, are some elegant useful objects, almost abstract pink and blue walls. They look as if they can be moved from one part of the building to another. The building itself is conceived of as a means to an end. It is also meant to look—and this is very important—as if it had been made in a factory. It was not, of course, made in a factory, and the techniques at first admired because of this look of impersonal precision have been abandoned in the postwar years. The Villa Savoye, along with many other buildings by Le Corbusier, was an effort to find durability in geometric form. It was a perfectly respectable effort, one with sufficient Platonic precedent to put Le Corbusier in the mainstream of the Mediterranean tradition, but an effort that has proved to be altogether ineffectual. There are few buildings that look as dated today as does the Villa Savoye.

In the 1950's a second great effort was made to find the form of duration. This was the effort made by Mies van der Rohe, who in abandoning his earlier experiments with modulations of space decided that architectural truth reside in structure, that the structural fact was the unchanging, unalterable fact of architecture. All formulations based on principle and executed with a degree of clarity and precision must indeed end by compelling some or even most of us for a considerable period of time. Certainly this has been true of Mies's formulation, but we do know that, when Mies says that structure is the truth of architecture, he means a particular kind of structure. Mies's logic is the logic of structure, but it is the structure of inhibition. Mies proceeds by excluding separate and, for his purposes, irrelevant truths. There are other kinds of structure. They do not lend themselves to Mies van der Rohe's view of the order of the universe, and so they are declared outside the realms of truth. This is a very familiar attitude; we encounter it all the time, even in the familiar argument between the scientist and the artist. The scientist who feels that last week in the laboratory hope was discovered to be a logical fallacy, and has the proof of this, is operating on a different set of truths from the artist.

There are alternate attitudes that have been explored. Le Corbusier himself abandoned in his postwar work many of the specific forms that he had earlier developed. He did not abandon, incidentally, his sense of the town as a collection of discrete objects spotted on the landscape, tastefully arranged. He did abandon the limitations of geometric form and expanded his vocabulary of shapes and textures to restore to architecture the sense of weight, of density, of substance, the immediate reality of physical presence.

Buckminster Fuller has presented yet another intensely principled, extremely compelling alternative. Buckminster Fuller has, in a way, carried the architecture of inhibition, if I may use this phrase, much farther than Mies would have dreamed possible. We must, according to Buckminster Fuller, imitate in our building forms what we consider to be the actual physical structure of the universe. Not the universe as we structure it in our minds, as experience, but the actual processes by which particles cohere. The injunction to do this depends to a great extent on the fear of being irrational. The idea is that, once you know this is the way particles are arranged in nature, you cannot do otherwise than imitate. If you don't, you are being deliberately archaic, willfully ignorant of the facts of the artistic universe. One of the most compelling aspects of his point of view is that technology itself evolves in this direction, specifically in the direction that we can do more and more technologically with less and less. We can, indeed, do more with the little technology we now have than we can do with the technology that Buckminster Fuller assumes will ultimately be at our disposal. The ultimate end of the Fuller view of the uses of structures is that architecture should disappear. It is necessary, finally, only to enclose the sky with a heavenly vault of man's own making. We have then the Garden of Eden. Architecture, other than as a frivolous act of self-indulgence, is unnecessary. I think that this is true. I think it can be done right now, and it does not have to be done with octahedrons.

There is still another alternative. It is, I think, the most compelling view of architecture at present being heard in the United States and in the world, because it makes architecture possible for you and me. It invites us to participate in something that seems to have a future. I accept, I believe everything that [Louis] Kahn describes, but I also observe a specific form sense that I cannot always relate to the purposes and motives that Lou Kahn describes. There is a Lou Kahn image of a building that I can summon up to the mind's eye. It has physical weight and density, enormous presence. It seems to me to suggest—and this is what I personally find most compelling about it—the purposefulness of human activity. It does this by drawing out of the building some particular element that will lend itself to being physically present before my eyes. It matters not whether this element is a stair, an elevator, or a pipe. And the exact weight of this physical presence is perhaps not always determined by the thing so enclosed. This is to me an entirely viable and human interpretation of the idea of utility, because it suggests to me that process, the means to the end, is itself subject to the aesthetic decision. It suggests to me that the world is not merely a dump heap to be ruined by factories making things, but that the process by which things are made is at least as important as the thing itself, perhaps more important.

I have so far tried to describe what seemed to me to be the major and most compelling, convincing, hopeful views of architecture in the years since the war. Obviously many other views are finding their practitioners and their audience. For instance, there is the view that the problem really is how to restore plastic form, sculptural modulation of mass, through an architecture which, because of the nature of technology, has become planar and linear. But we have one kind of escape. From time to time we can select a building program, whether it be a church, an airport, or a theater, and explode it into a form that will be understood to mean emotional response. Such forms are usually curvilinear, at least in this country and in the Mediterranean. They are also voluptuous, and often vulgar, because they do require that the architect have some capacity as a sculptor. This, alas, is not often the case.

Another attitude is that all of these form systems are rationalizations, that we can intellectually perceive the limitations of each of these systems, these attitudes. If this is so, no single one of them has a claim to our allegiance. In that case, the honest, educated man is under no commitment to any particular form system, nor is he under a commitment to invent one of his own. This I find disturbing. I am aware, I think, that things are relative, that nothing is absolutely good or absolutely bad. But I do not think that I am thereby disobliged from behaving myself according to limitations that it is not too difficult for myself and society to agree upon. In the arts something else happens. When this point of view or nonpoint of view prevails, we often observe the history of architecture regarded as the source of wonder. We see the beginnings of a new eclecticism, of tasty and tasteful forms. We see also the milliner's attitude toward architecture, or perhaps the cosmetic attitude in which a veil of tiny tiles is wrapped around what one must suppose is a frightful face. This kind of architecture gives us, instead of music, a pleasant humming sound, a kind of anesthetic.

Technology today is still something that happens in the factory. It doesn't happen on the site here; it happens there, wherever "there" may be. And "there" may be in every direction at once. The parts converge on the site, but the parts have been predetermind. They happen in the factory. All of the formulations I have described are dependent on this view of technology. Obviously there are gradations to this, and some exceptions. But I believe that it is accurate to describe the present uses of technology as the preparation of materials in a work place, and that architecture is the assembly of these materials at a certain position in space. The architect is the man who runs back and forth between all the places. He coordinates these things. He tells the client that he coordinates them. Once in a while he tries to get one of the factories to make one of the parts differently, and at that point he has the kinds of problems we are all familiar with.

Factories, you know, are really outside of reality. Real life doesn't happen in factories. Factories are exempt in the present world view except, of course, in the world view of people like Lou Kahn. But you know they are eccentric, they are marginal to what happens in the world. The whole world is becoming a factory. It's very hard to find nonfactory space to occupy. This means that we have a harder and harder time distinguishing ends from means. It also means that nothing endures, nor are many things meant to endure. Suppose that it were possible to invent an imaginary architecture. Suppose that we could think of architecture not as a thing but as a process of perfecting the earth. If you try to think of architecture this way, it may perhaps occur to you that, if you think of most buildings as a process of perfecting the earth, most of them are simply unnecessary. They need not exist before our eyes as discrete objects, as things set in the landscape. They simply need not be there.

Some years ago I was asked to meet with a group of designers at the Bell Telephone Company in New York. Ostensibly they wanted me to give them two or three deathless phrases about design, but really they wanted to show me their latest telephones. And I gave them several deathless phrases, and they gave me telephones, and we were not satisfied with each other. In the course of this encounter, one of the gentlemen said: "We have a problem. In many towns across the United States we have to build relay stations, and we can't afford to put these things in the center of the town because land costs too much, so we put them outside the town, and usually we put them on streets that have houses. Naturally, in most small American towns, these are colonial, ranch-type, multilevel things. We have to go to some expense to get all this humming and throbbing equipment inside these colonial-type houses, and we have to hide the fact that the building is actually a relay station. If we don't hide it, the people on the block get very upset, and this is not nice for the Telephone Company."

Well, the gentleman wanted me to tell him that his problems could be solved if he would hold a competition for good design of relay stations, which ought to yield a batch of manageably conservative modern things that you could set on the block without disturbing the neighbors. Instead, I told him that I thought there wasn't any reason why they should put these relay stations in buildings. I said it didn't make any difference to me what style he used, I thought they were all dreadful, modern as well as colonial. He thought I was joking, because you don't say that if you are from the Museum of Modern Art. And he was quite suspicious. I suggested instead that what they might do is put the whole mess underground. All that was required was that some-

153

body visit it once a day, if that often. It took very little space, was quite convenient when you put it underground, and then you could build a nice park on top of it.

To get back to the idea of an imaginary architecture, which is seen as the process of perfecting the earth. From time to time I go to visit students at various schools on the Eastern Seaboard, and I love to do this, because whenever I walk into a studio the tables are covered with models. The students, of course, make beautiful models of their buildings. This is very important. The stages of the construction of the model are to me the most significant part of the education and the mis-education of architects. Invariably, I have to walk past a model on my way to the project under discussion; I have to walk past a model that is merely a contour study of the site before the thing has been set down on top of the model. This topographical model—you know how they're all done, they're tiers, and tiers, and tiers of cardboard or balsa wood, or whatever it may be, cut out to follow the contours of the land. They're extremely beautiful. Why shouldn't they be? Often the land is very beautiful.

Those contour maps—those models of the earth—are already architecture. Nothing else is needed to make a building except to pull out one or two of these layers and make a space between them. Think how many thousands of buildings in the United States could slip into the earth. Instead, the students think of architecture as the making of things in opposition to the earth. Good design is considered to reside in the decisions made by the student in how he places the box in relation to the contours. The correct placement—and some placements are more correct than others, indeed—this correctness of oppositions is expected to yield an improvement to the environment. Ultimately, it is expected to yield the thing we call architecture. Well, I don't like that. I like to look at photographs, aerial photographs, of rice fields in Asia. And I have often wished that I could persuade architects visiting the United States from Japan or elsewhere that there is an attitude toward the earth that is in itself a guide for technology. They need not necessarily imitate us in the endless manufacture of little things and big things; cheap use-ful objects and useful objects over $10 million, all shiny, all expendable. In such a view of architecture, technology would develop somewhat differently. It obviously would continue to be largely the manufacture of things in factories; but it would also call for a technology of the earth, of making and doing on the spot. One would really have to design the process, and that is another proposition altogether. We don't have to think of technology as we do think of it. We don't have to think of the world as a scrap heap. There might indeed be an architecture process like that I have tried to suggest to you—the perfecting of the earth.

# All That Glitters Is Not Stainless
## Reyner Banham
## 1966

Two of the most important resources of modern design are about a hundred and twenty years old now; one is the plastics industry, the other is the tradition of worry about the state of the art. As far as plastics are concerned, celluloid molding dates from the work of my countryman, Alexander Parkes, in the middle 1850's, and the vulcanizing of rubber dates from the work of the brilliant American, Charles Goodyear, a decade earlier.

In the divided culture in which we live and work, we have to remind ourselves who founded plastics, but I don't have to remind you that design worry was founded by old John Ruskin and young William Morris, not to mention stylish Gottfried Semper in Germany and functional Horatio Greenough in the United States, in those same middle years of the last century. Yet, if you cast eyes on the visible scene or lay hands on the tangible environment, you will know that the effect of the plastics industry has been vast and all-pervasive.

But what has the tradition of worry about the state of the art done for design that can be compared to the avalanche of new materials and products that the plastics industry has emptied over the face of the earth?

One thing it has done is to worry about new materials like plastics, new materials that drive out old familiar ones because their performance can be more accurately specified than any ancient craftsman could select wood. Such materials can be more accurately specified by the designer, but remain totally inscrutable to the ultimate consumer.

So, John Q. Public, the well-known car buff, looks at the badge on the front of the 1967 GT Supremo Saddlestitched Hodad Fastback and can't tell by looking whether it is an exquisite specimen of the goldsmith's art sealed under crystal glass or just crafty vapor gilding on the back of one-shot styrene molding—though he has his suspicions!

Or another instance: The red minicar in which the Banham family used to thread its way deftly through the wild, swinging, miniskirted London scene was protected all around its lower perimeter by a strip of what was implied to be stainless steel but proved to be metal foil sealed under clear plastic. It glittered like stainless, but it wasn't. What is more, it did a better job than stainless could have done by not introducing certain risks of snagging, tearing and spearing that make steel dangerous in an accident. Yet the classic tradition of design worry would insist on genuine stainless and denounce the plastic trim as a cheap substitute or a trick. To satisfy the conscience of design (a monster on which I shall have much more to say), we have to be impaled by genuine stainless steel.

155

Fortunately, design worry offers other precepts to guide us: For instance, the plastic trim would be OK if it didn't pretend to be something it isn't. But that would deprive us of some things we all clearly love: Glitter, high finish, and shine. These are visual qualities that plastics have democratized, so that the average parking lot or appliance showroom bounces back the light in a way previous ages probably saw only on the serf-polished armor at aristocratic jousts and tourneys.

And this love of glitter is not just a vulgar dream of the silly and underprivileged. The greatest generation of design theorists, who flourished from 1910 to 1930, all loved glitter and taught us to love it too. Frank Lloyd Wright rejoiced in the lights of Chicago by night; Marinetti saw the new age reflected in the light bouncing back from control-consoles and electrical plants; Gropius called for buildings like crystal symbols, and Mies van der Rohe built them; Fernand Léger was struck by the magic of light on metal on a field gun; Le Corbusier and Marcel Breuer put that magic into production on furniture; Sir Herbert Read invited us to admire instruments and vessels of stainless steel.

Industrial design rides upon the back of an industrial complex that exists primarily to satisfy such desires of man as universal glitter. But why does the heart of man desire it? Why did the great masters of modern design teach us to echo, in life, Goethe's dying demand, *"Mehr Licht"*? What is the source of this modern desire that plastics above all can supply?

Philosophers, semanticists, psychologists, historians (and *there's* a bundle of resources every progressive design office and school increasingly employ) can all shed some light on this. The hypnotic effect of glitter and brightness caught up even Saint Thomas Aquinas, perhaps because "shining" is a word that rings with virtue throughout Holy Writ; the face of Moses shone, and the house of a latterday patriarch was called "Taliesin"—Shining Brow. That old magic still works today for copywriters pushing toothpaste and for poets pushing the millennium, asking the Almighty to "look shining at new styles of architecture, a change of heart!" And that stunning phrase from W. H. Auden sums up exactly what modern design has done for the ancient magic of glitter. The great source of our preoccupation with the shininess of modern design is that it symbolizes the fresh start, the clean new way of life that was, and is, to replace the miseries of those dark satanic mills in which industry and its arts of design were born.

The generation of great gray eminences who presided over the birth of modern design as a responsible profession grew up in the grubby, coarse-textured world of late-Victorian industry. They saw that industry's main product—soot—irremediably caking the unpolished and unwashable surfaces of its main structural materials, brick and cast iron, and they complained, in the words of a great visionary of light, Paul Scheerbart: *"Backstein-Kultur tut uns nur Leid* (brick brings us only hurt)." No wonder that Adolf Loos wanted the walls of the heavenly city to be flush and smooth from top to bottom and that his generation saw the task of design in Augean terms; a total, global cleanup. And not just a physical cleanup. In the writings of Le

Corbusier, for instance, words like "health" and "morality" frequently turn up in adjacent phrases of the same sentence as twin attributes of modern design. One of the great intellectual resources of our times, the concept of moral improvement through design, is also one of its most powerful sources of intellectual confusion. I suppose it goes back to that lovable Victorian nut, A. W. N. Pugin, and his implied proposition that the revival of truly Christian, or pointed architecture would bring back the Age of Faith he supposed to have been in full swing when pointed, or Gothic, architecture appeared for the first time round.

Ever since, the design theorists and worriers over the state of the art have insisted that style betrays the moral intention of the designers: Art Nouveau equals decadence; Expressionism equals selfishness; white walls and flat roof equal care for functional performance; redwood and roof overhangs equal care for human values; glass boxes equal inhuman disregard for people; chromium brightwork equals commercial swindle; and so forth.

Not one of these propositions is demonstrably true, yet each has been (and many still are) passionately believed in or persists as unrevised prejudice. Yet we know that many flat-roofed and white-walled modern buildings were indifferently designed for functional performance. Or again, when General Motors came up with the neat, sweet, almost chrome-free body shell of the first Corvair, moralizing design critics congratulated Detroit on mending its wicked ways. Yet this is the model that Ralph Nader and all the litigants assert is a deathtrap sold by General Motors with full knowledge of its instability. It seems that the glitter of a morally sound style does not guarantee a stainless reputation to the product in use.

Yet the moral reassurance seems to be remarkably necessary in all branches of design, and professional designers go to camp meetings in the mountains to be told what's right and what's wrong. No other profession, not even those bound by massive oaths of probity like the Hippocratic oath of the medicals, has this rage to keep itself morally pure by public self-examination. A man sitting next to me at a particularly bitter session of an architectural conference in England some time ago said incredulously, "Do dentists have meetings like this?"

This moral preoccupation is one of the principal driving forces of modern design and could be a great guarantee to the general public were it not so self-regarding. That line of W. H. Auden I quoted earlier reminded me of something contemporary from Louis MacNeice:

> Our freedom as free-lances
> Advances towards its end;
> The earth compels, upon it
> Sonnets and Birds descend;
> And soon, my friend,
> We shall have no time for dances.

The concept of the freedom of free-lances coming to an end is sure to strike a familiar note, if only because it has been said so often at places like Aspen. Year after year, men have stood at the microphone and preached hellfire, the population explosion, and the sands of time running out. We love it, gladly agree that our time for dancing has come to an end, and resolve to go out and do better by taking the situation more seriously.

Better? What's so good about a world where the designers have salved their consciences by taking everything so seriously that poetry falls flat, the birds are all grounded, and nobody dances. One of humanity's main motives for surviving the bomb, the baby boom, and the final solidification of the freeway system into a coast-to-coast parking lot will be to get the birds and the poets back into orbit, revive the watusi and the pavane, and clip on the optional equipment generally. Humanity is not going to survive just so designers can work up a high polish on their consciences, nor will it thank them for being less autarchic and more systematic in their thinking if the products don't get any better.

Any person in his right mind will know that conscience divorced from function helps nobody, yet the design profession at large is chronically prone to elevate the demands of private conscience. Why? The answer again lies in the source from which modern design has sprung: the concept of the designer as some kind of artist. On the one hand, this idea descends from the traditional view of the architect as one who imposes cultural values on the mere construction of buildings; on the other hand, from the William Morris fiction of the designer-craftsman as an artist in the sense in which the nineteenth century understood the artist, that is, as a free spirit answerable only to himself. If the public didn't understand the artist's work, so much the worse for the public, especially as they still owed him a living.

Morris himself took a more socially responsible view than this, but my reading of many of his professed followers is that they believed the only good product was one that brought pleasure to its producer. You will hear this proposition usually in the guarded and inverted form that mass production is evil because it brings no pleasure to the worker, but which ever way you phrase it, the whole conception is antisocial and perverse. No more in design than in dentistry can society accept that the first responsibility of its servants is to please themselves. And so to the big crossup: The public conscience of the design profession tells it that it cannot give absolute allegiance to the promptings of its private conscience. The designer as a social being confronts the designer as a creative individual in an unresolvable dilemma, and he is glad to have any hellfire demographer or revivalist cybernetician come and hand him a ready-made answer to this problem or any of the others.

For the conscience problem is no more than typical, in its inner contradictions, of the situation that modern design has inherited from its historical sources. Whereas most of its physical resources have unequivocal value—new materials, new production methods, etc.— many of its psychological sources bear signs of the confusions and misdirections that have resulted from trying to keep up with the physical resources and failing.

Take the concept of the basic design course, the *Vorkurs*, or what have you. There is a great primary source if you like! As a concept, it has a noble simplicity to it; the student is to be returned to zero and made to begin again with the elementary materials and primary relationships of his craft. The sophisticated shall be brought low, the honest and humble shall be lifted up.

Yet all over the world the "Bauhaus system," as this kind of teaching is often called, is in disarray and contention. Most design educators seem not to know where else to start, even while admitting that the system doesn't work. What has gone wrong? Firstly, and obviously, it never was a system, it was a body of teaching methods under constant revision from 1919 to 1933 by a body of remarkable men. And it was the men who mattered—the system never went wrong while it was administered by men who had been through the Bauhaus mill. It never went wrong on Joseph Albers, for instance.

But the other thing to note is that these old *Bauhausler* kept the methods under revision. There is startlingly little resemblance between what Moholy-Nagy was doing in his last years at the Institute of Design in Chicago and what he and Albers had been doing in Weimar in 1923. And I suspect the driving motivation to change everything was that one of the chief justification of the original Weimar course invented by Hannes Itten had disappeared—it was no longer necessary to disabuse students of ingrained visual prejudices, and it is even less necessary today.

A lot of things have happened to people since the Bauhaus was young, things like junk sculpture, hand-held movies, Batman, action painting, Hell's Angels, surrealism, custom-car shows, Op art, Henry Moore, Cinerama, and so on. As a result, people have become sophisticated—remarkably so—and far less visually prejudiced. Beady little eyes that can tell stainless from spray chrome at fifty paces and prefer the latter because it is more jokey clearly need a very different type of education from what suited the mystical peasants who crawled out of the Biedermier woodwork to join Gropius at Weimar.

Something else that has happened to people since the Bauhaus is, of course, the Bauhaus—and industrial design generally. It has not gone unnoticed, either; the public has picked up some famous names and even a few fairly far-out tastes. A top New York design pundit told me how he observed suburban housewives admiring some Barcelona chairs in Macy's. His comment: "God, it was horrible!"

My own comment on that comment would be: "When they stop throwing rocks at your head and throw a lifebelt instead, have the decency to say 'thank you' as you drown." But plenty of other design people would have responded in the same way. After a hundred years or more of regarding the bad taste of the public as one of design's major problems, it can be difficult to adjust to the idea that they may now be on your side and may have stopped throwing rocks.

159

Furthermore, a lot of design people seem not to want to adjust. The belief that design is a thankless task definitely appeals to the martyr complex that design has inherited from the artistic forebears. And furthermore yet, being out of step was a guarantee to their consciences that they were in the right, for design is also part of the great progressive do-gooder complex of ideas based upon the proposition that the majority is always wrong, that the public must be led, cajoled, sticked, and carroted onward and upward.

This evil backside on the face of public concern is one of the nastier aspects of worrying about the state of the art. It leaves behind some unpleasant questions, such as: Is the shine on the brow of the designer as he hands out the tablets of his lore the true stainless glitter of Messianic inspiration, or is it just the spray chrome of self-righteousness? Too many of the great unquestioned assumptions on which modern design is based have begun to peel and flake of late; neither they nor their advocates appear to be quite such stainless representatives of the shining new world as once we thought. It is high time we checked to see which ones have rusted through and must be junked, which need to go back in the plating tank, and which only need a wipe over with the silvercloth.

# XV Optimists Sometimes Look Silly . . .

. . . said Richard Farson of the Institute for Behavioural Studies in his new bill of rights and went right on, in his typically Southern California way, to propose a set of strenuously optimistic futures far more disturbing than the most pessimistic doomsaying. John Cage's paper, addressing many of the same problems, is, of course, a classic—but why so rarely reprinted?

# Design Diary: How to Improve the World (You Will Only Make Matters Worse)
## John Cage
## 1966

I. Continue: I'll discover where you sweat (Kierkegaard). We are getting rid of ownership, substituting use. Beginning with ideas. Which ones can we take? Which ones can we give?

*Disappearance of power politics.*

Nonmeasurement.

*Japanese, he said: We also hear with our feet, I'd quoted Busoni: Standing between musician and music is notation. Before I'd given the history: Chance operations, indeterminacy. I'd cited musics of India: notation of them's after the fact. I'd spoken of direct musical action (since it's ears, not interposing eyes).*

2:00 A.M., Jensen said, "Even if you didn't like the results (Lindsay, etc.), we hope you liked the telling of it." Telling (?) of it! We were there while it was happening!

II. *Minimum ethic: Do what you said you'd do. Impossible? Telephone. No answer?*

My idea was that they wanted to fight (human nature and all that), they should do it in the Antarctic, rest of us gambling on daily outcome: proceeds for world welfare. Instead they're cooperative down there, exchanging data, being friendly.

April '64: U.S. State Department man gave Honolulu talk—"global village whether we like it or not"—cited fifty-five services which are global in extent. Mountain range dividing Oahu, formerly crenelated (crenelations for self-protection while shooting arrows), is now tunneled, permitting population circulation, cars, etc., part of dying political-economic structures. Social work equals increasing number of global services.

III. As McLuhan says, everything happens at once. Image is no longer stream falling over rocks, getting from original to final place; it's as Tenney explained: A vibrating complex, any addition or subtraction of component(s), regardless of apparent position(s) in the total system, producing alteration, a different music. Fuller: As long as one human being is hungry, the entire human race is hungry.

City planning's obsolete. What's needed is global planning so Earth may stop stepping like octopus on its own feet. Buckminster Fuller uses his head: comprehensive design science; inventory of world resources. Conversion: the mind turns, no longer facing in its direction. Utopia?

Self-knowledge. Some will make it, with or without LSD. The others? Pray for acts of God, crises, power failures, no water to drink.

*IV. We see symmetrically: canoe on northern Canadian lake: stars in midnight sky repeated in water; forested shores precisely mirrored. Our hearing's asymmetrical: noticed sounds surprise us: echoes of shouts we make transform our voices: straight line of sound from us to shore's followed by echo's slithering around the lake's perimeter. When I said, "Fifty-five global services," California Bell Telephone man replied (September '65), "It's now sixty-one."*

The seasons (creation, preservation, destruction, quiescence): this was experienced and resultant idea (no longer is: he flies to Rio). What shall we wear as we travel about? What about Stein's idea: People are the way their land and air is?

V. When I said that culture was changing from Renaissance to what it is now (McLuhan), Johns objected to what he said was an oversimplification. But Johns was speaking according to our non-Renaissance experience: total field, nonfocused multiplicity. We are, are we not, socially speaking, in a situation of the old dying and the new coming into being? For the old—paying bills, seeking for power—take the attitude of play: games. For the new—doing what isn't necessary, "moving sand from one part of the beach to another" (Buckminster Fuller)—take the religious attitude: celebration. (It celebrates). The people have left. The cat and kittens were taken to the SPCA. The house is full of fleas.

VI. They say totally determined music and indeterminate music sound the same. I visited Hamada. Getting up from the wheel, he said, "I'm not interested in results; just going on." Art's in process of coming into its own: life.

*The lake is undefined. The land around resists upon it obscuring its shape, shape that needs to remain unrevealed. Sung. "Floating world." Rain, curtain of windswept lake's surface beyond: second view (there are others, he tells me, one with mists rising.) Yesterday it was stillness and reflections, groups of bubbles. An American garden: water, not sand; vegetation, not stones. Thunder.*

Without intending to, I'm going from lake to lake. Saltair. Salt Lake.

VII. Hugh Nibley. I hadn't seen him since high school days. I asked him what he thought about other planets and sentient populations. Yes, he said, throughout the universe, it's Mormon doctrine. We'd said good-bye. I opened the door of the car, picked up my attaché case and everything in it fell out on the grass and the gutter. His comments: Something memorable always happens.

Things we were going to do are now being done by others. They were, it seems, not in our minds to do (were we or they out of our minds?) but simply ready to enter any open mind, any mind disturbed enough not to have an idea in it.

*VIII. The daily warmth we experience, my father said, is not transmitted by Sun to Earth but is what Earth does in response to Sun. Measurements, he said, measure measuring means.*

Basho: Matsutake ya shirano ko no ha no hebaritsuku. The leaf of some unknown tree sticking on the mushroom (Blythe). Mushroom does not know what leaf is sticking on it (Takemitsu). Project: Discover way to translate Far Eastern texts so Western men can read orientally. Communication? Bakarashi! Words without syntax, each word polymorphic.

He wanted me to agree that the piano tuner and the piano maker have nothing to do with it (the composition). The younger ones had said: Whoever makes the stretcher isn't separate from the painting. (It doesn't stop there either.)

IX. Looking in all directions not just one direction. Housing (Fuller) will be, like telephoning, a service. Only circumstance to stop your living there: someone's there already (it's busy). Thus we'll learn to desire emptiness. Not being able to say "This is mine," we'll want when we inquire to get no response at all.

4:00 P.M. throughout the world. Whether we like it or not (is what he said), it's happening to us. Advertisements are all good; the news is all bad (McLuhan). But how we receive bad news can change: we're glad to hear unemployment's increasing. Soon, all that will be required of us will be one hour's·work per year (Fuller).

*X. They ask what the purpose of art is. Is that how things are? Say there were a thousand artists and one purpose, would one artist be having it and all the nine hundred and ninety-nine others be missing the point?*

Arcata Bottom sign said: Experiment endlessly and keep humble. "Write to Center for the Study of Democratic Institutions; they'll know about the global services." I did. They answered they knew nothing, suggested writing to State Department. Books one formerly needed were hard to locate. Now they're all out in paperback. Society's changing. Relevant information's hard to come by. Soon it'll be everywhere, unnoticed.

XI. ELECTRONICS. Day comes, the day we die. *There's less and less to do: Circumstances do it for us. Earth.*

Old reasons for doing things no longer exist. (Sleep whenever. Your work goes on being done. You and it no longer have a means of separation). *We had the chance to do it individually. Now we must do it together: globally. War will not be group conflict: it'll be murder, pure and simple, individually conceived.*

Curiosity, awareness. They returned to the fact we all need to eat to explain their devotion to money rather than music. When I spoke of the equation, work equals money equals virtue, they interrupted me (they didn't let me say that nowadays there's no equation), saying, "How can you speak of money and virtue in the same breath?"

XII. Where there doesn't seem to be any space, know we no longer know what space is. Have faith space is there, giving one the chance to renovate his way of recognizing it, no matter the means, psychic, somatic, or means involving extensions of either.

People still ask for definitions, but it's quite clear now that nothing can be defined. Let alone art, its purpose, etc. We're not even sure of carrots (whether they're what we think they are, how poisonous they are, who grew them and under what circumstances).

She was indignant when I suggested the use of an aphrodisiac. Why? Naturally she considers TV a waste of time.

XIII. The purpose of one activity is no longer separate from the purpose of any other activity. All activities fuse in one purpose which is (cf. Huang-Po Doctrine of Universal Mind) no purpose. Imitate the Ganges's sands, becoming indifferent to perfume, indifferent to filth.

*Influence. Where does it come from? Responsibility? Sick ones now are heartsick. Narcissi, they became entranced with emotions, purposes, mystified by living in the twentieth century. We've invented something else, not the wheel. We extended nervous systems. McLuhan: Agenbite of Outwit (Location. Spring '63). (The inability of people to be inactive. As Satie said: If I don't smoke, someone else will in my place. Audience participation, active passivity.)*

XIV. Since the Spirit's omnipresent, there's a difference in things but no difference in spirit. McLuhan was able to say, "The medium is the message," because he started from no concern with content. Or choose quantity, not quality (we get quality willynilly): i.e., we'd like to stay alive, the changes that are taking place are so many and so interesting. Composition'll have, he said, less and less to do with what happens. Things happen more quickly. One of the signs you'll get that'll tell you things are going well is that you and everyone else you know will be inhabiting lightweight Dymaxion houses, disengaged from ownership and from unalterable Earth spot (read Fuller).

XV. Smiling, she said, let the old ones walk out: there's not much to be done about them in any case. Distractions? Interruptions? Welcome them. They give you the chance to know whether you're disciplined. That way you needn't bother about sitting cross-legged in the lotus position. Phonetics.

*He was a physicist and a computer-composer in his spare time. Why was he so stupid? Because he was of the opinion that the only thing that will engage the intellect is the measurement of relations between things? When told that his mind could change, his response was, "How? Why?"*

Conflict won't be between people and people but between people and things. In this conflict let's try to arrange matters so the outcome as in philosophy will never be decisive. Treat redwoods, for instance, as entities that have at least a chance to win.

XVI. He wanders through markets as though they were forests and he an exploring botanist (throws nothing away). Lake.

Take what you're working on with you, if, that is, you have something to do. Gaps.

What a pity that she should feel obliged to take matters in her own hands! (There's practically no kitchen, he says, and it's already been figured out that money's being saved.) Mexico.

Europeans are still up against it. They seem to require a center of interest. They understand tragedy but life itself (and any art that's like it) puzzles them, seems unsatisfactory.

We're starved for entertainment (thanking the two women).

XVII. By becoming angry I simply altered my biochemistry, bringing about a two-hour recovery. Meanwhile circumstances continued characterized by habit.

*Going in different directions we get instead of separation a sense of space.*

Music as discourse (jazz) doesn't work. If you're going to have a discussion, have it and use words. (Dialogue is another matter.) Acts and facts. Straw that breaks the camel's back: their saying No (they advertise they'll say Yes).

*Principles? Then all's intolerable. No principles (which doesn't mean we fail to become furious). So? We swim, drowning now and then. I must write and tell him about beauty, the urgency to avoid it.*

XVIII. Hearing of past actions (politics, economics), people soon won't be able to imagine how such things could've happened. Fusing politics with economics prepared disappearance of both. Still invisible. Arriving, realizing we never departed. He mentioned heads on the ceiling. Seeing them, noticed him too. Fusion of credit card with passport. Means of making one's voice heard: refusal to honor credit card. End of the month? That too may be changed: the measurement of time, what season it is, whether it's night or day. In any case, no bills, just added information.

"Take it easy, but take it." What'll we do? (Before lunch). "Wing it."

XIX. Wanting list of current global services, how'll I get it? Long costly correspondences? (Pentagon advises telephoning.) I'll write to the President (of the U.S.). Time passing, I'll ask those I encounter whether they've any information (McLuhan hadn't any.)

I'll write to Fuller. Should have done that in the first place (Pope Paul, Lindsay: Take note). Amateur (used to say, "Don't touch it!") now speaks of audience participation, feels something, anything, is needed, would help. Develop panopticity of mind (listen).

What'll happen when intelligence is recognized as a global resource (Fuller)? Political organizations—giving up involvement with play (partners, opponents), involvement with unattainable goals (victories, truths, freedoms)—will simply fade out of the picture. Image coming up is that of the utilities (gas, electricity, telephones): unquestionable, emotionally unarousing.

XX. What is a drawing? No one knows any longer. Something that doesn't require that you wait while you're making it for it to dry? Something on paper? Museum director said (Tobey, Schwitters), "It's a question of emphasis." Thanksgiving.

Transportation plan (eventually at no monetary cost, conveyances recognized for what they are: extensions of each human being and his luggage): short distances costly (to taxi for one block is a luxury), long trips cheap as dirt (crossing continents, oceans). Effect of videophone on travel? That we'll stay home, settling like gods for impression we'll give of being everywhere at once?

XXI. *Everywhere where economics and politics obtain (everywhere?), policy is dog eat dog. Take taxi tolls between cities. Those in one town higher than those in the other. Driver going from one to the other must drive home alone. Relaxation of rules, ties (take marriage) is indicated.* Now that we've got the four-lane roads, we won't have any use for them. (Good for roller skating, he said.) Refuse value judgments. Since time lags were inordinately long, change's now welcome. Advertising's discredited itself. When they advertise something, avoid it.

*There's nothing we really need to do that isn't dangerous. Eighth Street artists knew this years ago: constantly spoke of risk. But what's meant by risk? Lose something? Property, life? Principles? The way to lose our principles is to examine them, to give them an airing.*

XXII. Heaven's no longer paved with gold (changes in church architecture). Heaven's a motel. She changed part of the loft: wall-to-wall carpeting, mobile TV. No conflicts.

Twenty-two telephone calls were made by Betty Zeiger "disrupting efficiency of federal agencies . . . dedicated to pursuit of peace." State Department said Hawaii speaker was a woman. Fifty-five (now sixty-one) global services are in area of humanities "beyond mere provision of food/shelter." Not technological services.

*State Department: Global village developed from "Literary Villages" (plan for the betterment of life in India).*

"We are packages of leaking water." "The next water you drink may be your own."

XXIII. Let's call it the collective consciousness (we've got the collective unconscious). The question is: What are things everyone needs regardless of likes and dislikes? Beginning of answer: water, food, shelter, clothing, electricity, audiovisual communication, transportation. Form of answer: global utilities network.

Do not fear that as the globe gets utility organized your daily life will not remain (or become as the case may be) disorganized, characterized by chaos, illuminated anarchically. You'll have nothing to do; so what will you do? A lifelong university (Fuller)? In the lobby after La Mont Young's music stopped, Geldzahler said: It's like being in a womb; now that I'm out, I want to get back in. I felt differently and so did Jasper Johns: we were relieved to be released.

XXIV. *Knowing-seeing, conforming with reality.*

*Anscombe's a feminist, insists on wearing pants. Obliged to lecture dressed in a dress, she took one with her, changed into it, lectured, changed back, walked home (teaching all the time) in pants. As was said, "When will you undress yourself of your ideas?" No escape.*

Billy Kluver said decision of judge in South America (e.g.) is taken as precedent by judge in Sweden. Brown's work *(Life Against Death)* is prophetic (also De Kooning's remark: we no longer have tragedy; the situation an individual may be in is only pathetic): society as a mass is what needs psychoanalysis. (Thus polymorphous perversity, necessity of Utopia.) Looking at billions, unlike Nehru, we must treat them as one person.

XXV. She says life is like a blank wall, impassive. Correct deduction: She is in love. Kluver: ITU lists many international agreements re Morse code, telegrams, telephones, radio, television, emergency signals, meteorological information frequencies and powers of stations, means to prevent static. "How would it be if these agreements didn't exist?" (ITU asks.) "No press news, no pictures in the papers, no exchanged radio programs, no static-free radio reception, no meteorological prognoses, no storm warnings, no security at sea, in air."

*Kluver reports: ITU (International Telecommunication Union) was established in 1865 (nine years older than UPU—post—and seventeen older than railroad agreements).*

XXVI. The truth is that everything causes everything else. We do not speak therefore of one thing causing another. There are no secrets. It's just we thought they said dead when they said bread. Or that we weren't tuned in when transmission took place. Being told about global services, Barnett Newman emphasized the importance of the arts.

Society has tape recorders, radio broadcasts and also copyright laws (which it considers extending). (Gets in its own way.) Get rid of copyright (this text is copyright). We're making nonspecialist interpenetrations.

Automation. Alteration of global society through electronics so that world will go round by means of united intelligence rather than by means of diversive intelligence (politics, economics). Say this idea has no basis in fact but arose through brushing of misinformation. No sweat. It arose (the idea exists, is fact).

XXVII. Do not imagine there aren't many things to do. We need for instance an utterly wireless technology. Just as Fuller domes (dome within dome, translucent, plants between) will give impression of living in no home at all (outdoors), so all technology must move toward way things were before man began changing them: identification with nature in her manner of operation, complete mystery. Fuller prophecy at end of Tomkins's profile of him editorially *(New Yorker)* eliminated. Subject: global network for electrical power (including China, who'd participate in a spirit of practicality). Fuller's remarks considered laughable in view of November blackout. (We need another blackout, one that isn't so pleasant, one that'll suggest using our heads the way Fuller uses his.)

XXVIII. We've poisoned our food, polluted our air and water, killed birds and cattle, eliminated forests, impoverished, eroded the earth. We're unselfish, skillful: we include in our acts to perform—we've had a rehearsal—the last one. What would you call it? Nirvana? "Not only was instant universal voice communication forecast by David Sarnoff, but also instant television, instant newspapers, instant magazines and instant visual telephone service . . . the development of such global communications system would link people everywhere . . . for reorientation toward a 'one world concept of mass communications in an era marked by the emergence of a universal language, a universal culture and a universal common market.' "

XXIX. POPULATION.

Art's obscured the difference between art and life. Now let life obscure the difference between life and art. Fuller's life is art: comprehensive design science, inventory of world resources (if enough mined copper exists, reuse it, don't mine more: same with ideas). World needs arranging. It'll be like living a painting by Johns: Stars and. Stripes'll be utilities, our daily lives the brushstrokes.

*McLuhan: Work's obsolete. Why? Work's partial involvement in activity. Activity is now necessarily total involvement (cf. work of artists, work not involved in profit). Why total involvement? Electronics. Why everything-at-once? The way we-things are. Vathabhutam.*

Where there's a history of organization (art), introduce disorder. Where there's a history of disorganization (world society), introduce order. These directives are no more opposed to one another than mountain's opposed to spring weather. "How can you believe this when you believe that?" How can I not? Long life.

## A New Bill of Rights
## Richard E. Farson
## 1966

One of the embarrassing questions that is often asked me is, "What in the world ever made you want to become a psychologist?" I have never had a very good answer to it, but I did hear a coroner answer the same question once. When someone asked him what made him want to become a coroner, he thought for a moment and replied, "I don't know, I guess I just like people."

Sometimes, when I'm interviewing someone for a job and the interview isn't going well, I stop and say: "Let's pretend that the interview's all over, you've left my office, are driving home and talking to yourself about how the interview went and what you wish you had said. What would it sound like?" It's remarkable what a good interview can result from that kind of role playing. Well, I tried that on myself, with respect to this talk. I knew that I was to meet with a group quite different from any I had met with before. So I told myself that the conference was all over. What did I wish I had said to those designers in Aspen? And my next thought came through very clearly. "I certainly hope you will turn your design talents to the design of human relationships."

This is not such a crazy thought, after all. It turns out to be very much in the mainstream of what others here have been saying. I thought you were only interested in designing things, but now I find out that as you talk to each other here you reflect a concern not just about designing things, but designing things in relation to people—so that in effect you are designing events, experiences and relationships. You should also design for the improvement of human relationships, so that they can be more fun, more exciting, more romantic, more sexy, more intimate, more loving, more open, and more honest.

In case the need for this is not immediately evident, let me discuss with you what I think we are learning about human needs and human potentialities and how these needs may be fulfilled and these potentialities realized in the next few decades.

It's very easy, I think, to take a pessimistic view of the future of man. After all, there's a great deal of evidence of man's inhumanity to man—that he has created a technological juggernaut about to crush him; that present trends, if continued, will produce a dehumanized, depersonalized world. These arguments are certainly persuasive, and it often seems rather difficult to take a hopeful view of the future of man. But I am going to take such an optimistic view because as I assess the trends—in relation to human potentialities—the future does look quite hopeful.

Unfortunately, optimists often look foolish; pessimists look smart. Have you ever noticed, in a committee meeting for example, that the people who are pessimistic seem realistic, hardheaded, down-to-earth, while the optimists sound grandiose, foolish, and naive? So, at some risk, let me present what I think is an optimistic view of our future.

Any women in this audience who may be pregnant are going to have babies who will be in the high school graduating class of 1984. That gives you pause, doesn't it? If we try to imagine, as George Orwell did in his book *Nineteen Eighty Four* what life is going to be like then, about all we can be certain of is that it will be vastly different from life today. We find it difficult to think about change at all—it is even more difficult to realize that changes are becoming increasingly frequent. In our generation, we have been able to make a change and then coast for a while, then rest on a plateau before we have had to make another change. But if we plot the curve of innovation, we can see that it is an accelerating curve, and this means that all the plateaus are being evened out, smoothed out, so that in fact *change will be a way of life in the future*. It's hard to imagine what that will really mean. There will be new developments, new concepts, new values, and new problems all the time. And people will be making new demands. These new demands are what I would like to talk about today. They have to do with the right to fulfill our human potentialitics.

In order to discuss human potentialities, one might talk about the limitless possibilities of the human brain; or one might talk about current experiments that attempt to evoke high-order behavior from people. But I have decided to talk about what I think are the realistic, practical demands that people will be making in 1984, or sooner, that have to do with realizing their potential as human beings. So I might subtitle this talk, "A New Bill of Rights." By this, I certainly don't mean a replacement of our constitutional Bill of Rights, which is concerned with living under a rule of law protecting our civil liberties. Rather, I want to talk about what might be thought of as an addition to it—an addition which deals with human potentialities and with the achievement of the "good life."

I am, on the other hand, not simply describing dreams for our society. I do believe that, like it or not, we will actually see these rights appear in legislation, political platforms, union contracts, governmental policies—and in the not-too-distant future.

People are never satisfied. Once they meet their needs at one level, they move on to higher-order needs. When we meet our survival needs, we begin to have needs for freedom and democracy and education and so forth. This means that we will never see an end to the developing, maturing needs of people and that, the more we satisfy them, the more new needs will appear. So my suggested Bill of Rights can only be an interim measure, based upon needs that we can now foresee.

*Leisure.* All right then, my first item in the new Bill of Rights is the Right to Leisure. That's a safe one to start with, because we already have leisure. But leisure, to us here today, means time off from work. If you can imagine a society in which leisure will not mean time off, but will mean the *right not to work* and still be thought a worthy human being, that's the kind of leisure I'm talking about. Work, to us, means performing a service, making a product, and receiving pay for it. But soon that kind of work will be done by a relatively small percentage of the population, perhaps only 10 per cent. And that means the chances for any of us to have jobs in the traditional sense—to "bring home the bacon"—will be quite limited. This poses a serious problem: How are people going to feel worthy without feeling useful?

For the past couple of hundred years, we've been thoroughly imbued with the idea that the way you achieve self-esteem is by working hard, by denying yourself, by being of service to others. Work has become an end in itself. We are caught in that value system, deriving from the Protestant Ethic, and because of that it's going to be difficult for us to imagine that we could feel worthy *just because we are fully human.* All this asks the question: What are people for anyway? People do not exist to serve the state, they are not here to be just cannon fodder, they are not here to make comfortable the life of a privileged few—that's not what people are for. I would suggest rather that people exist in order to exercise and enjoy their humanness. But in our society we don't feel that we can achieve self-esteem on that basis. The basic problem is whether or not we can in time develop a value system that permits people to experience feelings of self-worth simply because they are realizing their potentials for humanness.

I think that in the world of post-technical man the whole idea of the usefulness of things and of people will be quite changed. We may be asking the wrong question when we ask of something or of some process whether it works or is useful. Curiously, we don't seem to ask that about the things that are most important to us. We never ask that of a romance. We never ask that of a sunset. We never ask that of a symphony. We don't even ask that of a college education. We believe that these experiences are in some way enriching, of value in and of themselves. We only ask the "Does it work?" question of things we don't really care much about—products, training programs, things like that. It is my guess that we will ask this utilitarian question less and less.

In the future we are going to see a fusion of work and play. Work won't be anything like what we have always thought of as work. It will be something like what we are doing right here today in this conference. Is this work or is this play? Whatever it is, it is probably very much the kind of activity that people will be doing in 1984. And play won't be the same either. The kinds of things we do for play— bridge, bowling, television—just aren't fulfilling enough. We will have to look for play activities that involve our whole selves in the way children get involved in play. Play will be our work, just as it is for children. It will have to be similarly fulfilling. It will have to be something that we can cry about and laugh about and work at for many, many hours at a stretch. Hopefully, our homes, buildings, cities will be designed not just for work efficiency but for leisure, for delight, for romance and for play.

*Health.* The second right is the Right to Health. By health, we have always meant the absence of illness. But we are going to have to redefine this term to mean not the absence of illness but the opposite of illness. In the future we will think of health as a positive condition of well-being, with peak moments of vigor strength, coordination, ease. One can't help but wonder: What will be the treatments; what will be the procedures; what will be the experiences; what will be the drugs we will use to create these peak moments of health? And I ask you: What will be the situational *designs* that will help to make us really healthy?

The same case can be made for mental health. We are no longer talking about the mere absence of symptoms; we are talking about emotional *wellness,* episodes in which our emotions are integrated with our behavior, giving us a feeling of potency, of euphoria. In our mental-health activities, we will be increasingly concerned with the normal problems of normal people, the problems of everyday life, the problems of loneliness, superficiality, frustration, fear, guilt, despair, anxiety. And we will deal with these problems not only in clinics but in the basic institutions of our society—in schools, in churches, in homes, in neighborhoods, in industries. But this job can't be left to physicians and psychologists. We will have to make use of the therapeutic resources that exist in all human beings. People are very good for each other; they can be enormously helpful to each other, if we can arrange circumstances where they can really reach each other. How are these circumstances to be designed?

*Beauty.* The third right is the Right to Beauty. I think that right is already beginning to be recognized today, with new legislation to remove billboards, to establish green belts, to hide junk yards, and so on. We *need* beauty. It's much more important to live in the midst of beauty than we ever thought it was. People are beginning to demand it; they are claiming their right to it. And how ironic that at just about the time people like you are beginning to succeed in convincing your clients that good design is also good economics, the argument becomes superfluous; we will be required through legislation to make things beautiful. The *right* to beauty will be more important than the economics involved.

*Truth.* The fourth right is the Right to Truth. A friend of mine suggested that the new generation might be characterized as the "Honest Generation." If we were the "Silent Generation," this one is the honest one. The kids of this generation seem to want to be in on things. They seem to be much better able to share with each other.

Some sociologists talk about the behavior of people in relationships as being one of two basic styles: presenting and sharing. You can either "present" yourself to another person—that is, you try to see to it that the person forms a favorable impression of you, or you can *share* yourself by letting him in on what it's like to be you at this moment. Practically all of our relationships—at work, at home, at school, at parties—are of the "presenting" kind. We are forever presenting ourselves. We do very little sharing. It's quite rare. But I believe this sharing of oneself is much more common in the younger generation, where they don't censor so much of what they are saying. They seem to want more of the truth from themselves and from each other.

When I think of how much we censor our thoughts before saying anything, I am reminded of a little experiment conducted by a friend of mine, Alex Bavelas of Stanford University. In the experiment he asks the people he interviews to wear earphones that feed them white noise, which is something like a jet airplane going over. You can't hear anything else at all; it's the noise that dentists use to anesthetize patients. Well, when you feed in a lot of white noise, people can't even hear what they themselves are saying. A special wrinkle in this experiment is that Bavelas arranges it so that the noise only comes on when his interviewee is talking; it is activated by the person's own voice. So you see how it is possible to hold an interview with a person in which *you* can talk to him and *you* can hear what both you and he are saying, but *he* can only hear what you are saying. That is, he literally can't hear himself talk.

In this situation, some interesting phenomena develop. For one thing, people lose some of their ability to control and censor their speech. As an example, if a person's native tongue is not English, and he has difficulty policing his articulation of English, under this white noise condition he will fall back into the old patterns in his speech.

I think that our demands for a right to truth are more and more evident as we move toward an open society. We seem less willing to go along with the deceptions and secrets we have tolerated for so many years. We are unwilling to let manufacturers make product claims that they can't substantiate. We are concerned about truth in packaging and advertising. We are alarmed about investigating agencies and wiretapping.

The problem is accentuated because, for the first time in the history of the human race, man will soon have control over practically every one of the life processes. Science has provided us with a significant amount of control over heredity, over thoughts, over behavior. Many troubling questions are being raised as to how we are going to deal with this new power. I believe that we must deal with it by keeping things open, by reducing deception and secrecy. For example, I doubt that eventually people will permit information about themselves to be collected and stored in thick personnel folders that will be kept in some file to which they have no access. Further, I doubt that people will submit to psychological testing when they are unsure as to whether or not such tests are designed to benefit them. People will resist giving personal information to anyone or subjecting themselves to unclear procedures as they become more aware of the controls that can be exercised over them. I believe there will soon be sweeping legislation that will radically change our practices of record keeping, testing, experimentation, investigation, and communication.

*Intimacy.* The fifth new right is the Right to Intimacy. This busy, urbanized, crowded society of ours has made life extremely complex for us. Our complicated relations with so many people seem inevitably to lead to superficiality. Relationships in modern American life are appallingly superficial. Physical proximity has paradoxically brought emotional distance. We practically never have a feeling of emotional intimacy even with those who are closest to us. Millions of Americans have never had, and never will have, in their entire lives, one moment of intimacy with another human being—one moment in which they could be honestly, authentically, genuinely themselves. Now I think we've got to do something about this. People have to get acquainted with their own feelings, and they have to be able to share those feelings with other people.

We need new designs for living that will make emotional intimacy possible, that will encourage it—not force it, but encourage it. We don't have those designs now. As a matter of fact, we are actually embarrassed about intimacy. We don't like to think about it or talk about it. We have the idea that intimacy should take place only in the privacy of the family circle. The trouble is that the shared-feeling kind of intimacy seldom takes place even there. But that fact hasn't yet convinced very many people that we should try to make it happen elsewhere. It will eventually. I think that we will desperately search for authentic intimate relationships, and be relatively satisfied with relationships that may only be fleeting, transient ones. We need such experiences to remind us of our membership in the human race, to give us a sense of community, to help us be less afraid of each other, to give moments of humanness, to permit us to laugh and cry with each other. To accomplish this, we will need new arrangements, new designs for human relationships.

Now when I say we need new designs to make this possible, that must seem like at tall order for people who feel that they have their hands full just trying to select an appropriate type face or convince a client that he ought to landscape his parking lot. But it doesn't seem too ambitious to me. It doesn't sound any crazier to me than the idea of a person from the fine arts turning to designing tractors and telephones. That's what you've done, and you've done it with great success. We now need your help in the design of human situations that will encourage intimacy. I believe that the real problems in this for you are not technical but emotional, because its largely a problem of overcoming one's emotional resistance to the concept of planning for intimacy. We all have deep within us the idea that human relationships should happen by chance, that they should be random, that it's somehow wrong, unnatural, unromantic, to suggest that relationships should be arranged.

So the basic philosophy in our culture holds that chance relationships are OK, arranged ones are not. But that philosophy is simply not working. People select marriage partners by chance now, and consequently we have a high divorce rate; in my community in Southern California, there are six divorces for every ten marriages. Now that assumes the proportions of a national calamity. Maybe it's time to get over the notion that something's wrong with arranging relationships. Actually, in many of our social practices we seem quite willing to design relationships. In business and industry, for example, we have organization charts, which must be considered arranged relationships. We don't hesitate to plan so-called intimate dinner parties, which are certainly arranged relationships. They just don't happen to be intimate, that's the problem. Far from it, I'm afraid. Such designs in order to be successful must make use of the best that behavioral science has to offer, and the best that people like you have to offer.

For another thing, I imagine you would feel, as I often feel, that there is something presumptuous and naive and perhaps a little utopian about the idea of making social arrangements, designing society, if you will, for personal relationships. Maybe such ideas were interesting in the 'thirties but are passé now—even a bit corny. But mostly we are encumbered with the idea that it's just not right to meddle in human affairs. But look around you—we've *got* to meddle in human affairs.

*Travel.* Right Number Six: the Right to Travel. Soon travel will be so inexpensive and so delightful and so rapid, and the exotic places of the world will be so accessible, that people will insist on the right to travel. I can foresee the possibility of union contracts' being written in the coming decades that will demand as a fringe benefit the right to travel.

An inevitable consequence of large-scale travel is that we shall develop a new kind of citizen, a citizen of the world. He will return from his travels different in many ways. Take the Peace Corps volunteer, for example. One of the major benefits of the Peace Corps is the changed attitude of the returning volunteer. Quite apart from what he was able to give to the country in which he worked, it is clear that the experience in that country has had tremendous impact on him. It is probable that the most important changes being wrought by the Peace Corps are within the volunteers themselves. They are returning to the United States as knowledgeable citizens of the world.

*Study.* Right Number Seven is the Right to Study. Now, I'm not talking about basic education; we already have that right pretty well pinned down, the right to go to school and learn basic skills. I'm talking rather about lifelong study, the enriching experience of learning as an end in itself. In the future, education will be our full-time occupation. We'll be studying and learning all the time. But education will no longer simply serve as *preparation;* it will have to stand as a worthwhile *experience* in and of itself. It won't be preparation for something, any more than listening to a symphony is preparation for something. It may be enhancing, but not preparatory.

I was talking with someone from one of our major foundations the other day, and he was saying that they have spent millions of dollars on education, on improving the intellectual, cognitive aspect of education. But the newer concepts of education are much broader in scope and the objectives are much more ambitious. Education now means *human development*. So it must include the affective, emotional, interpersonal dimensions, as well as the cognitive, intellectual ones.

We are beginning to realize that unless we start educating along all these dimensions, the people who will be graduating from our schools in the 'eighties and 'nineties are *not* going to be fully human, able to cope with increasing change, able to enjoy themselves, able to live creatively, able to meet the problems of that world. So some of us are wondering now about how to go about the education of the emotions and the senses, how to educate for awareness, how to bring people in touch with their feelings and how to help them improve their own interpersonal competence.

*Sexual Fulfillment.* All right, now here's the right you have all been waiting for—Number Eight, the Right to Sexual Fulfillment. We are the last generation, hopefully, to settle for less than our full sexuality. We have been so plagued by ignorance and fear and guilt that we really haven't enjoyed our sexuality nearly as much as we could. I was speaking to a group of sex educators recently and told them that, in my work as a psychologist, I probably encounter an unusual group of people; on one hand, I am impressed with the vast amount of sexuality that seems to go on in the high schools and in premarital relationships, and on the other hand, when I meet with married couples I am impressed with how little sexuality there is in marriage. I was only joking when I said that this led me to another definition of sexual intercourse, namely, what people do before they get married. Well, I thought that would be very funny, but nobody laughed.

Sex mores have changed, are changing, and will change much, much more, and we might as well face it. We have a real sexual revolution coming. As the saying goes, we should probably relax and enjoy it. It could mean a lot more fun for everyone. I don't know if it's a good enough issue yet to be part of a political platform. I suppose I had better leave to your own inferences just what the designer might do in response to these new developments.

*Altruism.* The ninth right is the Right to Altruism. People always seem to want what the aristocracy has. People have demanded freedom, education, leisure, all of which used to belong only to the aristocracy. If I'm correct in my interpretation of events, people are beginning to demand beauty, travel, and the chance to study, also rights that have belonged to the aristocracy. As people move to higher-order needs, it makes one wonder if we aren't eventually going to demand the right to be altruistic, to be philanthropic—still pretty much the private reserve of the aristocracy. I think we will. We will demand legislation that will permit us to extend beyond ourselves, to be of help to others, to love others, to care for others. This is a genuine need, and I think we need arrangements by which we can fulfill this need—a need that many of us don't even realize we have.

*To Be Different.* Finally, I think we will demand the Right to Be Different. We all experience enormous pressures toward conformity, and these pressures will becomes even greater. It is an inevitable consequence of living and working in groups. The war on poverty has been called the war of the middle class against the lower class. It appears that the middle class might win, leading to a kind of homogenized society, everything the same. It will wash out our differences, and I think we will be very sorry. Here is a striking example. Some sociologists have recently studied skid-row society in Denver and Chicago. We are used to thinking only of the failure and misery in that unfortunate segment of our population, so it's surprising to discover in conversations with the returning sociologists that they really liked it there. Apparently there's something that is *really* true about skid-row culture that we only *say* is true about our middle-class culture. People do care about each other, on skid row. They go the distance with each .other, they work together, they will help each other out in a difficult circumstance. They do regard themselves as their brother's keeper.

As we redesign our cities, our problem will be not only what to change, but what to preserve. I don't mean only historical landmarks. There are other places—charming, quaint, romantic, sentimental, highly valued, and highly functional places. What dingy book shops, what smelly delicatessens, what smoky taverns, what meeting places for old people do we want to keep?

We will in addition certainly want to preserve some customs, practices, cultures, ethnic differences—but in depth, not just as traditional pageants that we revive once a year. But how can we enable people who are caught in ghettos to improve their lives and enjoy full citizenship, and at the same time help them retain for the benefit of all of us the richness of their culture? I think that's a very serious problem and one to which I hope you will give your attention. It may be that celebrating these ethnic variations rather than pretending to ignore them will do more to achieve full citizenship, full humanity, for all of us.

*Designing for Human Potentialities.* It's not easy to talk about the human potential, because there's probably no limit to it. The human potential is not only what it *is* but is also determined by what we *believe* it is. What we want it to be has a lot to do with what we find it to be.

Although the subject of human potentiality demands a great deal of study, for some reason we give it very little study. We seldom seem to be studying man when he is at his best. We study people in prisons and in clinics, and when we run out of white rats we study college sophomores, but we don't study man when he is realizing his full potentialities. Quite to the contrary, we bring him into our laboratories and ask him to do things he never does in his life and doesn't understand. We tend not to go out into the "real" world and observe normal people doing things that are natural to them. We should be studying them when they are full-functioning at their creative best. We simply don't know much about the conditions that evoke this potential. This kind of research is unfortunately meager.

We do know that the environment, the situation in which a person finds himself, is an important determinant of this potential. As a matter of fact, probably the best way to predict what a person's behavior is going to be is to study the *situation,* not the person's life history. For example, people don't smoke in church. It doesn't make any difference what their histories are, nobody smokes in church. The situation has determined their behavior. I think we have overemphasized the importance of individual differences, and consequently we haven't really taken the environment seriously. It comes naturally to you. It does not come naturally to a psychologist.

Designers are beginning to look more and more at total systems. I applaud this new direction. I believe it will turn out to be a potent way of dealing with human affairs, of evoking the human potential. Systems designing is probably a better way to solve problems than by responding only to individual differences, to psychodynamics.

As we design systems, as we design society, really, we need to remember that the fundamental element in all these designs is that they must be self-designed, self-determined, self-renewing. We must make it possible for the people who are the *components* of the system to be the *designers* of the system. That's the difficult part. But that, I am sure, is a fundamental prerequisite.

Let me close with a paradox: The more progress we make, the more we must make. Perhaps that's the most frustrating fact of life. Making improvements inevitably brings higher expectations and insistence upon more improvements. And that's not easy to accept or to understand. We have the same problem in the civil-rights movement, for example. We must, as a result of our successes, step up the pace even more. People become increasingly anxious as they get closer to their goals. That's why this business of trying to make life better is an endless and frustrating task. You think you've really accomplished something, and then you not only receive no credit for what you've done, you don't even get the chance to coast. People even become angry with you because you are not doing something more and better. But don't feel devalued or feel something is wrong with people when that happens. It is simply the inevitable consequence of being a leader, of being good at something.

Similarly, when people feel that their potential is not being actualized, is not being realized, they grumble about it. But that's not to be understood as ordinary griping and complaining. Instead, these grumbles should be valued because they reflect high-order motivation. Actually, we should feel lucky—we wouldn't have such grumbling if it weren't for the fact that the future of man and the quality of life are for the first time within our control. I think we can have that better life if we can understand that the real barrier to a better world is our own resistance to change.

# XVI  The Orders of Freedom

Ben Shahn's "Defense of Chaos"—an epitome of his love of creative freedom—is unique among Aspen papers in having specifically set the theme for the next conference, where it was played back at the beginning as a keynote address. Of the many papers delivered on the ensuing days, that of the distinguished biologist Paul A. Weiss represents the most direct response at Shahn's own philosophical level.

# In Defense of Chaos
# Ben Shahn
# 1966

As a guest and interloper during the past week of enlightenment, I carry with me a heavy sense of guilt. I have heard and seen my environment being built around me and above my head; I have seen the doors closed and the windows locked. I have faced my diet of plankton; I have seen the linens replaced by paper—all to be well ordered for me by benign and unseen forces—and I have said not one word in defense of Chaos!

I love Chaos; it is the mysterious, unknown road. It is the ever-unexpected, the way out; it is freedom; it is man's only hope. It is the poetic element in a dull and ordered world!

I am sure that you think that I am only amusing myself; well, that too, but I am serious. And I would like to communicate to you some little notion of what I conceive Chaos to be, and why I think it is our unsung and uncelebrated human friend.

Insofar as I know, Chaos is utterly disallowed by science. The very notion of Chaos runs counter to acceptable logic. Every object upon which we place our hands is part of some physical order; every object has its evolutionary history and its future existence either of long endurance or of predictable decay. And every part of this is orderly. Every act of ours and every notion of the mind has also its history of impulses, exposures, and connections. And all of this is order. The macrocosms and microcosms obey their physical laws. Where then is Chaos?

Even as any order of being—including you as an order, and me as an order—unfolds through space and time, absorbs and reflects and digests its environment, as any such order pursues its own way, developing its individual shape and form, so there are other orders, thousands and millions of them, unfolding too, independently of each other. All are ordered within themselves and to their environment. But their paths through space and time may be completely unrelated—each one following and making its own rules. The disorderly element, the unpredictable, the unforeseeable item, is the moment of impact between two such orders. That is pure accident. It is the moment of Chaos. And it can also be an act of Chaos. It may be deliberately undertaken by a conscious individual.

In nature, out of such conflicts between orders, the great changes have been born—geologic revolutions, earthquakes, volcanic upheavals, and continental movements. In life, the mutations in species have probably been due to such conflicts between orders. In the processes of thinking, the great social changes, the revolutions, the overturns of tradition have been brought about by conflicts in order—between orders.

None of these calamities has any particular quality of being good or bad; they may be either beneficial or harmful to man; if they are sufficiently inexplicable, we call them "acts of God."

But within the area of man's life and his thinking there are fierce conflicts of orders. And here is fierce conflict between order and disorder. All such conflicts have what are called "value" aspects. Some prove to have been good; others prove to have been bad; and all claim to be good.

Among the thousand varieties of classification that might be applied to the fierce struggle between order and disorder in the human arena, there is one that I find interesting. That is the division—the conflict—between omniscience or tyranny on the one hand, and Chaos, or the breaking-out-to-freedom, on the other. I have had to name this breaking-out-to-freedom "Chaos" for the simple reason that a break for freedom is always a disruption of established order.

I am certainly not condemning order as such; we could not live or breathe for a day without it. But neither can I accept it as an unqualified good. Sometimes we cannot breathe within it! However generous it may be in its intention, omniscience is a dangerous quality in us. Let us say that a designer has designed a living space so perfect in all its dimensions that no one takes issue with it. It has everything; extreme thoughtfulness and understanding have provided for every one of the dweller's needs. There are the conveniences; there is beauty everywhere; there is equipment for ministration to the sick; food is provided, and entertainment; there are paper for the writer and paint for the painter and aphrodisiacs for the poor in spirit. Nothing is wanting. The occupants move around, function smoothly; time glides along.

No one wants to break out of this perfect place; there is no reason to. Through the days and the nights, the bolts gradually slide into place along the windows; the locks rust on the doors. All exits, unused as they are, become sealed.

But no one actually notices this condition until the ever restless poet exclaims, "Let's let a little air into this place, I'm suffocating!"

He is roundly condemned; the place is air-conditioned; who wants the hot, humid outside air? The poet insists; he begins to wrestle with the doorknobs; he tries all the windows. He is a troublemaker, a dissident element. He picks up a chair and throws it through the window and makes his break for freedom. A few people follow, but "The Society" stays inside. Not until he comes back with a bouquet of mountain flowers clutched in his hand do the occupants of the living space begin to question their condition. (The planner, through an oversight, had forgotten to install mountain flowers.)

The people climb out; they look around themselves—what a heavenly world! They are refreshed; they think of all sorts of things that they can do in the newly revealed world. They have broken out of the perfect place; they can grow. The poet dies, of course; he has fulfilled himself. He isn't really much mourned; he was such a chaotic element!

I said somewhere, I think, that Chaos is not—even to my mind—an unqualified good; certainly the poet is not the only deliberately chaotic element among us. So is the criminal—and psychologists, omniscient as they are, have frequently aligned the two elements of our society as being essentially the same individual, sharing the same characteristics of temperament.

But there is a difference between them so profound as to put them at the opposite ends of the social scale of good and evil forces. Each one is, within himself, an order, evolved, predetermined, and self-determined, and self-determining. The criminal strikes society with the impact of an order—an organism—built out of cruelty and hatreds. His vision is narrow; he is without compassion. His dreams and images are antihuman. He strikes against, not in behalf of, the other person.

The poet is motivated—almost always—by pro-human visions. These may not be acceptable to the society within the closed room; they may not even be particularly good for it. But the poet seeks freedom, fresh air; he has to breathe; he cannot stand suffocation; he cannot be shackled either by bad design or by good design; he just cannot be shackled. And, in seeking freedom for himself, he sees in his own act liberation for other people, for his society.

There is a very antique legend (it is the oldest one known) that holds Chaos to be a dragon named Tia-Mat. According to this legend, a certain god, Marduk, was chosen to destroy the Dragon of Chaos. There was a historic battle and Chaos, Tia-Mat, was vanquished. But, significantly, she was not actually destroyed, she was chained by Marduk, who then proceeded to place the North Star in the zenith, arrange the heavens, separate the water from the earth, and create the planned society under which we have been living ever since. (And incidentally Marduk in time became Mars.)

Tia-Mat reappears from time to time—almost anyone can see that—and she is quickly quelled again. But she is the dark genius of the artist and the poet, the musician, the dissenter, and about three philosophers out of every ten thousand. I don't propose to release Chaos and just turn her loose upon the human race—we still must have banks and plane schedules. But I think it would be nice if we just made a pet of her and let her go free from time to time to get a breath of fresh air and romp around a little bit among the Planned Society.

# We Are Not Clockwork
## Paul A. Weiss
## 1967

Science is frequently blamed for the wrong things. Science is neutral; science is trying to give a human replica of the universe in the human mind with all the limitations of the human mind. It presents the facts, the data, the conclusions, and interpretations and passes them on—not to man, but to men. The decisions are made by men, and if men want to make foolish decisions they cannot blame science for not having shown the facts of life. A knife is neutral, whether it is used in the hands of the surgeon for better or in the hands of the assassin for worse.

One of science's benefits is technology, and I must say that C. P. Snow largely has technology in mind when he speaks of the antithesis between science and humanity. I would like to take you in the opposite direction. I have noticed a remarkable symbolic feat, which is basing problems of practical life (like business, design, and so on) on a solid underpinning of a unified cultural basis. This basis rests in philosophy, understanding what the universe is all about, what it can demand of us, and what we can actually implement. Because we are limited by our senses and our logic, we are living in a box out of which we cannot escape. We are trying to escape, and our mind is built so that we strain to the extreme to escape from the rigid framework of the world within which we live as natural beings.

I would like to tell you a few ground rules which are the base rules within which all life exists, which make us up as individuals and build up our group societies and nations. These groups all work through the agencies of people, just as a human individual operates only through the agencies of the particular cells that compose him, as each cell operates only through the agency of its component molecules, and as each molecule operates only through the agencies of its atomic and subatomic constituents. If you want to, we can say man and his society are no more than ninety odd elements in various reshuffled combinations. This is not the true story, however, and this is where science has to raise its voice.

I would like to explain a little about what a living system is and what it is not, what man as a living system is and what he is not, and what he can do and what he cannot do by virtue of his powers as an organism.

The universe is given to us as continuum. We have to break it up into parcels because we see certain complexes within the universe that retain some degree of stability and don't fall apart every second. The mere fact that we give a name to something like a cell or an individual means it is a recurrent complex phenomenon in our experience that we respect and regard as something worthy of our interest.

Let's look how science views a complex like a cell or organism or society. One level of this hierarchy may be completely unrelated to another level.

Somebody said the other day that order is a property of collectives. I would like to emphasize this, because otherwise we have only ninety odd elements in all their various interactions, and these interactions are not random chance movements as they used to be regarded. They are grouped; they're ordered; and any disorder is essentially an artificial simplification. We established the term disorder, but it doesn't exist. What we do deal with is order at different levels and, as the mathematician calls then, "orders of magnitude." There may be order on one level and complete disorder at the next level with regard to that particular property we are considering.

Let's take a cell. A cell is recognizably the same for a certain length of time, although it's never the same for two seconds. Within you, you're not only changing the population of cells all the time, but you're changing within each cell; the inside is changing, being reshuffled, redone, turned over every moment in your lives, and still as a whole, the cells remain in their pattern.

We have order in the gross, with infinite variety in the small. This order in the gross at the higher level couldn't exist if the individual components each had infinite degrees of freedom. Their interactions, the ways they behave, are under the dominance of the system as a whole, so when any one of them makes too far an excursion in one direction, the others compensate (regulate) in the opposite direction. They do this without circuitry, thermostats or control mechanisms. How they do it is in many cases still unknown. There are chemical regulatory mechanisms and so on, and these limit what a man can do; what his brain can do. These limits are the boundary between freedom of the individual excursion and freedom of action. These systems are stabilized, although that stability is temporary. They move in time through evolution—constant genetic evolution in the case of animals. This frame of reference limits the degree of freedom for the excursion of the individual. And it is these restraints that we have to respect in all we can do in human affairs, whether in our own practical affairs or in their extrapolation into the world of fantasy, into the world of actual art, creation, creativity.

The term "evolution" should never be used without its opposite, which is stability. The average citizen doesn't realize that, when we speak of evolution in animal and plant kingdoms, the basic processes have been the same and are still the same for the most elementary protozoan and for man. There has been remarkably little innovation in the basic ingredients. They have only been reshuffled, and the new combination has given rise to other emergent creative capacities.

In evolution, it is not true that "anything goes." What can go is strictly limited by limitations placed upon man and his brain by being an organic structure. It is *not* limited, however, by a micro-precise clockwork mechanism that leads from the genes (as it is now being presented in popular literature). It is *not* all predetermined in the sense of a live, prestabilized harmony, a clockwork that merely has to work itself out, with us as puppets pulled by strings not of our own making.

As a scientist in full consciousness of my responsibility, I say that biological science nowadays can validate the right to freedom of decision, the right to exercise ingenuity and foresight. We can validate this, and therefore, the gap has been shrinking and has broken down.

Let me say now why I lay so much stress on this freedom of self-decision, freedom of operation, scientifically validated, within a scope of orderly relations. The question, as you can see, is not "Is there order?" or "Is there disorder?" or "Should we plan for more order or less order?" We should plan for the proper balance between the two, because thermodynamically we are in a universe that is *supposed* to run down. But if you take smaller samples you'll find some of them run down fast, and some of them don't run down at all but run up. The rundown is a statistical average, and the human mind is given the instrumentalities to counteract the running down. It can create order out of chaos, but does it?

You have to counteract thermodynamic rundown by spending energy, which you take from somewhere else, from solar energy. You build it into organic beings, using that solar energy to do something creative.

Motion takes energy. If you take the energy needed to run a machine through fuel and by restraining its free dispersion, guide this energy into useful channels, it is the same amount of energy needed for a match to blow up a machine. What would be lacking, though, would be restraint, the guidance of the energy toward a goal, a design.

This is where we have to draw the line between order and disorder. We can use our energy to make creative decisions, or we can escape the decision-making process by merely spending energy in destructive ways, energy that deplores the old order, not realizing that order is a moving thing, an evolution that goes on all the time. Nobody who speaks of order should have the Establishment in mind, because thermodynamically free dynamics has a tendency to encrustate itself in structural, firmly set channels. A river grooves its bed when it first forms, but it isn't long until the bed forces the river to flow down that way. It is here that the freedom of human effort—design—keeps us from getting trapped in the ruts and deep channels of prescribed motion. We use design to build our own channels for progress with purpose.

I'd like to close with a plea that we build things that are symbolic representations of some degree of order, having not rigid order but some degree of regularity.

We learn far more subconsciously by our perceptual environment than by verbal analogy. The question is not order versus disorder or any of these antitheses, but how much of each will save us in the precarious balance between running down to a thermodynamic death (regimentation) and free exercising of the powers that are given to any organic building from the cell, through the organism, through the race, the nation, and, perhaps one day, the world.

# XVII  A Dialectic and an Overview

The formal four-part statement of views by Moshe Safdie and Christopher Alexander is the staid reflection of a bitter disputation between two of the culture heroes of young architects in the 'sixties—Alexander, the author of the intellectually probing *Notes on the Synthesis of Form;* Safdie, the builder of the heroically scaled Habitat at Expo '67 in Montreal. Each seems to be professing an exclusive doctrine—but are they not both subsumed within the Olympian view of René Dubos: that the designer's task is to help make it possible for human beings "to live and function effectively on this earth"?

Almost alone of all the speakers who deliberately set out to address themselves to the mood and condition of their particular conference as they found it, Dubos produced a document more enduring than the paper on which it is printed. This wise and wily old French biologist, with uncanny intuition, revived and reactivated themes that had run through the whole history of Aspen, and breathed into them the life of heartfelt commitment. The result transcends the merely timely comments on current dialectics that form its ostensible subject matter, and delivers a statement that could have been given with profit in any year and to any audience.

# Complete or Incomplete?
# Moshe Safdie and Christopher Alexander
# 1967

MOSHE SAFDIE

The concept of order and disorder implies a world of dualities, a need for balancing order by something mysterious, unexplainable, and a need to complement order.

Uniformity versus randomness, rigidity versus looseness, regular versus irregular, good versus evil—all are dualities. They are in contradiction, as Lancelot Whyte puts it, with "unitary thinking." As we pause and say, "We need disorder, randomness, chaos, arbitrariness," we must observe that what we feel is because the prevailing order is incomplete. It omits something basic, and so we strive to explore what is missing. Where has integration failed?

The missing mountain flower in Ben Shahn's poem is a demonstration that an aspect of structure has been overlooked, and order is incomplete in that environment.

This is not a play on words, a semantic exercise. It is the essence of thought in the process of increased human integration, unitary thinking, the rejection and suspicion of the arbitrary in favor of exploration and integration.

By arbitrary, I include much that is done today in the name of art. If I am to be honest, most of today's "painting/sculpture" means absolutely nothing to me. It does not affect my environment or my mind. I see escape behind it; it seems out of context. At its worst, as Pop painting, it is nothing but a joke, an expression of perversion and decadence.

Fashion is arbitrary. We wore pointed shoes in 1965 and square-ended ones in 1967 to fit a foot that has not changed. Fashion varies directly with arbitrariness in the design of an object.

Nature is all order, so integrated that it permits variations and local adaptations of the system. Two plants in identical environments are identical, but the asymmetrical cedar on the Pacific shores is only an adaptation of order.

The leaves of the maple spiral and spread to absorb light, and the cactus rotates perpendicularly to the sun to preserve its moisture. The nautilus spirals to permit ordered growth, and the bee seeks to store honey with the least wax. We build buildings of glass and frame and talk about "expressing" structure, and what we mean is one iota aspect of structure, which is what holds the thing up. Structure is more than that. It is order, it is organization; it is system. Total structure is the

191

structure of light and air and growth and reproduction and stability and all aspects essential to the survival of an organism. It is that which we must explore and satisfy, and it is that which will give us order that will not need to be balanced.

Man's environment has a total structure, so as we consider the concentrated, dense, three-dimensional environment we explore these structures, which have to do with the grouping of things. We group dwellings in the cold north so they absorb the most sun, or in the desert to shade each other in space, so they are different as the maple is from the cactus. To permit growth, as the nautilus can, or to enclose the most space with the least material, or to distribute services and allow for mobility and so on, we consider each aspect of structure.

But these are all physical aspects of total structure, and the environment of man also has its psychic structure—the aspects of sense of location, social relationships, sensations and fixations, identity, and privacy.

We know less about these things, so we tend to mystify them. These psychic needs are not arbitrary. They vary from culture to culture, from time to time. They are dynamic, but they are psychic structures.

We have decided to explore one aspect of the psychic structure, that of identity. Identity gives us:

1.  a sense of location within the urban organism;
2.  a sense of community;
3.  a sense of personal or family identity; feelings of possession and security.

Identity, too, is dynamic. The culture of the sari, the tarbush, and the adobe village has a different attitude from the culture of Levittown and *Vogue* magazine. Today we feel threatened. Identity, we feel, decreases as the concentration of humanity increases. Identity decreases as mechanization and systemization of construction and method increase. But does it have to?

CHRISTOPHER ALEXANDER

Under circumstances where mass adaptation is being handled very efficiently, how can personal adaptation be maintained?

We all know a man's character extends well beyond his physical body; it extends to his choice of material possessions, his clothes, his house, his car, the games he likes to play, the way he likes to talk to people, the way he reads a book, the way he stands, the way he makes love, the way he likes to entertain his guests.

Now almost every one of these distinguishing characteristics is reflected by certain physical configurations in his material possessions, which facilitate life as he lives it.

Even though it is extremely hard to define this in specific detail, we can tell a great deal about a person's character by looking at the material world in which that person lives. The child's swing hanging in the living-room doorway is specific to a special attitude of parents toward children. Can you lie down in the living room or only sit up? Are the evening lights adjusted for reading or for conversation? Which objects are placed in the kitchen, which in the living room, which in the bedrooms? Are there pictures on the walls or travel posters? Can several people sit in a circle in the room; is the kitchen open to the living room; are the books kept at head height or waist height? Each of these things tells us a great deal about the people living in the house, because whatever choice has been made has been made to facilitate expression of some special personal need, and therefore reveals the need because it is adjusted to it. The most highly developed form of this fine adjustment is found where the same family has been living in a house for many years. In these cases, we often find a special kind of harmony between the people and the inside of the building; the fine adjustment is very highly developed.

If we ask a realtor how his clients choose a new house, one salient fact emerges: Most clients are unable to state what sort of house they want, except in the most general terms. However, when the realtor shows them houses that conform to the general description they have given, they reject many of these houses immediately, without hesitation. Then, all of a sudden, he shows them a house they like, and they recognize it immediately as being "them." Even though they couldn't put it into words, they are aware of this relationship between their life and the house they live in. Given individuals or families, even when they move from one apartment to another or one house to another, manage to re-create almost the same atmosphere, time after time.

The trouble is, this kind of fine adjustment is becoming very hard to get. First of all, the gross adjustment provided by technology tends to crowd it out; second, people move so often that they never manage to bring this adjustment to any very high degree.

In the past, this fine adjustment was very easy. Houses were built of plastic materials, and people lived in them for a long time. If you live in a house made of mud or wood, and you live there for a long time, the fine adjustment is made incrementally, as a result of a long process of piecemeal adjustment, made with hands or hammer and awl. However, both these conditions are disappearing. Houses are made of less and less malleable materials, like four-by-eight-foot sheets of plasterboard, aluminium window frames, prefabricated kitchen and bathrooms. People are on the move. They rarely stay in one place for more than a few years, often for no more than a few months. As far as we can tell, both these trends are going to increase. People will live in dwellings largely made of prefabricated parts, and they will be moving more and more often. Under these circumstances how can fine adjustment be made successfully?

Basically, there are two ways in which the fine adjustment can be made. It can be made by choice, and it can be made by action. In other words, you can choose a dwelling that fits your life, or you can change an existing dwelling so that it fits your life.

On the one hand, there is the school of thought that believes fine adjustment can be made by choice from a preselected range of parts, which may be put together in many different ways. This is essentially the idea behind the variety of extras provided on automobiles; it is the idea behind the use of different façades on tract houses; and it is the idea behind the concept of flexible architecture.

The difficulty here is obvious. So long as you choose from a finite range of preselected alternatives someone else has made available to you, the choice is very limited indeed. You never really manage to create a truly personal environment; you never actually escape the system.

The idea of architectural variety's being built into a housing scheme by a designer is equally trivial; it is obvious the variety of shapes and sizes that architects create in such schemes always look mannered, contrived, and artificial. Above all, it never really manages to provide the fine adjustment I am talking about; people are just too different from one another; there is little hope that one man could design enough variety for all of them.

On the other hand, there is a school of thought that believes fine adjustment should be made by the inhabitants of buildings—do-it-yourself buildings. Certain elements, like structure and services, are to be provided in advance, and the rest of the building built by the inhabitants. This is essentially the idea of Le Corbusier's Algiers scheme. The trouble with this school of thought is also obvious. People want to move into finished buildings. Most people are not willing to undertake major construction in their own houses; and this is especially true when they are moving constantly.

To solve this problem, I believe the fine adjustment must be made in both ways: by action and by choice. These two processes of adjustment are designed to complement each other. Buildings must be constructed so each building has a kind of cumulative memory; each inhabitant makes certain very minor fine adjustments in his own dwelling, and as the character of the dwelling develops future inhabitants choose those dwellings whose accumulated fine adjustment and personality are suitable to them.

There is nothing very revolutionary about this concept. Yet most modern buildings—tract houses, row houses, and apartments, as they are made today—do not permit this process. They are so constructed that the inhabitants cannot leave their mark on them. The only fine adjustment possible is in the furnishings, with the result that these dwellings never become highly differentiated from one another.

Let me repeat, then, the specification. Dwellings must be so designed that they have a kind of built-in cumulative memory in them. As individuals or families pass through, they leave their mark upon the dwelling, with the result that over time we create a stock of buildings with very great variety. This variety, unlike the arbitrary designed-in variety, is specific to various types of human personality and life-style. It offers future inhabitants a truly rich opportunity to make their own fine adjustments—first by choice, then by further incremental changes in the building itself.

194

We have chosen identity as one iota aspect of structure, that which usually is assumed to be achieved by disorder. What are the issues of identity in the concentrated three-dimensional urban environment?

First, there is the aspect of greater hierarchy and rhythm, which gives us a sense of location and defines communities. We depend on hierarchy—rhythms and variable asymmetries. A pianist would have difficulty playing on a piano that has no black keys, only one continuous row of white keys; he would not know where to start, where A or C was. Then we come to individual and communal identities. They are interdependent. One could look at it as a graph of classifying identities in various culture:

The Beehive is all communal identity.
The Mesa Verde cave community is mostly communal identity.
The Greek Aegean village is a fifty-fifty balance.
Levittown is mostly personal identity.
Isolated farms are all personal identity.

There is a difference between the culture that groups houses to make a village and the one that spreads them isolatedly along the road.

Let us look at it in the context of our society. We want much personal differentiation, but mass production means repetition. How can we preserve identity, give selection, permit adaptation? Also, the less arbitrary a solution to housing is, the less differentiation there will be.

It is possible to have specific system solutions that do result in differentiation and variety, however.

In Habitat I use one repetitive modular cell.

It offers identity through selection, say, twenty house types. But it could be said that, even though there are twenty house types, they are all the same spatially, they appear to have the same "personality."

Let us consider a cube 23′ × 23′ × 23′ within a seven-foot three-dimensional grid. Walls and floors can be placed anywhere by the tenant. Here, too, true differentiation is not achieved, even though hundreds of permutations are possible.

Finally, we propose a system made up of six repetitive elements: a cube and five accessories selected by the tenants. The cubes group in space to satisfy requirements of sunlight, distribution of services, stability, etc., but the five components can be placed to produce *hundreds* of different houses that have truly different spatial character and are capable of adaptation and change by individuals.

CHRISTOPHER ALEXANDER

Let me say a little more about the way in which individual differences among dwellings are felt by their inhabitants. In other words, where does the personal character of a building lie, which part of the building is it that must be especially open to fine adjustments and personal adaptation?

Let us separate this question sharply from the question of where the over-all functional character of a building lies—obviously this lies throughout the spatial organization, and we could not succeed in localizing it. Our question concerns merely the personal aspects of the dwelling. Can we identify any particular physical part of the building that contains the bulk of its personal character and identity?

I believe we can. Most of the identity of a dwelling lies toward its edges and surfaces, the three or four feet near the walls, floors, ceilings.

As evidence for this I would bring forward the following points:

1.  Almost all a family's belongings are placed on or near the walls.
2.  We can identify only with things that have a rather fine grain.
3.  The definition of the shape of rooms is given by the local contour of the walls, floors, and ceilings.
4.  It is these surfaces where we can most easily make changes—hence this is where it is easiest to make a building personal.

The problem is that in most modern buildings the walls, floors, and ceilings have no surface depth or thickness. I propose, then, that the space near the walls, floors, and ceilings be designed in such a way that all personal adaptation takes place within this thickness, and that this thickness be specially designed to give the maximum opportunity for personal adaptation.

All space walls, interior and exterior, should be very deep—say, three to four feet deep. Floors and ceilings should be only slightly less deep, two feet, six inches.

These walls and floors should be of material that is easy to manipulate (three-dimensional sheet frame, like wood, fiberglass, or styrofoam), and the people should be able to cut pieces out of it without weakening the structure. As time goes on, each family will be able to work these wall surfaces, in a very gradual, piecemeal, incremental manner. After a year or two of occupancy, each dwelling will begin to show its own characteristic pattern of niches, bay windows, breakfast nooks, seats built into the wall, shelves, closets, lighting arrangements, sunken parts of the floor, raised parts of the ceiling. Such houses would go a long way toward solving the stated problem. Though the gross spatial organization is identical and each house contains the same mass-produced kitchen and bathroom components, it is no longer able to dominate the individual and drive out his personal idiosyncrasies.

Each house has a memory; the characteristics and personalities of different human individuals can be written on these houses. The houses will become progressively more and more differentiated as they grow older, and the process of personal adaptation—both by choice and by piecemeal modification—will have room to breathe again.

# The Spirit of Design—Period
## René Dubos
## 1969

I come from a world very different from yours. I have never seen any of you before and do not expect to see any of you ever again. Not that I do not wish to, but our paths are different.

I have come to this conference because it deals with a problem at the heart of my profession as a biologist. Like you, I would like to learn how human beings and all other living things can live and function effectively on this earth. I say "on this earth," because, despite what may happen next month when astronauts will land on the moon, man has not been designed to live and function anywhere but on this earth. Furthermore, each and every one of us becomes so shaped by the environment in which he has been born and in which he functions that he cannot deny his origins and reject his past without suffering and without losing a part of his essential biological and mental being. I'm going to speak about design as seen by a biologist.

I have had a feeling during the past three days that we are attending not a conference on design but an antidesign conference. Why is it antidesign? This comes to the heart of my talk. It is antidesign because a very large percentage of the speakers so far have concerned themselves with what I regard as trivial and often destructive aspects of our society rather than with the constructive spirit that we must inject into it if we are to make life worth living.

Our conference has been largely antidesign in a more subtle manner. There has been a tacit agreement in our discussions that, if we could correct a few of the ills of our society, then everything would be all right. We seem to accept the idea that society and technology can proceed on their own course without a positive and creative intervention through which human beings determine what they want the world to be. Since I evoke the image of what we want the world to be, you will sense that I take a very positive and personal attitude toward design. I would define design as the physical embodiment, the incarnation—the world "incarnation" implying here putting flesh on ideas—of one's faith in a vision of the world. Design implies that a person wants to create a world that fits his own genius.

I shall probably use the word "genius" several times in the course of these remarks. I shall apply it to human beings, I shall apply it to animals, I shall apply it to the landscape and to nature, because I shall use it in its etymological sense. In the traditional Greco-Roman sense, the word "genius" means the array of attributes that defines the person, makes the person be what he is or rather should become—also the attributes that make a landscape different from other landscapes, and that impose constraints upon what we can do with that landscape. Design in my view implies the recognition that each person, each place, each time has its own genius defined by the array of attributes that makes him or it different from anything that has happened before or that will happen again. Design also implies a conscious attempt, which demands courage, because it demands the willingness to integrate these attributes into a new structure that reflects the genius or spirit of the designer.

Let me restate that I am not using the word "genius" to denote some extraordinary quality but only to denote the courage to be oneself, to put one's signature on one's own life and one's own creations. And to acknowledge one's allegiance to whatever one believes in. A corollary of this attitude is the need for humility, so as to grant other persons the right to be what they are and become what they choose to be. Throughout all my remarks I will affirm who I am and what I want the world to be. But in a complementary way, I must manage my life to encourage you to do the same, even though I disagree with you.

This concept of design implies on the part of each and every one of us an attempt to isolate and separate from the immense welter of experiences and impressions that impinge on us those experiences and impressions that fit our genius, our personality, and that we can integrate into some kind of picture, some kind of reality, which is our individual reality. Whoever will organize another conference of this sort should have in mind some mottoes or phrases that seem to me to symbolize the willingness to engage in individual creation. Two of these mottoes come from William Blake in *The Marriage of Heaven and Hell*. One is that "Every thing possible to be believed is an image of truth," and the other is, "What is now proved was once only imagined." These statements affirm that man's dignity and power come from his ability to imagine the world so as to have it become what he wants it to be. The world can become what you want only if you have the courage to act on what you imagine.

Another motto is derived from Shelley's *Defense of Poetry*. "We want the creative faculty to *imagine* that which we know." The word "imagine" as used by Shelley has a very powerful meaning, namely, that we must organize the facts as we know them into an *image* of our own—in other words, into a design.

One can readily develop a philosophy of design out of these mottoes, but it must be based on the unchangeable biological nature of man and on the ecological characteristics of the earth environment. One tenet of this philosophy of design dictates that we must, at all costs, respect the identity of each individual component of the system with which we work. We may select among those components, but we must respect their individuality. This is essential to mental sanity as well as to biological sanity. It imposes the recognition of variety as an essential component of design.

There is another aspect of design, which appears in contradiction with the need for variety and variability yet is equally valid because complementary. No system is viable unless it has an inner unity and logic. No system can survive, whether it's a human society or an animal society, without achieving the kind of unified structure that makes every component relate to the other. There has to be some kind of internal coherence that imposes constraints on the designer, whatever he is concerned with.

In passing, there comes to my mind, as I speak, another phrase that might serve as a useful guide for the planning of a conference on design. It comes from Marianne Moore's definition of poetry. According to her, the poem is "an imaginary garden with real toads." The imaginary garden is that concept of reality that we create out of the bewildering confusion of events; the real toads are the actual components of life with an individuality of their own that we introduce into the garden to make it a living structure.

Now, why have I felt so disturbed by the discussions of the past three days? Perhaps I can explain it to myself and convey it to you by calling to mind the poster announcing the conference. If you recall, it shows a pyramid, a cube, and a sphere—in other words, well-defined structures—covered by a cloth that half-conceals their form. I take this poster as a symbol of the illusion—an illusion that has been expressed time and time again during the past three days—that the rest of our lives, the future, the world in which we live our own lives is more or less predetermined. Those cubes, those spheres, and those pyramids represent the structure of our society, and all those little men standing on top of the cloth are there just to lift the cloth so that the future will be unveiled before you. We, the speakers, are assumed to be the men whose task it is to lift the cloth and unveil the future.

Those structures under the cloth can be destroyed by those who have conviction enough, courage enough, to state what they do not like and what they want to happen. The slogan "Make love not war" may be getting a little thin and worn out, and I wish somebody would invent another one just for the sake of variety. Nevertheless, it will remain important in the history of mankind not for what it means literally but because it is proving right now a powerful factor in determining international politics, as powerful as Einstein's formula for the equivalence of mass and energy. The slogan "Make love not war" is a force that the Pentagon has to take into consideration just as much as the use of nuclear weapons. It provides a telling example of how human beings who have convictions can change the course of events against all the power of technology and the power of political structures.

The shapes under the cloth are irrelevant to the future of our lives for other, more concrete reasons. Those who speak about the future— and I shall not quote anybody, there are so many against whom I would love to quote!—assume that the mechanical, technological forces that have been set in motion will inevitably shape our lives. I have already mentioned that it is not the way things happen historically. There is another aspect of this problem that is perhaps even more convincing, namely, the fact that man's needs, potentialities, and limitations have not changed for 100,000 years. The genetic endowment of man that determines what he needs and how he functions has not changed since

199

the late Stone Age. Each and every one of us, whatever the outward expressions of his daily mood may be, nevertheless continues to function with the same inner forces, the same biological needs that existed in the Paleolithic hunter and the Neolithic farmer.

Most of the problems that disturb us today—the college crisis, the fact that the natural world is being degraded, the environmental pollution that spoils everything around us, the disturbances in human relationships—have well-defined biological components that are rooted in man's unchangeable nature.

If human life, our societies, and the quality of our environment are to be saved, it will be through mechanisms very different from those described by the futurologists who pretend they give a picture of what the world will be like in the year 2000. I have mentioned the year 2000, because I have in mind the most scholarly book recently published by Herman Kahn and Tony Wiener. It is a scholarly work except that it deals only with the trivialities of our times. It does not touch at any place on any of the problems that concern you now and will concern you in the future, the problems that have to be solved in order to make the world really different from what it is today, not just more of the same. The book does not even touch on any of the obvious environmental problems that have to be solved within the next twenty years if we are to survive.

I am irritated at times by Tony Wiener's statements, as I have been immensely irritated by his book with Herman Kahn. But I acknowledge Tony Wiener must share many of my concerns, because every phase of his presentation expressed doubts as to whether the facts he was reporting were really as important as is commonly thought. You will recall that at the end of his presentation—as, by the way, at the end of his book—he made an explicit statement that, after all, all the technological miracles he had predicted might not be very important, because human beings are more deeply concerned about other things.

Now to return to that poster. The cloth that covers the pyramid, the cube, the sphere looks like a shroud because the structures underneath are dead or dying at least. I hope the young people among you are going to destroy them.

Why should it be that so many intelligent persons that have spoken on this platform during the past three days have made statements that seem to imply acceptance of the fact that the rest of our lives is going to be what futurologists tell us? I think it's because nobody tells the truth. Not that the speakers have lied, but those who have provided them with so-called information have not told the whole truth. Let me select a few examples.

For my first example, I shall take exception to what Mr. Knapp stated Monday evening when he showed his beautiful medical illustrations. He told you, because he had been told and almost everyone in this room probably believes, that medical progress has improved health immeasurably. Mr. Knapp's graph, based on some kind of expertise, gives the impression that we can expect to live an average of eighty-seven years in the near future. But the truth is very different. The

United States, and I shall limit myself to this country for obvious reasons, has one of the worst infant mortality rates in the Western world. Of all the countries for which there are good statistics, it ranks fifteenth or sixteenth in infant mortality! In this rich country, with an immense and sophisticated medical establishment, we cannot even manage to deal with fairly simple problems about which much is known. More important, do you realize that the United States has one of the worst life expectancies past the age of forty-five of all the countries of Western civilization? Countries that are almost as bad are Sweden, West Germany, and other highly technicized and rich countries. If you are forty-five or thirty-five, your chance of living a long life in the United States is less good than it was twenty years ago, less good that it is today in Ireland, in Spain, in Israel, and in many other poor countries. Thus, it is not even true that we have improved significantly our state of health or our longevity. If you don't believe me, consult statisticians in insurance companies. Insurance companies know much about expectancy of life, because it's important for them in dollars and cents, and that's why they know it so well. They know that the expectancy of life past the age of forty-five has not improved and may be decreasing. The worst expectancy of life, in fact, is among physicians. As Dr. Kantrowitz made clear to you, this is due in large part—although not exclusively—to the increase in vascular disease.

Dr. Kantrowitz will have to sacrifice not 7,000 dogs, as he has already done in his experimental studies, but another 700,000 dogs if he is to develop techniques good and economical enough to replace the hearts of all the men and women, including many among you, who are going to suffer from cardiac disease in the near future.

Let me now move to a statement made by Reverend Coffin. He spoke about manipulation of man's genetic endowment. What one can do, or rather what one might be able to do on a small scale, will be to correct a few obvious genetic defects in certain individuals. But this is very different from changing the nature of man through manipulation of his genetic endowment. If we were able to do this, it would be not only changing the genetic endowment of man, but changing his very nature and creating a different kind of creature. No one, but no one, let me assure you, has the kind of knowledge that would even permit an approach to a real genetic manipulation of man. Yet the statement has gained currency that we shall soon be able to change human nature.

Other statements that were made on several occasions deal with population projections into the future. We should, of course, be all very much concerned with this increase in the world population. But the problem is far more complex than indicated by the popular picture of teeming Asians and Latin Americans. In French Canada, the birth rate has decreased so markedly during recent years that it is now lower than in English Canada. I understand that in central Harlem also there has been a definite decrease in birth rate during the past two or three years. Why do I mention these examples? Because they provide such a striking illustration of the fact that when human beings decide to take certain courses—for reasons that I shall not discuss here—they immediately change the future projections of population size which would-be prophets use to make their plans. The problem goes far beyond making contraceptives and sex education available to all people. Some of the highest population increases in the world are among the inhabitants of wealthy suburbs in large American cities, including New York, who certainly cannot be accused of ignoring contraceptive techniques. It is not only ignorant Catholics, Hindus, or Negroes who have large families, but also the most decorative members of the Protestant ruling classes. So the problem of population explosion is not stated honestly.

Another example I cannot ignore is the possibility mentioned by Tony Wiener of manipulating the so-called pleasure center in rats and of making them at will function in a certain way. The fact is correct; the laboratory manipulator can do all that he says. But I cannot believe that any one with common sense does not realize that the use of the term "pleasure center" or the word "pleasure," with reference to a certain brain area that can be stimulated by electric stimuli, has the same meaning that the word "pleasure" has in human life. Who is it among us who is not aware of the fact that pleasure is an extremely complex concept in human beings, who through a long process of acculturation have learned to substitute all sorts of satisfactions for those that can be elicited by electrical stimuli in rats. By the way, I know a good deal about experimental animals, and I can assure you that rats also have ways of experiencing pleasure that transcend what can be achieved by electric stimulation of their brain. In my judgment, it's an insult to human beings (and to rats) to identify the so-called pleasure center with the real determinants of life and its enjoyment.

Why should there be all these errors of fact and misuse of words among intelligent people? First of all, there is the fact that, contrary to what is being said, intellectual communication has not improved and, in fact, is breaking down. The technology of communication has nothng to do with the ability of human beings to perceive and to integrate the information that they receive through mechanical means. What the technology of communication does is transmit certain signs devoid of all the rich connotations and overtones that any one of those signs should have. Then there is certainly a great deal of intellectual dishonesty in the transmission of knowledge, as was alluded to yesterday.

It is an intellectual dishonesty that takes the form of making promises which are not warranted, only in the hope of stirring up interest and also—as was said yesterday—of obtaining a handsome research grant from some office in Washington or some wealthy foundation.

Even more dangerous and more universal is intellectual escapism, looking for anything that disengages you from the real problems around you. Typical examples are the endless discussions among scholars—humanists as well as scientists—concerning manipulation of man's genetic endowment. This is a wonderfully entertaining, titillating kind of science fiction. We organize meetings about it in all sorts of pleasant places and we talk about it and that saves us from the responsibility of walking across the street where 100,000 children are being poisoned every day by lead in paint. A large part of mental retardation in our cities probably comes from something as trivial as lead poisoning from paint. Something can be done immediately about this problem, but it is not being done because it is not of sufficient interest or as exciting intellectually as talking about changing the genetic nature of man.

Since I'm coming to the end of my presentation, let me restate in a few simple words what I regard as the biological determinants and constraints of designs. The first point is that man has not changed genetically and will not change in the foreseeable future. His biological equipment is still the same as that of the Paleolithic hunter and the Neolithic farmer. Through cultural processes the activities of man's brain have changed, but not his genetic constitution.

If Stone Age man were to come back from the Dordogne country, to be raised wherever Henry Wolf has been raised, and have the same kind of education and occupation, he would be just as witty as Henry Wolf is.

The second point is that each person is a unique specimen in the entire world. Each one of you certainly believes that he is different from everybody else in this room, but biological and mental uniqueness goes even beyond what you realize. Each of us differs from other human beings in genetic constitution, except in the case of identical twins, and I shall come back to them, because they are not as much of an exception as is usually believed. Equally important is the fact that it is statistically impossible that at any time in the past there has been anyone identical with you genetically, or that there will be any one identical with you in the future. Each person is unique, unprecedented, unrepeatable. When she received the Aspen award a couple of years ago, Martha Graham made a similar statement based on her perception of the world as a sensitive human being.

I was just mentioning the possible exception of identical twins. It is true that identical twins are endowed with the same array of genes. What a person becomes, however, is not determined only by the genes he inherits from his parents. Genes govern the person's responses to environmental stimuli. But the effects of these responses on individuality are different, because stimuli differ from person to person. Even the Dionne quintuplets, who were genetically identical, became different persons because they occupied different places in their mother's body during gestation. In practice, therefore, each one of us becomes a different person through the responses he makes to the environment and to all the stimuli that impinge on him throughout his life. Most important are the environmental forces that act on the child during the first five or six years of life, including prenatal life. This fact imposes on us an enormous responsibility to learn more about the manner in which the environment shapes young people and thereby influences their future. It also has large implications with regard to our concept of freedom.

203

I believe in individual freedom, in free will; each one of us believes in it. Freedom, however, is something that you can exercise only if conditions are right. The child born and raised in slums has in theory as much freedom, free will, as you or I have. But in practice he is conditioned, both in a negative and in a positive way, by the slum environment that shapes the expressions of his genetic endowment. The slum child is not entirely free because he does not have the chance to develop at the critical time those components of his potential individuality that would make it possible for him to become something else, to choose something else.

In fact, I am not thinking only about slum children. The most deprived child in the world today may be the child born and raised in the pretentious suburbs of New York City, where the range of his stimuli is so narrow, and especially where the quality of those stimuli is so cheap.

As you see, I'm beginning to link the total environment, the way we design it, with what human beings become. I have spoken of the genius of each person, that which is unique to him. But there is also the genius of the place. All ancient literatures have embodied the concept of genius or spirit of the place in the forms of gods and goddesses. The spirit of the place determines what the place can become. The formal gardens of Italy and France fit well in certain parts of Italy and France, whereas the magnificent parks of England would not do well under the same conditions.

Let me try to convey to you the sense of what I'm trying to say by quoting a letter of Horace Walpole, who, as you know, was very influential in formulating the theory of the English park. Horace Walpole had gone to France at a time when it was fashionable in France to imitate everything in England. Walpole noted that the French were trying to create parks imitating the English parks, and this is what he says in his letter. I quote from memory: "The French will never succeed in having trees, parks, and lawns as beautiful as ours until they have as rotten a climate." This is a very profound sentence. For each type of country, for each type of climate, for each type of landscape, we must learn to recognize the genius of the place, and we must work with it. If there were time, I would now discuss the feedback from environment to man. It is this constant interplay that permits us to discover what we are, discover what the environment is capable of becoming, and thereby create an integrated structure, which is the mark of all great civilizations.

I hope you understand why I am not entirely pessimistic. What we need is faith in ourselves, the ability to create that image of which I spoke that demands not only intelligence and knowledge but also courage. And because I have mentioned the word courage, I shall end, in acknowledgement of my French past, by quoting a message of hope and an invitation to courage from Albert Camus. It comes not from his novels but from one of the newspaper articles he wrote immediately after the war when everything appeared so dark in France: "It may be the attitude of a fool to believe in the human condition.

But it is the act of a coward to despair of events." The word "events" is of great importance here, because what Camus wanted to convey was not just a literary expression of faith in man but a sense of commitment, the willingness to do something concrete for what you believe in.

# XVIII Polarization

In 1970 the long preoccupation of IDCA with the larger social aspects of design came to what that year was prone to describe as a "crunch point" and revealed a gulf across which only shouting, not dialogue, was possible. The gulf divided those who believed that rational action was possible within "the system," and those who wanted out. In the latter camp were the student activists who forced the conference to vote on a twelve-point resolution covering every current "problem" from abortion to Vietnam and the abandonment of design for profit. But the same camp also included the French delegation, who dismissed all environmental action as a new "opium of the people." Against both such gut-felt dissent and Olympian superiority were those who believed something could be done—could *only* be done—through the system. Though many such could be dismissed by their opponents as "running dogs of decadent capitalism," it was difficult to set aside the English geographer and planning theorist Peter Hall, with his claim that the British Establishment had already delivered the reforms the environmentalists were demanding, or those others who could show some measure of success achieved by working around or through the margins of the system. Few could claim successes as widespread as that of Peter Hall's English New Towns, just a housing scheme here, a constructional system there, or a ghetto improved. Cora Walker's paper on the Harlem Co-ops is not reproduced here, but it is impossible not to praise her achievement, a triumph of practicality, patience, and humanity over the impotence of the professionals to deliver what they had been trained to produce.

# The Environmental Witch-Hunt
## Statement by the French Group
## 1970

The French group, which has been invited to this conference, has decided not to bring a positive contribution.

The group believes that too many matters, and essential ones, have not been voiced here as regards the social and political status of Design, as regards the ideological functions and the mythology of environment.

In these circumstances, any participation could not but reinforce the ambiguity and the complicity of silence which hangs over this meeting. So we prefer to present you a text expressing our positions.

The burning question of Design and Environment has neither suddenly fallen from the heavens nor spontaneously risen from the collective consciousness: It has its own history. Professor Banham has clearly shown the moral and technical limits and the illusions of Design and Environment practice. He didn't approach the social and political definition of this practice. It is not by accident that all the Western governments have now launched (in France in particular for the last six months) this new crusade, and try to mobilize people's conscience by shouting apocalypse.

In France, the environment issue is a fall-out of May, 1968, more precisely a fall-out of the failure of the May revolution. Ideology, which the political power tries to divert onto rivers and national parks, could happen in the street. In the United States, it is not a coincidence that this new mystique, this new frontier has been developed during and parallel to the Vietnam war. There is in France and in the States a potential crisis situation. Both here and there the governments restructured their fundamental ideology in order to face this crisis and surmount it. We see that ultimately the real issue is not the survival of the human species but the survival of political power. In this sense, environment, design, fight against pollution, and so on, pick up the torch in the history of ideology from the great crusade of human relations which followed the great 1929 crisis. At that time, the capitalist system succeeded in reviving production and in restructuring itself by means of an immense injection of publicity, of services, of public relations into consumerism, enterprises, and social life.

Today, when new and larger contradictions affect the internal structures of the overdeveloped countries and force them, all together, on a world scale, into opposition with the underdeveloped countries, the system comes up with a worldwide ideology that could remake the holy union of mankind, beyond class discrimination, beyond wars, beyond neo-imperialistic conflicts. Once again, this holy union created in the name of environment is nothing but the holy union of the ruling classes of the rich nations.

In the mystique of human relations, it was a question of recycling, readapting, and reconciling both individuals and groups to the social context given as norm and as ideal. In the mystique of environment, it is a matter of recycling, readapting, and reintegrating the individual in the context of nature given as an ideal. Compared with the preceding ideology, this one is even more regressive, more simplistic, but for that reason even more efficient. Social relations with their conflicts and history are completely rejected in favor of nature, with a diversion of all energies to a boy scout idealism, with a naive euphoria in a hygienic nature.

The theory of environment pretends to be based on actual and evident problems. But pollution, nuisances, dysfunctions are technical problems related to a social type of production. Environment is quite another problem, crystallizing the conscience on a Utopian model, on a collective enemy and, moreover, giving a guilty feeling to the collective consciousness. (We have met the enemy and he is us.) The crusade of environment goes from technical problems and technical solutions to simple and pure social manipulation. War and natural catastrophes have always been used to unify a disintegrating society. Today, it is "la mise-en-scène" of a natural catastrophe or of a permanent apocalypse which plays the same role.

In the mystique of environment, this blackmail toward apocalypse and toward a mythic enemy who is in us and all around tends to create a false interdependence among individuals. Nothing better than a touch of ecology and catastrophe to unite the social classes, except perhaps a witch hunt (the mystique of antipollution being nothing but a variation of it).

Problems of design and environment only look like objective ones. In fact, they are ideological problems.

This crusade, which puts again, but on another level, the themes of Kennedy's New Frontier, as well as the fighting against poverty as the theme of the Great Society (in France, the New Society), constitutes a complete ideological structure, a social drug, a new "opium of the people." In one sense, it would be too easy to compare napalm bombing in Vietnam with the loving care with which people here protect flora and fauna—one could make a fabulous list of all the evident contradictions in which this new idealism is sinking. But there is here a misunderstanding, and the opposition between chlorophyll and napalm exists only in appearance. In fact, it is the same thing. In Vietnam, the fight is against communist pollution. Here the fight is against water pollution. To lock Indians and black people (in France, Algerians and Portuguese) in reservations and ghettos, that is also a fight against pollution. It is the same logic that organizes all these aspects, the ideological process consisting in disguising in humanistic values some practices (such as the fight against pollution) to oppose them formally to other practices (such as war in Vietnam), which are then considered only as a deplorable reality and an accident. We must clearly see that there is a same policy, a same system of values fundamentally operating here, and that everywhere the established power has always fought against pollution, evidently against the pollution of the establishment itself. This enemy that each of us is invited to hunt and destroy is all that pollutes social order and production order.

It is not true that society is ill, that nature is ill. The therapeutic mythology which tries to convince us that, if things are going wrong, it is due to microbes, to virus, or to some biological dysfunctions, this therapeutic mythology hides the political fact, the historical fact that it is a question of social structures and social contradictions, not a question of illness or deficient metabolism, which could easily be cured.

All the designers, the architects, the sociologists who are acting like medicine men toward this ill society are accomplices in this interpretation of the question in terms of illness, which is another form of hoax.

In conclusion, we say that this new environmental and naturistic ideology is the most sophisticated and pseudoscientific form of a naturistic mythology, which has always consisted in transferring the ugly reality of social relations to an idealized model of marvelous nature, to an idealized relationship between man and nature.

Aspen is the Disneyland of environment and design. We are speaking here about universal therapy, about apocalypse in a magic ambiance. But the real problem is far beyond Aspen—it is the entire theory of design and environment itself, which constitutes a generalized Utopia, a Utopia produced by a capitalist system that assumes the appearance of a second *nature* in order to survive and perpetuate itself under the pretext of *nature*.

# The Liberal Conspiracy
## Peter Hall
## 1970

You need to do two things:

1.   Realize that there's no "environmental problem," that there is a series of environmental problems, some big, some small, and that each needs hard work. You want to remember Banham's warning against the "pinhead" mentality of tackling the problem without the necessary information to work on. What I'm stressing here, like him, is the need for simple old-fashioned academic rigor.

2.   Realize that when you've got a solution worked out, the thing is to achieve it. That means political action. Good will won't achieve it. There's a danger of behaving like a religious community, of believing that faith alone will move the mountain of bad environment. While we good people are talking up on this mountain, some less good men called politicians are acting down on the plains on either side of us. I suggest that after we've analyzed the problems, we get out and engage in some political action to realize the answers.

That's my message to you. Now to press it home, I want to illustrate it by our British experience. I'm going to do what I would never be seen dead doing at home: I'm going to tell you that in some ways I think we did pretty well. I think that our strengths may be your weaknesses, just as much as I think your strengths are very much our weaknesses. Let me therefore tell you something about environmental planning in Britain in the last quarter century, its successes and its failures, above all where it now needs to go. Let me suggest some lessons for you—lessons from our failures as well as our successes. If I annoy and goad you sufficiently, that will be my recompense and I hope, yours.

First, let me tell you what I think is the outstanding characteristic of British planning. I want to tell you this, because I think it offers you an interesting parallel with your own present concern. It is above all land-use planning, based on the notion that land and the natural resources that go with it are inherently precious because they are unreproducible. This is a concern that became an obsession with us in the 1930's, as I believe it did with you. (In many ways, your current obsession with the problem is only a rediscovery of that debate of the 1930's.) With us, in particular, there was a belief that land was being squandered and that it must be saved. This belief was mystical, not rational. It was presented as an absolute, quasi-religious dogma that any right thinking man believed in. That was the basis for us in the late 1930's, as it is with you, now, in the 1970's.

There were two other beliefs, not either of them really capable of rigorous proof. The first was a belief that the big city was inherently a bad place, socially as well as economically. It gave no feeling of belonging, no feeling of social cohesion to its people; they were lost. And it imposed economic costs on its people, costs that were social (in the sense that they were borne by the community at large or by groups within that community). The other belief was that certain regions of the country then in economic decline—chiefly in the northern part of our country, that part which is farthest from London—should be revivified. This belief was basically similar to the one that animated area development programs in the United States in the 1960's.

These three beliefs came together in a report by a Commission of Inquiry, a so-called Royal Commission, in 1940. That commission declared that urban areas had become too big, that their growth should be controlled, and that the use of land should be brought under effective public management. Now, the interesting thing for an American audience was this: The government, quite simply, acted on the report and on a series of supplementary reports that directly followed from it. At the end of World War II and immediately afterward, they passed a great series of Acts of Parliament. One of these allowed the government to set up New Towns to be run by public non-profit-making corporations with the right of eminent domain. Another provided for the creation of National Parks. A third provided for complete and effective control over the location of industry—new industry anywhere must seek government permits. The most basic of all—the famous Planning Act of 1947—made land-use planning mandatory across the whole country. It nationalized the right to develop land while providing that private title to land should remain. This right was then transferred to local planning authorities, who were to prepare and regularly revise development plans. These were no paper plans. They were enforceable because no development could take place save in accordance with the plan. At the same time, in accordance with the nationalization of development rights, the act provided that speculative profits in land development should be taken for the state. This was the provision that was later repealed by the Conservative government in 1953.

Now, there are several outstanding features of this history that I would commend to your close attention. The first was that the basic religious belief was fortified by a series of dispassionate—well, nearly so—public inquiries into the facts. The second was that the conclusions were then embodied in legislation of an extremely practical and comprehensive kind. The problem in each case—there were a number of interrelated problems—was identified and a precise solution found. This was then embodied in legislation, which set up whole new agencies charged with specific responsibilities. The third was execution. It was done by an extremely tight ruling class, or oligarchy: the British Establishment. This is partly an aristocracy of birth and partly an aristocracy of talent. The point about it is that, for a reasonably large nation of 50 million, it was (and is) extremely tight.

It is small, it consists of people who know each other very well (they are mainly Londoners) and who share each other's thoughts and systems of value. In this case, it includes propaganda and politicizing agencies of a special sort—the Town and Country Planning Association—and more generalized intellectual political organizations, like the Fabian Society, which was founded by Sidney Webb and George Bernard Shaw and which to this day has been the real powerhouse of ideas for legislation of any Labour government. Virtually every major Labour politician, including Harold Wilson and almost every member of his Cabinet, has been and is a member of this society. Its symbol is a tortoise, and its motto is, "When I strike I strike hard." This was supposed to be the symbol and the motto of the Roman General Quintus Fabius, after whom the society is named. It has proved a very acceptable recipe for successful political action in the eighty-six years since the society was founded. Let me commend it to you.

The essential features of the approach are, I believe, best illustrated by two of its best-known features: the new towns and the green belts. Essentially, these are very concrete design solutions to specific problems, and they are intended to achieve specific objectives. The green belts surround the big urban agglomerations, limiting their growth and providing for easy access to the open countryside, as well as preserving agricultural land. The new towns provide for the overspilled population from the cities, in communities small enough to be recognizable and real to their inhabitants. Both ideas can be traced back to that signally practical utopian, Ebenezer Howard, who developed them in a little book, *Garden Cities of Tomorrow,* in 1898. The point about Howard is that not merely did he have a sense of the problem, but he developed a specific, readily grasped design solution to the problem and then showed in detail how it should be carried out. His scheme was ready to hand when the recognition of the problem became general, half a century after he wrote and over a decade after he died.

But equally interesting is how this specific solution was applied. The government, spurred on by the Town and Country Planning Association, appointed a commission on the subject in 1945. It was chaired by Lord Reith, the man who single-handedly created the BBC, and a man not best known for his democratic views. (He insisted on announcers' wearing dinner jackets to deliver the news on radio, and refused to employ people who were divorced lest they lower the moral tone of his shows. The BBC got unhung up since those days and it has at least one disc jockey who broadcasts wrapped in an Indian blanket. But I should mention that he's the son of a Hollywood film producer.) The point about Reith is that within about three months he had terrorized his committee into signing his report showing exactly how the new towns were to be run. (Naturally, they were to be run like the BBC, by independent public corporations accountable to virtually no one except vaguely to Parliament through an annual report.) It was almost completely undemocratic and a few timorous souls faintly said so. But Reith was greatly respected in the Labour Party, and his views prevailed. Thus it was, as in many other respects, that a party which called itself a Democratic Socialist party ended by setting up a series of wholly undemocratic bureaucracies. But they *worked*. How they worked! A quarter-century later, nearly a million people live in more than twenty new towns, one in fifty of the population. It just illustrates the fact that in the last resort the British sacrifice democracy to efficiency. Compared with the Americans, in practice they pay scant regard to the power of the people. You could call it a liberal conspiracy!

Today, even in undemocratic Britain, this would be one of the main criticisms of the approach that was symbolized in the new towns and green belts . . . that they were design solutions *par excellence* arrived at too hastily on the basis of a superficial analysis of the problem and of the objectives of society, among a group of people whose arrogance was matched only by the limitedness of their knowledge. There is a particular feeling that the obsession with land and its use excluded consideration of more important social objectives like income redistribution and the granting of better social and economic opportunities to the poorer sections of the population. It's argued, for instance, that green belts in practice mainly helped existing exurbanites preserve their way of life and that new towns reduced the range of job opportunities for those overspilled from the big urban agglomerations with their rich range of different types of employment. There is a feeling—I think facts support it to some extent—that the objectives of the "Class of 1947" were at one remove from the problems of most of the people. This ought to be a lesson for our latter-day environmentalists. It's argued that, before we know we need more new towns, before we know where and how big they ought to be, we want a closer examination of these objectives and of the alternative ways of achieving them. We need in other words less of what Mel Webber of Berkeley has called the "design method" and more of what he has called the "economizing method."

I believe that Mel's charge is right. We are more conscious now that society has many different possible objectives, that they may come into conflict, and that the first job is to resolve the conflicts by deciding how much of this thing we are willing to trade off against how much of that. The English Class of '47 ignored this. Their design solutions took all too little cognizance that such clashes existed. The problem is whether Mel's criticism means that city planning, in the old design sense, is dead. I don't believe it is. I believe that there comes a stage in every plan where design, the realization of objectives in some tangible form, is essential. The problem is to decide how much time to spend discussing fundamental aims before getting to that point. I feel that the British could do temperamentally with taking more time than they have up to now, but I think you need much less. I think you need a few autocratic men of action, a few Lord Reiths. Perhaps when they bring the generals back from Vietnam, there might be a job for them there. At least that's what we did with many of our retired World War II officers: We put them in charge of new towns, and by and large they did well at it, believe it or not.

# XIX  Now, to Sum Up

For the reason that they must inevitably be directed to the immediate and local, Aspen summing-up speeches are extremely perishable. Inspiring at the time, they wither even before the year's papers are sent out to conferees. Only fragments endure. Here are a part of the discussion after Jivan Tabibian's stirring summation of 1968 and the illuminating *jeu d'esprit* with which Jacob Bronowski opened his summation of "Order and Disorder" in 1967. None of the great summers-up seem to have been designers—Bronowski is a scientist at the Salk Institute and an expert on Leonardo da Vinci and William Blake, Tabibian a Lebanese political scientist turned futurologist and planning consultant—and there may be some significance in this. But would these summers-up be any good as designers?

# The Alienated Professional
## Jivan Tabibian
## 1968

BANHAM: Now, what I have found strange, and extremely instructive in getting the professionals up here on the platform, is that when they look into one another's eyes, when they look really deep into one another's psychological eyes, they don't like the view. They always start saying that one should have had the developers, or the politicians, or the tax experts up here on the platform, and not us. As if they could not ultimately take the blame or responsibility for their actions. There was always some other guy who was to blame, some other guy who really initiated the action. Maybe this is true. The designer's task is almost always initiated by somebody else, and that's one of the reasons why a designer can never be an artist and probably one of the reasons why many a designer has decided to get out of being a designer into a field where he could be his own man and do his own thinking. When designers, so to speak, look into the professional mirror, they are not enchanted with the view; all they seem to see are the pock marks and blemishes on their own professional face. They are very good about being gloomy about their business in public. This, I found instructive and disturbing. I was certainly provoked to wonder whether, for all the skills of professionalism, for all its pride, for all the value that someone like Dick Latham says he gets out of the admiration of his colleagues, there might not be something hollow in the whole business of being a professional, that when you get right through to the heart, so to speak, its a situation that has no content.

Whether in formulating a professional position in so many words, say, in the constitution of a major professional body like the American Medical Association or the Royal Institute of British Architects, whether in codifying the rules of profession somehow, you get alienated from the ultimate business of doing that job.

TABIBIAN: There are several reasons why I agree with your observations. I find them also very, very disturbing. On this problem of alienation, there is a view that a good friend of mine has been peddling, namely, that a good professional is one who makes himself obsolete. I really, honestly, sincerely, believe in this. And, if this is so, anybody aware of this problem is by definition an alienated man. He is about to do a job, no matter how well, that he knows should have been done in such a way that he should not have been the one that had to do it. Namely, the moment you have to face a problem, simultaneously you are both necessary and superfluous. When you start solving it, you have already put in it the seed of your own obsolescence. That's why,

216

by the way, people come up with new labels to describe their old professions.

Since I got here, I have discovered that there are label fads. The word "environment" is a very *in* word. Even the most environmentalist still remain architects, but the point is, it's a way of acting out this self-destructive wish, professional self-destructive wish, so that by being an environmentalist you're putting an end to being an architect, and by so doing you've tried to go beyond the alienation of being an architect. Until, of course, you become a professional environmentalist, and there are very few of those around, and those who are really professionally recognized as such are really high-priced. But this alienation, it is very true, is a professional's common lot. Now, you designers are very fortunate people, but you are not really blissful. The blissful ones are the medical doctors, because they are the most ignorant of the problem. They are so ignorant of the problem of the necessity of their own obsolescence, that those who realize it could only go one place, to an African jungle. In the case of medicine, you are a real doctor if you have eradicated a disease, and then you have really made being a doctor an obsolescent phenomenon. If any doctor deserves my real respect, it is when I don't need him.

Being alienated means being broken off from, or not connected to, disjointed from, my collectivity, my society. The fundamental require-ment of our communal cohabitation is not fulfilled, namely, each one's dedication to the other's freedom of action. And alienation, when explicit, is put in those terms. When implicit, it is walking into an office and wishing you were back home. It's going home and wish-ing that you hadn't. It's driving in the street and not feeling like turning to the guy in the next car, and not smiling. In Los Angeles I spent a lot of time on the freeways, and, believe it or not, when I see somebody really alienated in the other car, I stick my tongue out. And you do not know what that does, even for about ten seconds. For ten seconds, you see, you have consciously increased the op-portunities of freely motivated action for the other individual. He can stick his tongue out at you or not. You also get interesting luncheon dates with attractive young women. The freeways are the new com-munity, the new neighborhood. I have made more friends on the free-way just because they are at their peak of alienation, so that even the slightest opportunity to get out of it is extremely welcome.

# Shall I Compare Thee to a Su?
## Jacob Bronowski
## 1967

I propose to summarize the conference by posing some questions that most of the speakers touched on at one time or another.

It would be simplest if we took these questions in the context of some work of art, so I thought I would talk about Shakespeare.

The first question is, "How far can the artist get with chance or random processes?"—with the subtitle "Shakespeare was impossible." The second question is, "How does nature succeed in being inventive?" —with the subtitle, "Shakespeare was not a bee." The third question is, "How does the inventiveness of nature find its echo in human innovation?"—with the subtitle, "Well, Shakespeare wasn't just anybody."

Arthur Eddington, discussing physical reality, made the casual remark that if you put a monkey in front of a typewriter and simply let him hit the keys, sooner or later he would write out in sequence all the plays and sonnets of Shakespeare. It's a good statement for randomness or chance, and I thought I would calculate how long it would take a monkey to write part of Shakespeare's wonderful sonnet that starts, "Shall I compare thee to a summer's day. Thou art more lovely and more temperate . . ."

[Dr. Bronowski then illustrated that by the known rules of probability, the monkey would not have gone as far as the tenth letter in the first line of the Shakespeare sonnet in the 15 billion years or so that the universe has existed.]

It is a thousand million years before the monkey comes to print once, in the right order, the letters of the first three words as far as the "e" in "compare." It would therefore be 25 thousand million years before he correctly hit a sequence which went on to the next letter, "t." But the universe is not 25 thousand million years old. It's only between 15 and 20 thousand million years old, and life is only between 4 and 5 billion years old. So the answer is that Shakespeare couldn't happen. In the universe as it is, picking at random, you can't get beyond the first three words, "Shall I compare," in the time it has taken from the beginning of the universe until now.

Now, if you substituted a computer for the monkey, I calculated that the most powerful computer, typing one letter at random every millionth of a second from the beginning of time until now, could conceivably have reached the letter "u" in "summer."

That really shows that by random processes you could not yet have written any poetry. The world hasn't been going long enough.

Also, "Shall I compare thee to a su" simply is not where there is any poetry. The poetry doesn't really begin until the word "temperate" at the end of the second line—roughly speaking.

What is to be concluded from this is that the processes of nature are indeed designed to write poetry, and for that purpose they have found it convenient to invent human beings, because they are much more economical in time than monkeys with typewriters.

In just the same way, if nature has any design to make honey, for instance, it has turned out to be convenient not to use monkeys with typewriters or chemists with flowers, but just to use bees. The invention of the bee and the invention of the human being are indeed the important things in the creative ability of nature, because they lead to worthwhile products, which the chance processes do not. The path to poetry is by making a man; the path to honey is by making a bee.

The second question I'd like to pose is, "How does nature manage to be inventive?" After all, she has to do with atoms what we have been doing with letters. How is the creation of things made by living creatures possible?

Two million years ago there was a smallish ape man with a brain weighing one pound. He was rather smaller than men are on the whole, and he was barely able to walk upright. He had no speech, no writing, no symbolism that we know of, but he did have a certain amount of foresight. And in the fantastically short time of 2 million years, here we are sitting in a tent, flying kites, recording everything electronically, dressed the way we are. I would like to make a comparison with you. Long before the prototype of a human being even got as far as having a brain weighing one pound (ours weighs around three pounds), the bee had already finished with its evolution.

What are the processes of nature that create the bee and say, "Perfect!" You can't improve on bees, and you certainly can't improve on honey"—and then go off and produce human beings who produce poetry?

Piet Hein has said that art is solving problems that cannot be formulated until they are solved. I repeat this remark: Art and the process of nature consist of solving problems that cannot be rightly formulated until they are actually solved, and then you know what the problem was.

This is what distinguishes life from the computer. You see why my monkeys or computers didn't type very well? They were just programed for random numbers. But if I had programed them for the Shakespeare sonnet, then I would also have had to give them the plan. But, of course, there is no point in having a computer write a poem for me that I have already written.

The whole point about evolution and invention and creation is that they follow a program that has not been written, and yet they come out with poetry—and it doesn't stop at "Shall I compare thee to a su."

How does evolution do this? First, nature works by using words, not letters. What was wrong with the monkey was that he kept trying to make words out of letters, a thing that dictionary-makers had already done for him. Nature works constantly by a series of hierarchies, so every step of evolution rests on the conclusion of some previous level. Each step is complete in itself but in time can serve as a base for the next higher form of organization. You don't try to write poetry until you can make paragraphs, and you don't write paragraphs until you can make sentences. You don't make sentences until you can make words, and you don't write words until you've learned the letters. You don't try to jump from the letters to the poem, and life doesn't try to jump from the atoms to Shakespeare.

The second thing about nature is that at each level of evolutionary processes you make units that are stable, that stick together, and that act as a foundation for development of the next higher level. In dead nature, for example, in which the second law of thermodynamics operates, you shuffle cards for a bridge hand, and the ace, king, and queen of spades do not stick together. But in evolution, once ace, king, queen of spades come together, they form a unit that sticks together. You could really say the basis of life is that it waits for the accidental formation of the word "compare" but, by Jove, from then on it knows that c-o-m-p-a-r-e is going to spell "compare."

The next important level is to make things like poetry. Poetry is different from honey because the bees that make honey today make exactly the same honey as the bees that made honey 20 million years ago. But Shakespeare's poem could not have been written 200 years earlier.

The fourth and most delightful thing about nature is that it makes mistakes, and these errors are productive. It is exactly the chance of random alignment of an atom in a gene that starts a new step in evolution. Not every time. On this sort of scale, most of the time we have nothing at all. But just once every so often what looked like a perfectly good finished creature, the little tree shrew from which we all started, suddenly has some mutation that makes something go wrong with his toes and he can't climb very well. From the point of view of the tree shrew it's a mistake, and if the other tree shrews were half as intelligent as human beings they would kill it. But they don't know this tree shrew with this mutation in a matter of a hundred million years is going to start the monkeys and the human race, so they let it live and it limps about in a rather unsuccessful way. The mutation takes over, and a new level has been started.

Why are we sitting here in this tent 40 million years after the ant, while the ants are running around outside in the cold? It's because they were better adapted to the cold. And here we are, with spectacles, false teeth, hearing aids, beautiful shoes, brilliantly colored clothes. All because, unlike the ant, nature didn't provide us with any of these things. An animal which is too well fitted to its environment remains unchanged almost forever, and does *not* progress. Man has progressed to his present state from a primitive ape stock within the last 2 million years exactly because he is not well adapted; he has to remake his environment in order to survive, and as a result he makes art and science—two dynamic processes that have the same open character that evolution has.

That brings me to my third question, "How does the inventiveness of nature find its echo in human innovation?"—or, "Shakespeare wasn't just anybody."

Shakespeare wasn't just anybody because when he came to the word "more" the second time, you could have taken every one of the Elizabethan poets and asked them to put in a three syllable word with the accent on the first syllable and none of them would have come up with the word "temperate." The line has this tremendous punch, what Leo Lionni called the "hook," because "temperate" has the miraculous quality of being unexpected but right. Until the word "temperate" was written there, the problem of what word should really go there didn't exist.

So, invention, or innovation, consists of exactly the same kind of unexpectedness which nevertheless creates its own fitness. This particular relation between the error that creates the new stability, the error that fits into the stable thing, this is "the living order." This is what we really mean by integrating the innovation into something which has a new order when an older order already existed. The integrated innovation raises the order to the next level.

# XX  Aspen into the 'Seventies

To sum up these collected papers is a different matter from summing up a conference. Preserved in print and packaged in a book they are not what they were when delivered *viva voce* at 8,000 feet of altitude to a living audience. They are the dry remains, not the breathing presence. They are not the Aspen experience and cannot pretend to be. For this reason the selection I have made may baffle, even enrage those who were there in the 'fifties and 'sixties and can remember uplifting or astonishing or enlightening or amusing speeches that are not here, and why the hell aren't they?

Well, time alters many things, and so does the transfer of speech to print. Some of the most famous orations, particularly the summings-up, have dwindled in content and stature. Others that once seemed dim, muffled by a halting delivery or an unresponsive audience, now come up bright and shining on the printed page. Good for them, but tough on golden memories!

Time has also altered IDCA. The conferences have changed by their own internal compulsions, and because of the changes in the world outside that charmed valley in the Rockies, and the changes of mood and attitude in the business of design—and as chairman of that stormy last session of the '70 conference I could suddenly feel all these changes running together in a spasm of bad vibrations that shook the conference. We got ourselves together again, but an epoch had ended.

Frustratingly, I have had to spend the subsequent two years as an offshore observer, relying on friends and globe-trotting members of the board to report the extraordinary scenes of 1971—masterminded by Richard Farson under the entirely appropriate title of "Paradox"—and 1972—"The Invisible City," under the chairmanship of Richard Saul Wurman.

Neither was anything like previous Aspens; these were the years of participation and workshops and be-ins, and they emphatically did not produce "papers" in the classic sense. Tape cassettes, yes—entirely appropriate electronic simulacra of verbal happenings, proof against effective transcription onto the printed page (though IDCA '72 finally appeared in massively edited but tangibly printed form as a double issue of *Design Quarterly* [86/87] in 1973). And even if later Aspens should revert to anything like the classic lecture format, it will never be the same —I knew that when I arrived there for the 1973 conference ("Performance," chaired by Jivan Tabibian and Milton Glaser) it would be an operation to which I was somewhat a stranger.

We can skip the hail-and-farewell routine—the new operation needs nothing from us men of the 'sixties—and we can skip the hearts-and-flowers bit as well, because there need be no tears shed over the Aspen that was. In its time, it did a tidy and productive job, appropriate to the times and adaptable to their changing, a workable and effective design in itself.

But it does mean that the present volume, originally commissioned as a twenty-first birthday tribute, is now a memorial of sorts, and if it exhibits a certain gravity and calm that seems at variance with the remembered hilarities and elations of the time, this may not be inappropriate to its unintended function.

In any case, these are the foundations on which the newer IDCA inevitably rests; the conference style of the 'seventies is the work of men who were around in the 'sixties and even the 'fifties. Among those of us who took part in the 1970 board meeting that buried the old-style Aspen, every generation of the conference was represented, back to and including Herbert Bayer, the originator of the whole concept. The break in form and method has been real and profound, but the chain of ideas and men is unbroken.